The Soul of Taiji: Zhang Sanfeng-Wu Baolin Taijiquan

by

Dr. Wu Baolin

and

Michael McBride

Original Artworks
by
Oliver Benson

Three Pines Press
St Petersburg, FL
www.threepinespress.com

9 8 7 6 5 4 3 2 1

Printed in the United States of America
This edition is printed on acid-free paper that meets
the American National Standard Institute Z39. 48 Standard.
Distributed in the United States by Three Pines Press.

Translations: Eric Di Wu
Illustrations: Oliver Benson
Cover Design: Cranes Flying to the Moon by Brent Cochran
Photo Sketch Art: Michael McBride

Library of Congress Cataloging-in-Publication Data

Names: Wu, Baolin, 1954- author. | McBride, Michael, 1965- author. |
Benson, Oliver, 1968- illustrator.
Title: The soul of taiji : Zhang Sanfeng-Wu Baolin taijiquan / by Dr. Wu
Baolin with Michael McBride ; original artworks by Oliver Benson
Description: St Petersburg, FL : Three Pines Press, [2020]
Identifiers: LCCN 2019058099 | ISBN 9781931483438 (paperback)
Subjects: LSCH: Tai chi. | Taoism | Zhang, Sanfeng, 1247-
Classification: LCC GV504 .W73 2020 | DDC 796.815/5--de23
LC record available at https://lccn.loc.gov/201905809

Contents

List of Illustrations

Original Artworks: viii, 50, 98, 111, 113, 117, 119, 121, 124, 128-142, 152-244

Photos: ix, 1, 3, 7, 9, 17, 22, 25 (Karen Kreiger), 28, 30, 33, 36-41, 43, 46-48, 52, 54, 57, 60, 61, 63, 67, 69, 72, 74, 76, 78, 87, 106, 108, 126, 245, 246

Diagrams: 15, 80, 89, 93, 94, 97,

Foreword

The cultural heritage of Asia represents a rich and colorful combination of science, art, literature, and health philosophies. The essence of a deep pragmatism manifests in the classical arts and sciences of China, among others in Taijiquan (T'ai Chi Chuan). It is through the practice of this ancient art that man comes to understand the movement and flow of energy. The ancient philosophers, shamans, Daoist (Taoist) and Buddhist priests, and warriors accomplished the task of ushering a race of peoples into modern times by teaching harmony through movement in nature. It is now in the 21st century that we can taste some of the fruit of this ancient peach tree. Access to Taijiquan is easy. The smallness of the world is ever apparent, as at any Chinese local restaurant, there is someone who knows just a "little" Taijiquan or where to study it. Most people have seen that slow dance-like movement exercise somewhere. While hundreds of years old, in the West it has only been discovered in the last forty years. It is a calisthenics close to the heart of many Eastern and Western people, a new yogic-like martial art and meditation that makes sense to those who are tired of treadmills, aerobics classes, and weight-training exercise. For the Taijiquan practitioner seeking aerobic training, lowering the posture an inch or two, or slowing down the movements while playing the form will accomplish this quite naturally.

When I heard that Dr. Wu Baolin was going to teach a class in the White Cloud monastery style of Taijiquan, I was really excited. This style developed by Zhang Sanfeng (Chang San-Feng) had previously seemed more legendary than real, and there was always someone claiming to be its inheritor. It made a lot of sense that it would have been archived in one of the centers of the Daoist arts. The White Cloud monastery, comparable in importance to the Smithsonian Institute, is a place where many treasures dear to Daoism have been preserved. I had heard of the White Cloud monastery many years before meeting Dr. Wu. Bai Yun Guan, as it is referred to in Chinese, was always revered as the highest temple for the learning of Daoist practices and the home of the Complete Reality and North Star sect of Daoism. I had heard of this great learning center for many years from several well-published martial-arts and Qi Gong experts, some of whom were masters in their own styles.

As a player of Yang-style Taijiquan since 1971, I feel very fortunate to have been able to support the learning and presentation of the Zhang Sanfeng temple style here in America. This form of Taijiquan has a special meditative and Daoist flavor: after all, the originator was a Daoist priest. Discovering the relationship between the stimulation of the acupuncture points and the Daoist hand gestures has deepened my understanding of this core and original style. Studying and communicating these arts is a very sensitive process, since the

v

deep cultural flavors are sometimes difficult to grasp, especially for those who aren't born in the same culture.

Kinesthetic proof of martial-arts ability is extremely valuable, even though the highest level of the art is perhaps to mentally humble someone so that he can see the way of peace. There is a particular instance that impressed me deeply about this style of Taijiquan that Dr. Wu Baolin has come to share with us in America. For me the proof of Dr. Wu as a master came unexpectedly. It had happened about eight years ago while I was standing on a bluff overlooking the ocean near San Diego in southern California. It was a beautiful, postcard-perfect day. A very accomplished non-Asian martial artist was demonstrating his art of Xingyi Quan (Mind Form Boxing), a highly respected internal martial-arts style (nei jia wushu). Dr. Wu and his translator were about twenty feet away observing this gentleman who was demonstrating a dynamic, powerful set of movements. It was explosive yet very internal and obviously well practiced for many years.

As Dr. Wu was standing across from me watching what I thought was an excellent demonstration, I felt this warm fluid energy flowing down the right side of my body. I had never felt anything quite like it. It was a warm comforting energy, as if someone had turned on a hot shower next to me and the water was soaking through my clothes. I looked over and there was Dr. Wu, looking pleasantly at me, half-smiling. Was this a challenge? I heard about "masters" issuing challenges and being able to emit Qi (energy) from their bodies. I had never experienced this myself, although I had seen some interesting phenomena. He was so nonchalant in his presentation of energy-force projection (fa jing).

I decided to embrace and test this sensation, so I shifted my weight to the leg that was feeling very warm at this point. As a matter of fact, I leaned quite directly into this warm Qi that was becoming more turgid by the moment. If this was a challenge, then I definitely must move in some way. I couldn't move. My body could not pierce through the energy. Dr. Wu had put up a wall of Qi and was not going to let me move. I looked directly at him with "soft focused" eyes; he didn't move and appeared to be rooted to the earth's core. Time froze for a moment. He turned and made a short comment to his translator. I begged inside for meaning to this event. All he said was: "You can tell a lot about people by the way they stand." That was it; the sentence ended, and I could move freely. It was as if Dr. Wu had exerted not even an ounce of effort. At that moment I knew I had met my martial-arts master. I was all tingly inside and didn't say much the rest of the day and have pondered the event deeply ever since.

It is rare that this level of skill and training is shared in the Western world. It is with hearty applause that I introduce this book. As many western Taijiquan enthusiast have known, there has always been a deeper philosophy behind the art. We have all struggled with the question of how to gain this understanding, aside from the "just keep doing the set and you'll find out"-type training. Here it is to be studied and put into practice for both the beginner and expert player. For the beginner, this book is an opportunity to put a toe into a vast ocean of learning and culture. For the more advanced student there are some brilliant ideas, concepts, meditations, and practices that will deepen the understanding of the essence of Taijiquan no matter what style is practiced.

The dawn of a new century is upon us. It is this sunrise that we raise our arms to in the opening of the set. Let the Zheng Qi (righteous) arise to greet the heavenly Wu Qi.

Roger C. Hirsh, O.M.D., Lac.
Doctor of Oriental Medicine
Los Angeles, California
Year of the Tiger, 1998

In Loving Memory of Feng Zhi Qiang, Dr. Roger Hirsh and Dr. Udd'hava Om

Member of China Martial Arts Association
Vice-Chairman of Beijing Martial Arts Association
President of Chen Taiji Research of Beijing Martial Arts Association
President of Hua Xia Martial Arts Club under
FESCO International Teaching Centre

Feng Zhi Qiang

No. 14, Chaoyangmen Nandajie   Tel : 5088287(O) 4660368(H)
Chaoyang District   Fax: 5088298
Beijing 100020   Telex : 210030 FESCO CN
China   Cable : 7571 (Local)
                                           FESCO (Abroad)

中國武術協會委員
北京市武術協會副主席
北京市武協陳式太極拳研究會會長
FESCO國際教學中心　華夏武術館館長

馮　志　強

中國・北京   電話：5088287(辦)　4660368(宅)
朝陽區   傳真：5088298
朝陽門南大街14號   電傳：210030 FESCO CN
郵政編碼：100020   電報：7571 (國內) FESCO (國際)

Dr. Wu Baolin

Laozi Transmitting to Zhang Sanfeng

Chapter One

Basic Training

"Jump!" Master Du Xinling commanded most insistently, addressing his young disciple, "or I cannot advance you any further into the internal secrets of Zhang Sanfeng Taijiquan."

On that day, Master Du's words echoed through canyons and valleys, where teacher and students reached the heights of the steepest and tallest peaks in Xinjiang, an autonomous territory of mountains and deserts in northwest China. As was often the case, Master Du's powerful voice would make Wu Baolin tremble down to his core. This was certainly not the first time the master commanded his undivided attention. Whenever the venerated teacher erupted at this level, the youngster felt the earth rumble underfoot, his breathing shattered by bolts of bioelectricity appearing before his very eyes without strain.

These were not uncommon occurrences during his training days as a fighting monk in the White Cloud Temple (Baiyun guan) in Beijing. The forceful air that arose from the bellows of Master Du's concentrated source represented over a hundred years of *qi* (life-force energy) cultivation inspired by a love of fighting. His brash method was not meant to rouse fear, although that certainly was a motivational feature. It was rather a didactic conveyance, a person-to-person charging system, signaling out and impressing upon a disciple various sought-after Confucian virtues—filial piety, wisdom, justice, integrity, loyalty, and continence—believed to be uniquely humane qualities, crucial to their enduring social customs and therefore dear to Chinese culture. Theirs was a mutual understanding and an unbreakable bond, a tacit agreement, which had evolved through a near-death hardship during their first year together.

Zhang Sanfeng Taijiquan is an internal martial art Daoists consider supreme when fully matured and developed within the dedicated practitioner. Beyond the general training and rehearsal of various forms of taijiquan, its highest levels require participation in a series of dangerously impromptu challenges and hurdles, intended to allow unfettered access to the nonphysical realms of the transcendent Chinese fighting spirit. As far as Wu Baolin was concerned, it was the golden key to the temple gates, something he had coveted ever since becoming a resident monk at the monastery in 1955.

Young Wu, without self-concern or emotional expression, unflinchingly turned away from his treasured teacher's penetrating glare. Fueled by divine impulse, his little feet beat the dusty ground and lifted plumes of fine powder that followed him as he ran full-sprint directly toward the cliff's edge. No one tried to stop him and no one followed. Without breaking stride and zero trepidation, he jumped off the mountain wingless, his last step displacing a scree that went cascading down the cliff's face along with him. Fearless! As he disappeared into the vast cerulean blue, gravity instantly embraced, escorting him to the valley floor thousands of feet below. The winds of change fluttered through his black monk garb as if insulated with butterflies. Another dare he refused to ignore. He had never been so far from home. He was convinced that this time was a dead end…

In the decade before making this grand gesture, Wu Baolin had come to be fully entrenched in one of the oldest religious institutions in the world, the White Cloud Temple, the northern headquarters of Complete Reality or Complete Perfection (Quanzhen), the major school of Daoism since the 13th century. The temple thus was a primary depository of Daoist knowledge, encapsulating millennia of Chinese thought, culture, and spiritual practice, vigilantly committed to safeguarding the delicate assemblage of Daoist, Buddhist, and Confucian doctrines that make up the core of Complete Reality teachings. Its administration was under the custodianship of the Dragongate lineage (Longmen pai), the leading line of the Complete Reality or Complete Perfection School, founded by Qiu Chuji (1148-1227), one of the Seven Perfected and leader of the school after its original founder, Wang Chongyang (1113-1170). Over the centuries, it attracted numerous masters of immense talent and capacity and supported the development of cutting-edge methodologies of spiritual cultivation and enlightenment.

In the 20th century, the school trained disciples in the main subjects of study, healing exercises (*daoyin*), energy work (*qigong*), martial arts (*gongfu*), and divination based on the *Yijing* (Book of Changes); the essential elements of taijiquan. The entire curriculum consisted of seventy-two classes, each of which was fundamentally grounded in the same philosophy as taijiquan—that is, seeking to balance the two polarized energies of the universe known as yin and yang. Another major center of the school, moreover, was in the Wudang mountains, covering the dense forest reserves of Hubei, which places dominant emphasis on the development of martial arts, both external and internal.

Master Wu Baolin spent twenty-three years at the White Cloud Temple, thus advancing in its most complete and comprehensive system of taijiquan. He learned all 464 movements directly from Master Du, lineage holder of both the Wudang sect and Nine Palaces Taijiquan. Master Du first taught him the classical form, then graduated him to the Zhang Sanfeng system through daily routines of advanced qigong exercises as well as the study of the *Yijing* and various martial arts. In addition, he had to endure the ten-thousand knife cuts of the Buddha. Young Wu's training meant that he constantly had to knock on death's door, storm through the doorway as and when his teacher unlatched it, time after time facing the worst fears of humankind. In the end, he attained the distinction to attach his name to the cherished practice, which came to be known as Zhang Sanfeng-Wu Baolin Taijiquan.

The form is quite unlike popular taijiquan undertaken by ordinary people in Beihai Park or on the grounds outside the Temple of Heaven. It is also different from the circulating style of taijiquan commissioned by the emperor to be taught to his concubines in the Forbidden City. In fact, it is a temple form, reserved for members of the Daoist order. Although Master  Du taught martial arts publicly around Beijing for many decades, he never shared this particular practice, reserving it for his most gifted disciples. Admittance required not only various unorthodox tests of Daoist and martial arts acumen, but also a degree of personal karmic affinity (*yuanfen*). Wu Baolin's life and growth present a good example of how karmic affinity and destiny work hand in hand in securing disciples a position in specific martial arts training with a monastic institution and show how the Daoist tradition conceives of taijiquan and its training as transmitted in the White Cloud Temple in Beijing and the Purple Cloud Temple (Zixia gong) on the Wudang mountains.

Encountering the Master

For Wu Baolin, it began at the age of four when his parents offered him to the temple. This was not a voluntary gesture but one born out of necessity and a state of emergency. Little Wu was suffering from a severe disease that even two hundred years of ancestral medical knowledge and good family connections could not cure. There were no solutions for his extremely volatile health condition in Beijing or elsewhere, so that the family came to make a plea to the gods. They would give up their son in exchange for the remote possibility that his life could be spared. Thus they surrendered their boy to the temple. Once taken in, the monks performed a medical assessment under the leadership of the incumbent abbot, Master Du, who in due course became the last leader chosen by the rank and file of the Daoist monastic community. Little Wu was found to suffer from whitewater blood disease, requiring admittance as an inpatient.

Medical treatments commenced, but for two months the child would remain in dire straits. After six months of round-the-clock biorhythmic acupuncture, herbal prescriptions, and qigong treatments, he was better yet not strong enough to lift his head and often fell into states of delirium. Still, the temple physicians persisted and kept up the good work, "treating the dead horse as if it were alive" and believing that anything was possible. While making all-out efforts, they were yet prepared to acquiesce to the will of heaven for the final outcome. Promises and commitments were made, and a silent agreement was reached that, should the child be cured its karmic affinity to the temple would be so strong that he belonged there. In the end, Wu Baolin had to choose his destiny, but he remained indebted to the Daoists. As the saying goes, "When a maiden contacts the blood of a man on her birthday, even if by extraneous circumstance, they are destined to marry."

One day, the dark brooding clouds of ill health began to dissipate, the shadowy mist and windblown smoke, as if scattering off a campfire, started to move away from Wu Baolin's frail ecosystem. Soon he experienced an emerging renewal of strength, like a phoenix rising from the ashes. He was able to walk and do moderate exercises, his appetite growing steadily. He was taught to mold clay in order to rebuild his strength, while continuing to take medicinal herbs and eat a unique steamed pork dish for the regeneration of blood cells— prepared specially by the temple chef. Unlike household priests of the Celestial Masters or Orthodox Unity School who eat meat, monastic Daoists are vegetarians, consuming animal products only for medicinal reasons. The method of preparation, moreover, was essential for increasing healing properties and effects, especially for neuron production in the brain.

In this particular case, using a switch plucked from a willow tree, a live suckling pig was whipped repeatedly across the upper portion of the hind legs and rump, until all the blood and *qi* of the animal rushed into that circle. Once the skin complexion changed color and muscle density softened, that slim portion of flesh would immediately be sliced off cleanly with a sharp cleaving knife and placed into the cooker. The animal was treated for its wounds and promptly reunited with the drift of piglets and their sow for feeding—its sacrifice considered a good deed, likely to lead to reward in a future life.

The healing of Wu Baolin is not unlike the transformation Buddhist monks undergo on Mount Wutai, both of the Chan (Zen) and Lama (Tibetan) schools, wearing vivid green and scarlet with gold robes, respectively. Before a monk can wear his robes, he must first practice fasting for forty days, living as a recluse behind the Buddha's altar in the main hall of the temple. He purges himself physically while renouncing the ways of the secular world, disconnecting from the matrix of illusion—what Daoists call the "ten thousand beautiful things."

Sitting in meditation on an elevated wooden platform, bordered by four white- or saffron-colored curtains hung from the vaulted ceiling, he recites sacred spells and scriptures, inviting the Buddha's blessing. Guards surround him for the entire period, since practitioners must not leave the platform. In the course of the ordeal, they pass through several near-death encounters, not unlike the disease that matured Little Wu beyond his years. Both the Buddhist and the young Daoist emerge in revisiting life as a new being, the feverish or ascetic journey to the cusp of the abyss in fact a rite of passage.

When his health was restored and the time came to go home, Wu Baolin returned to his family. They were ecstatic, gleefully optimistic, and showed immense gratitude and generosity toward Master Du and the Daoist institution. They handed over donations in the form of cash, land, food, and herbal medicines, hoping that family life would soon be back to normal. However, after living for a full year in the monastery and mingling with the monks and the many animals, both wild and domesticated, of the temple, Young Wu did not easily take to civil life. Rather, he missed the elements of austere living, increasingly coming to crave the monastic life, repeatedly returning to the temple—whether it was to visit Master Du, get help for a relapse of his condition, practice martial arts, or enjoy only for the special taste of the distinctive steamed cabbage doused with black vinegar and a dash of salt, there was always a reason to go back to the temple. For Wu Baolin it was the pulling of heartstrings and the inexplicable call of the wild.

Whenever he was in the temple, his life was simple and any questions about his future were relaxed. All seemed to coalesce fluently as he affirmed his place in the monastery, making himself the decision to stay and thus choose his destiny. With some reluctance his parents agreed to let him go, realizing that living and studying there would ensure his strong and healthy future. After all, their son had shown clear signs of advancing talent and compatibility with Daoist philosophy, and as the saying goes, "Every parent wants their child to become a dragon." Healthy and vigorous, Young Wu found the pursuit of a Daoist calling to be the opportunity of a lifetime. The decision was made to commit himself to the training absolutely and positively, leaving no way of getting out again.

Inside the Temple Walls

Wu Baolin began his Daoist training under the guidance of Master Du, a top fighting monk of modern China and a resident of White Cloud Temple since the early 1930s. This was one of several conditions stipulated by the Wu Family. If they were to permit their son to become a Daoist monk, Master Du would have to be his primary teacher and guardian, exercising meticulous oversight. Up until this point, Master Du had never indicated that Wu Baolin was a prospective student of the White Cloud Temple: he had just been an in-patient.

But it soon became clear that he had become Wu's leading spirit or *guiren*. This term indicates someone of high nobility in society or an affiliated fraternity, with a rank based on wealth, wisdom, or virtue, who has the means to make a serious difference in people's lives. It also has the implication of savior, a person who has granted, spared, or saved a life by virtue of his own merit. When Master Du cured Wu Baolin from his ailments and snatched him from certain death, he essentially earned the right to use him as he believed necessary. By the same token, Little Wu was indebted to him who had saved or spared his life.

At this point, when Wu Baolin's monastic education was getting started, Master Du had, at least on the surface entered semi-retirement, approaching the milestone of one-hundred years of age, a corollary of his dedicated training in taijiquan and the Daoist martial arts. When teaching the temple monks, he emphasized with more and more regularity returning to the source and embracing Dao by practicing the rainbow transformation (*honghua*), whereby the flesh and soul of the adept transform into pure light, bypassing the six realms of reincarnation in a dramatic departure using the Nine Palaces qigong practice, a solar energy purification system.

Master Du's goal, as he often mentioned, was to continue his edification at the feet of magnificent celestial immortals, most notably Laozi and Wang Chongyang, in the ninth level of the sun, the highest Daoist heaven. After turning eighty-one, he only practiced Zhang Sanfeng Taijiquan using his mind and his spirit body as his main focus turned to qigong. He spent increasingly lengthier periods of time deep in isolation and refinement, his sabbaticals becoming months long as he explicitly prepared for the rarest of feats. His schedule was not conducive to teaching anymore in the traditional sense. And besides, he had not taken on a new student in many years. To some insiders of the temple it clarified in part the end of a tenure—yet still unclear who would be his successor.

After a formal announcement, the temple registrar recorded the adoption, introducing Wu Baolin to the order of monks. Immediately, it was presumed he would be groomed to be Master Du's successor as there was no other justification for this grade of commission. It would have been utterly inconsistent with Master Du's well-known character, accountable position and his perfectionist attitude, ways and means to make any imprudent assessments, his approach to matters often circumspect.

Objections were founded upon this declaration by some of the temple council members. Most of the council members did not see there being enough time to impart Dao to Wu Baolin who despite his cleverness, had shown a penchant for questioning everything taught or applied, seen as obstinate and disbelieving in religious creed, and he was so young. There was genuine shock and surprise, followed by a great deal of speculation and heated discussion. It changed the entire climate at the monastery for a time. It was even eluded to that Master Du was thinking irrationally. Concerned opinions flooded and philosophical debates volleyed. The reactions were completely normal and necessary to objectively observe through the filtering lens of the *Yijing* every possible outcome, a Daoist trait invariably instigated.

Master Du valued the input but he was the *Yijing* expert and visionary fortune-teller at the temple, his skills exceeding other members of the council. Master Du was keeping to himself important secrets, which if revealed too soon could alter those secrets. Since he was the head abbot of the temple his unshared strategy needed to be adhered too. Master Du was never casual about the importance of any decision, so his approval of enlisting a five year old boy possessed the tenor of something greater and something premeditated.

Predisposed sociopolitical environments in China, most remarkably the recent introduction of communism, had prompted Master Du to "prematurely" make, what appeared to be at the time, an ostensibly reckless decision regarding the future of the Daoist association, but, social reform was in the air and Dao was the master of change.

A New Era

The changes to traditional Chinese culture in the 1950s were astonishing. Almost overnight, the Chinese way was modified and/or diluted with many western inclinations. The differences between producing traditional eastern medicine and modern western medicine illustrate one example the changes.

When traditional Chinese herbalists' produce medicine pills, the ingredients are rolled together into a ball using one accumulative direction, a procedure myriad centuries old. In this way, the medicine grows larger and larger as does a snowball rolling down a mountainside. The result of the snowball effect is a soft mud pill, which is quickly soluble, easy to digest, and natural in color usually browns and blacks. When making modern pharmaceuticals such as Western medicine the chemical process is more industrialized, pounding and pulverizing ingredients into slightly coarse powders and synthesizing them into large tablets or loosely encapsulated for quick release to facilitate entry into the bloodstream. These tablets are multi colored and signature branded with unique identifiers, usually cryptic symbols or number codes in order to responsibly track their recipe and dosage. This process results in a hard and dense substance, a stone pill, occasionally found difficult to swallow. They are the soft and the hard, respectively, yin and yang.

That is to say traditional Chinese culture goes with the flow of nature, a long-standing philosophical paradigm, which is in essence Daoism, a ten-thousand year old indigenous shamanic culture based on free association and mysticism at its very substance. In contrast, reaching the goals of a communist ideology requires the consolidation of human resource and of materials for a greater purpose, in this case growth through Chinese industrialization. After enduring over half a century of civil in-country fighting compounded by the invasion of foreign powers, China finally became thoroughly annexed by revolutionary theory with the forming of the People's Republic of China (PRC), established October 1, 1949. Despite any misgivings, it was a time to reunify China.

Master Du had calculated long ago the new springtime and turning over of Chinese soil. Although the country's new path and transitional methods initially unmelodic, he could not argue with the calculations arrived at by the *Yijing*—voicing imminent changes. In the new era he was witnessing interruptions to cultural resonance and a devaluation of traditional Chinese wisdom, the exclusion of ancient customs. There was the deconstruction and simplification of written language, a brilliant policy to expand literacy, but, by extracting vital formulaic radicals from the ideographs, by definition, eliminated key elements of the Chinese intellect, i.e., its unique reasoning in association with nature, putting ancestral knowledge at risk. Master Du wanted to prevent such an interruption in his own line. Master Du was already an immortal and his departure from earth was not long relatively. He was born to be a monk. Exchanging his black robes for a modern Chinese tunic suit did not fit the elder master.

When China centralized power, the White Cloud Temple lost its anonymity and began slowly moving with the changes. It was not decision by committee any longer in the way Master Du had been voted the leader of the Dragongate lineage in the 1930s as an example. His unanimous appointment to head abbot came after two weeks of examinations. Rigorous Daoist service testing covering all subjects of the Complete Reality School were administered, including fighting competitions where Master Du excelled. Over seven-hundred eligible monk entrants tested and interviewed for the esteemed position. Master Du had been the clear-cut favorite to preside over the affairs of the White Cloud Temple, however, everyone deserved a chance to compete. Formalities were absolutely necessary to remove all doubts and to mitigate the political fervor and argument that would ensue otherwise for such an honorable standing. That was and this was the "end" of autonomy. Master Du surmised that openly announcing the future of the Dragongate lineage during the new era would inevitably expose and possibly endanger the new link, risking the interruption of thousands of years of precious knowledge. The dragon would have to be hidden.

Master Du considering to train someone as young and not immediately obvious as Wu Baolin, was predicated on the changeability of a new social structure. Wu Baolin was going to be raised to adapt to both worlds, Old China and New China, to become their treasure chest. However explained by Master Du, it was none-the-less misconstrued by the Daoist council. Master Du never intended it as an insult to other candidates and their teachers though now he was being accused of basing his decisions purely on emotion because some years earlier he lost a true successor in Yanzi Li San, another master of Zhang Sanfeng Taijiquan. This heavily criticized historical figure whose erroneous judgments and conduct unbecoming of a monk, caused a massive scandal and loss of face for Master Du and the White Cloud Temple. There is a Chinese saying, "The teacher is only as good as the student they produce." For Master Du, it was the one blemish on an otherwise impeccable career and Wu Baolin was the student who could rectify this past humiliation. Master Du's leverage was his possession of the "Soul of Zhang Sanfeng," a sequence of thirty-seven secret movements in addition to the base form of Zhang Sanfeng Taijiquan, known only to him and his teacher. Never having taught the former meant the future was undecided.

A mandatory collective effort under the direct supervision of Master Du would be vital to the success of Wu Baolin's training, including the participation of seventeen Lama Buddhist monks from both the Temple of Eternal Harmony (Yonghe gong), Beijing, and also in Tibet. This decades long undertaking most adult men struggle to complete so there were no assurances that it would lead to readiness. The onus for achieving Wu Baolin's transformation was clearly falling on the shoulders of the entire village. Master Du could have chosen to focus on several other well qualified monks to become a 17th-generation master of the Dragongate lineage, but instead set his eyes on Wu Baolin. It was also the fact that Master Du saw himself in the boy, a reflection on his own boyhood, and the atypical path and identical age on to which he had entered the Daoist life. He had good reason to believe they were of the same ilk, but he was still waiting on a sign before confirming his choice.

Raised by a Tiger

> To possess Dao is to become an infant again.
> No wild beast will attack,
> No predators from the sky will snatch,
> And no insect dare alight and sting.
> —Laozi

When undergoing a program of Daoist esoteric study and exercise, it is not uncommon to extricate the phenomena of cellular memory from the soul. This is known as returning to pure yang and retracing the steps to a primordial or original level of being. Newly developed cell as well as genetic memory becomes equally accessible, either time-released or on demand. The process of the soul's passage through time stores these encounters at least subconsciously, in the brain and heart databases, although not exclusively, and embosses them on the soul. The highly specialized Daoist exercises can return to the practitioner full awareness of these memories, people, places and things long forgotten by the average person roaming the world. Master Du had achieved the highest level of perfection in Daoist *qi*-cultivation, earning him the title of Dao Master of Purple Yang. Not only could he access his own memory and lifetimes, past and future, but he could do it also for others by utilizing the *Yijing*, a skill set that allowed him to access information over and beyond 1500 years into the future and 1500 years into the past. His predictions were uncanny as well as his offered guidance, ideally determined by the subjects own destiny and *qi* reflections.

The mighty current of the mysterious Dao guided Wu Baolin to the White Cloud Temple several years after liberation in 1949. In the mid-1800s, Master Du had mysteriously found his own way to the front gates of the Purple Cloud Temple, a Ming-dynasty mountain enclave nestled high in the Wudang mountains, and the focal temple in the south. Between living with immediate family and his matriculation into Daoist study, a precipitous shift in weather abruptly ended Master Du's family relations, causing him to live for three summers among the best fighters and hunters of the forest. The physical and mental involvement of this invaluable course in survival and attrition was so deeply engraved that it set him apart from all comers for his lifetime. As he recalled significant cultural and personal events with the help of his teacher, he broadened the scope of his memories. This enabled them to ascertain the series of actions that parted him from his native place, placing him outside ordinary society. Here is his story.

The sky was in falling and a great flood swept through the hometown of the infant Master Du. In its wake there was out-and-out decimation, large patches of the human ecosphere disappearing without warning, his village buried in a watery grave. In an attempt to save their infant's life, Master Du's parents frenetically swathed and secured him onto a small rough-and-ready raft preparing to send him downstream—all alone. Letting go, they used their remaining breaths to say farewell and pray for their precious bundle to survive, themselves getting swallowed by the rising surge. Beyond his immediate survival of the turbulent waters, their greatest concern was that most strangers would never adopt a child that had been abandoned or lost for fear of attaching themselves to bad luck. Misfortune was thought to be contagious in the way that cold and flu viruses are seen today, and only a cursed child could have such tragic misfortune to be severed from his family by the destruction of wind and rain. In the seconds that remained of their lives, his parents wished their son to find his path, confident that, "heaven does not let children go hungry." Master Du recalled this moment clearly as it was so remarkable and pivotal that the experience took a deep hold in the cell's memory.

The forceful currents swept the child for many miles into wild territories until the waters became shallow and marshy. In the aftermath trees and vegetation lay strewn from days of heavy flooding, piling up where the waters slowed. His makeshift raft followed the current, pulling him to the shore near long tall green grasses where predators would normally crouch next to established animal runs, patiently waiting for their next meal. Laying on the raft and comfortably rocked by the constant current that slightly crashed onto the outer edges of the floodwaters, Master Du was out of sight from any passerby, a position that could only be given away by "a baby's loud cry, the only true sound of heaven." Master Du remembers massive pupils and eyeballs, non-human, coming into view through the shadows between the blades. These large eyes belonged to a mountain tiger, the vertical black stripes blending with the tall blades of grass shadowing the breadth of its shoulders. When the tiger fully appeared out of the greenery it stared down with affection and a mothering tendency toward what society might view as a hapless child, but, a tiger walking down off the mountain onto the valley floor is believed to be a hungry tiger according to Daoist astrology.

A special vibration emanated from the big cat, the inimitable sound falling somewhere between a purr and a roar, oddly, was contributing to lowering the stress of the infant. This special effect which emanates from the abdomen, thorax and throat of tigers' was used for healing patients at the White Cloud Temple, since tiger's yang force and body heat are an antithesis to disease when they come in contact with the patient. The tigress began to lick Master Du's face, her viscid aqueous fluid cleansing the orifices of any small debris and defense secretions, which had accumulated from the journey via rapids. She then gently freed him from his bindings, lifted him out of the raft and into her jaws, cradling him firmly with the thirty razor sharp teeth that tigers are known to have, the upper and lower canines enfolding his soft body so he would not slip away. The tigress moved cautiously up a mountain trail, her plans for the infant unclear.

Inside the mountain den was a welcome party of tiger cubs, anxiously awaiting their mother's return. They had not yet been weaned so the infant was not appealing as a meal, their instincts and curiosity instead leading them to play with the child. The tiger litter was small so there was always a teat free for Master Du to be suckled along with the others. Since most tiger cubs begin to eat solid foods roughly after six weeks, the human child eventually inherited the entire batch of tiger's milk for himself. As a result of living off of tiger's milk for the duration, his bone density was extraordinary, and the teeth, tendons and ligaments grew remarkably strong for a child his age. These healthy acquisitions were the very same sought-after medicinal properties and attributes that kept poachers of the forest king in business. This, along with the intensity of fiery tiger *qi* clearly accelerated his growth cycles. Through this yang *qi* enthused environment Master Du developed keener instincts. He was expected to be on constant alert around his tiger siblings who were continuously training for the hunt; spontaneously pouncing on the feral child in poised displays of recklessness. He learned to skillfully maneuver like them and fight impetuously.

Learning by osmosis, Master Du now had the facial expressions relating to tiger emotions and communications down pat. He lashed out in playful disagreement and his snarl was uncivilized and genuine. His eyes became big and round since tiger's milk contains special nourishment for the rods and cones of the eyes, contributing to their shape and acute night vision, six times that of humans. The pineal gland (heavenly eye) in the brain of tigers, is thought to be wide open in these creatures. The Chinese written character for "king" (*wang* 王) naturally shows between the eyes of some tigers, a symbol of leadership and intuition. This feral way of life was the foundation for Master Du's martial arts training and prowess born out of unrestrained fighting with the fiercest wild animals in China. In due time, he would be relocated back into the human world.

The Tiger Ascends

In the mid-19th century, when Master Du was running with the tigers in the forest, the chief abbot of the Purple Cloud Temple was on an extended walkabout in Hubei. Before leaving the temple, the abbot told other ordained priests that he would wander through the region, searching for rare herbs and gathering vital fungi. It was customary for Daoists to forage the hillsides for medicinal herbs and have impromptu meetings with other ascetics. The forests of the Wudang mountains grow over thirty percent of the medicinal herbs listed in the medical classic *Bencao Gangmu* (Compendium of Materia Medica). This wild pharmacopeia is sustained by the splendid waters that gush and spring from nearly every rock face, crevice and cave on the mountain. And since the mountain range is naturally protected by geographical guardians, it was chosen by the ancient masters as a suitable environment in which to invest in the earnest development of Chinese medicinal culture and in the trajectory of spiritual cultivation.

However, what the abbot did not reveal was a heart secret and unbreakable promise. The abbot often times kept his own counsel and after conducting scores and scores of *Yijing* divination in a special inquiry, reinforced by powerful dreams and visions, the abbot's conclusion was, expect a very special guest to arrive. A living Buddha. Following explicit instructions, he told nobody about the predestined meeting. Daoists believe when a secret is made known, even to just one other soul, it runs the risk of interference from the outside, whether accidental or by sabotage.

There was an arranged drop-off point where the tigress and the feral child would wait for the transfer of guardianship. The time had come for Master Du to return to the human world where he would progress among his own species, although his adopted tiger nature never allowed him to be fully human ever again. The parting was bitter sweet. Master Du was losing his second mother in four years, an early lesson in detachment and impermanence. Daoist masters prefer students to commence their training with the least amount of physical or emotional attachment as humanly possible. After all, the study of Daoism is in part a science of reduction. "Only when the cup is empty, does it become useful". Based on centuries of recorded history, emotional attachment can be burdensome, keeping the spirit restless and anchored to the earthly realm.

When the abbot found Master Du, his observations were that this was the pupil he'd imagined. The child's eye movements were spirited as were his physical actions, free, uninhibited, quick and responsive and the aptness for learning had no foreseeable limitations. The child's skin and aura had a glow, luster and radiance of proper *qi*, signs of good health in Chinese medicine. After their meeting, the elder led the child back to the temple.

The Wudang mountains are well named Martial Mountains, since they are an area where the potentiality of martial perfection is highly valued. Almost immediately, Master Du began his Daoist martial training and at no time was he ever at a disadvantage in this world. Though still under the watchful supervision of the Purple Cloud Temple masters, Master Du was walking into the wild animal enclosures undaunted. There was already a ferociousness instilled in him, an instinctual dominance and fearless spirit that he tapped into at will. As his hobby, he engaged in combat and most times emerged victorious. The uncanny emulations of what he had learned from the tigers in the wild was plain to see and his unique tiger *qi* was sensed ubiquitously. This was complimented with an equal amount of compassion for his animal friends. Much older monks were amazed at his boldness, crossing lines of danger they had not yet come to cross themselves or at least not without extreme caution. Even when overpowered, Master Du would find a way to win or escape the clutches of larger opponents even if it meant biting an ear or the nearest body part to escape defeat. He possessed fantastic courage and strength at every stage of development. His spontaneous and unpredictable actions made sure he was well respected even as a minor. His arrival to the temple raised the bar.

Master Du remained on at the Purple Cloud Temple until in his sixties when he was finally called upon to occupy the opening at the White Cloud Temple. The station of head abbot in Beijing is considered the most prestigious position in the Daoist network, comparable to the Vatican papacy or that of the Dalai Lama of the Potala Palace, but with a lower visibility. Master Du chose public anonymity and political avoidance whenever possible, because in order to dissolve into the Great Void, the ultimate test and goal of Daoist practitioners, distractions have to be kept to a minimum. Master Du's invitation to Beijing was actually spurred by a redistribution project of the Nine Palaces system, a branch of esoteric exercise considered a great treasure to both Daoism and particular sects of esoteric Buddhism. The effects of the Nine Palaces practice bode remarkable change for its practitioners as well as the environment, balancing yin and yang in the universe. As part of this system, are the Nine Palaces and Zhang Sanfeng Taijiquan sets.

When Master Du was entering office, China was falling into turmoil. Although in many of the larger cities, such as Beijing, Shanghai, and Hong Kong, the Chinese economy was stabilized after joining the industrial market, in rural China, there was less growth as many landholdings and cultural possessions were being swept away by vast other interests. Foreign invasion and the struggle for power and direction, politically, was waxing and waning between assorted parties, both domestic and foreign. Master Du's appointment was therefore also strategic, plugged-in to weigh and sort out tumultuous current events. This close proximity to centralized powers provided Master Du the necessary access needed to positively influence the country's affairs from behind a veil of ambiguity, as Daoism always walks side-by-side with Chinese history. This second-ary and less publicized purpose for Master Du's promotion to Beijing are close-ly related to the first set of actions, the Nine Palaces redistribution, which over time brought alliance and stability to the region.

The third reason for Beijing was to investigate an important prophecy recorded during the Tang dynasty by Master Wang Chongyang, who left behind a hidden message for future discovery.

Attempted Escape

The eight trigrams (*bagua*) are formed by a combination of double or broken (yin) lines and single or solid (yang) lines. Arranged in a circle, they represent the eight directions of the compass. According to Daoist cosmology, when human beings are born, they must enter the world through one of these eight cosmic gates, which also match number. The numerals of one's birth date are the original name one receives from the universe, superseding the names given by parents. They are the original code of the matrix, the coordinates on a base map from where individual destiny and fortune are launched.

The eight trigrams consist of combinations of yin and yang, so that everyone born into being must face a particular reality. This entails making personal decisions, which may have resounding effects on life, shaping past as well as future. Some choices occur naturally while others are made after lengthy deliberation. There is a Daoist saying, "One wrong step and all succeeding steps will be wrong too." Finding the proper gate to a different phase of life is crucial, and efforts make a huge difference.

What Wu Baolin could not fathom when he committed himself to Master Du and the monastic life was that his words and actions formed an everlasting bond. In hindsight, he regretted not asking more questions when he had the chance. When choosing to become a monk, he supposed the same set of cir-cumstances would apply as his last days as a patient, living part time with his family and reuniting with them on the weekends and during holidays. But this was not the temple's infirmary or a boarding school. There were to be no more free passes coming and going through the front gates without a guardian, be-cause the temple's security took precedence. Breach any of the temple gates without permission and risk severe punishment, or worse yet, be intercepted by the vigilant magical sword of the immortal Lü Dongbin, which without human intervention, unhinges with anything categorized as a forced entry or an un-scheduled departure by resident monks or their guest.

Wu Baolin was strong-willed, an exceptional trait when beginning the path of Dao, but the acclimation period posed challenges for his guardians. He was difficult to yoke, forming strong opinions and presenting clever arguments pertaining to rules. Wu Baolin's contention was that he was being given too much responsibility for someone his age. Sometimes he just wanted to play.

There is a saying in China, "Those who are in, want out; those who are out, want in.", a true statement applicable in any number of occupations and relationships. In old China for example, when aspiring child performers seeking fame and fortune joined the opera houses they first need to qualify by passing physical examinations and talent assessments, but once accepted, these children soon found themselves in shock when discovering the harsh reality of developing perfection in their field, pushed through mass amounts of physical exertion from the start. Corporal punishment came early on in their training if they struggled to attain absolute precision in their efforts.

There were evenings when Wu Baolin became terribly homesick missing his family and close friends of his own age. In contrast, the monastery was indeed strict and predominantly adults. Every time he asked to go home, he was met with the same refrain, "If you ever want to leave the White Cloud Temple, you will have to fight your way out and win decisively", but how could he ever overpower grown men he thought. In his heart and mind, he often thought to escape.

Sentry monks were posted throughout the monastery twenty-four hours a day protecting Daoist treasures against theft. The ancient relics, which had been magically enraptured by consecration ceremonies (*kaiguang*), including the burial ashes of the perfected Qiu Chuji, were abundant.

Wu Baolin believed he was clever enough to navigate through the sentries undetected and if he succeeded it would be considered an accomplishment. He studied the sentries patrol patterns, timed their rounds and one night attempted to abscond. He tip-toed quietly through the doorway of his sleeping quarters and patiently scanned all around. On the outside of his door frame, appearing like a war bonnet, were a plethora of bird feathers, each one wedged between the door frame and outer facade of the unit. The feathers had been gifted by all the other monks on the day he was invited into the monk order, each feather there to act as a talisman to defend Wu Baolin from any unforeseen dangers. Other gifts were a golden bell meant to be rung every morning to scatter demon spirits, and a piece of soft watery jade, to rub as a protective amulet, bringing sleep. These important pieces were part of a Daoist monk's living quarters along with a table and chair, ink brush set and paper. He was ready to leave it behind.

As he navigated one courtyard onto the next, undetected, he began to feel the rise of hope in his chest, and the stifling plum-pit sensation of nervousness caught in his throat descending. A genuine excitement was growing within. The front gate came into view, a symbol of liberty. He would escape the inescapable White Cloud Temple after all he thought. A major coup. His tip-toeing turned into a shuffle as he approached the last line of defense, his ecstatic feet moving nearer to the bridge that bends over the moat. Suddenly he saw low dark moving shadows projected along the wall, but they were not the decorous actions of man. He froze and carefully began retreating behind an incense urn planted in the exact center of the clearing, to avoid discovery. His hair standing on end, was sensing clear and present danger. He watched and waited, forgetting to blink his eyes for what seemed an eternity. His heart sank that night along with his dream of returning home and to the way things used to be. What he saw next he would not have imagined in a thousand years. The outer ring of security

charged with patrolling the inside of the temple walls was a team of hungry tigers and wolves, two animals compatible in Chinese astrology. In a complete reality check, Wu Baolin exploded back toward his sleeping quarters, dove into his room and locked the door behind him.

His pulse was racing. He felt caged, but in that same moment realized that the only way out of the monastery was to be the best fighting monk, bar none and there was no time to waste. He had taken notice of the style and behavior of the monks. They were stoic and endured hardship without complaint, supportive and encouraging of one another. They never showed displeasure and were always self-deprecating regardless of age, skill or rank. Wu Baolin followed their lead.

Often the perception of monks is that they live in perfect peace and solitude, but finding true separation and independence and spiritual prosperity, requires high degrees of suffering. If you cannot fight your way out of the monastery, you cannot leave. If you try to escape and are caught, you will answer for your transgressions. The sentries of the monastery are not human, and at night, when the sun sets and the torches are extinguished, the tigers and wolves are let out of their cages and allowed to roam and protect the temple grounds, subsequently, they prevent any attempts of escape. What boy does not want to play with his schoolmates? The animals eventually became his friends.

Truth be told, Master Du 's first impression of Wu Baolin was that he would one day make a fine fighting monk and perhaps a good doctor based on family background. He had no plans of ever teaching him *Yijing*, fengshui, or any of the other Daoist subjects. One day, shortly after Wu Baolin's failed escape, a meeting was called on a different matter. As Master Du began to sit on an old bamboo chair once belonging to Wang Chongyang, he felt one of the legs of the antique chair start to give, followed by a loud snap. While keeping his balance standing, the chair went crashing down to the floor. When Master Du looked down, a broken bamboo strip lying apart from the fallen chair, caught his eye, snatching it up. Carved on the broken piece was an important message from the past. He passed it around for all the senior monks to read. In that precise moment, Wu Baolin walked into the chamber to check on the big commotion. The only thing Master Du said to him as he handed him the bamboo piece was, "Read what is written on the broken chair leg you're now holding." Wu Baolin read it aloud: "I, Wang Chongyang, predict that on this exact date, Wu Baolin will arrive to the White Cloud Temple and become the 17th generation successor of the Dragongate lineage." Any doubts or reservations that Master Du or any of the other monks had had, were laid to rest. No one dared argue the wishes of the founder of the sect.

Wu Baolin was amazed. The date was correct. Master Du explained to him that Immortal Wang Chongyang had predicted his coming to the White Cloud Temple nearly one-thousand years earlier, and further explained that he, Wu Baolin, was one of the main reasons he came to Beijing. It gave Wu Baolin a sense of belonging, helping him to become more interested in the goings-on at the monastery.

Discovering Taijiquan

One evening after finishing his studies, Wu Baolin went exploring the monastery grounds for something amusing to do or see. He observed Daoist monks practicing an array of interesting forms and unusual activities such as standing meditations and animal based martial arts. On any given night, monks stood alone facing a different corner of the earth pertaining to their personal birth directions, by aligning themselves with the season to which they were born (Spring-East, Summer-South, Fall-West, and Winter-North). Some followed intuitive sensations not unlike a compass needle, finding their own magnetic north in some sector of the universe, while others chose a specific direction searching for a solution to a difficult problem or fulfilling a need or query in relation to *Yijing* knowledge. Most nights however, like a flock of cranes, together they faced toward the moon, poised to fly away in the practice of the Five Centers Facing Heaven, the primary yin-based practice of the White Cloud Temple.

After qigong, the monks engaged in auxiliary exercises designed to build internal power. The most common of these are water-based, submerging hands and arms in and out of water filled stone basins, forcefully slapping the clear surface, and splashing water high above their heads. Another practice involved pushing the water around the inside rim of the basin in one direction, alternating the hands to create tightly formed whirlpools with the building of speed deepening the hollow center. Another skill building favorite was snatching freshwater eel or fish out from large pottery barrels in the dark while blindfolded, using only their bare hands. This speed and dexterity skill was developed by watching the extraordinary *diao* eagles hunt. The eagle are famed for being the eyes in the sky and recognized army generals of the Yuan dynasty. After watching for a time, Wu Baolin wandered on

Various areas and chambers of the temple were used freely for cultivating exercise. However, there were other areas, which during designated hours were completely off limits except to the head abbot of the monastery, Master Du. Rules did not seem to stop Wu Baolin from going there anyways. His curiosity was protected by childhood innocence, and his own prerogative. He approached his teacher's private courtyard clandestinely, hiding partially behind a wall, and the camouflage of low hanging tree foliage. Between two branches, he quietly spied on Master Du who was immersed in a set of very slow martial arts movements, his balance progressing as carefully as a cat walking on ice. With each transition every single one of his joints in his body were connecting like a string of pearls, the luster of which surrounded Master Du. The actual speed of his exercise routine was almost imperceptible like the misty clouds that shroud mountain peaks. Other times he appeared asleep and not moving. His stillness method, known as *taiji zhuang*, generated static electricity that tangibly filled the air. Master Du could go on for hours and sometimes all night, never repeating the same posture, the extent of the form unending, denoting mastery.

Master Du had a keen sensitivity of his surroundings, since enemies of the temple often lurked in the darkness and shadows. His ethereal body sensed Wu Baolin watching and normally he'd have no qualms issuing corporal punishment for breaking temple rules, but he wanted to entice his young student so he let him continue on before casting out his thousand mile stare.

Wu Baolin observed some very interesting effects surrounding Master Du's practice. Far-out things he had not noticed with other monks. He noted that the longer his teacher practiced the larger the moon's halo grew, reaching down forming a giant ring of ethereal light around the practice grounds, discharging up to three rings, thicker than the Great Wall. After certain movements, the trees rustled forcefully, the leaves turning over one-hundred and eighty degrees on an otherwise tranquil evening. The electricity in the air was palpable, manifesting in concentrated and expansive expressions; sometimes heavy, condensed, and full and other times light, diluted, and transparent, the characteristics of yin and yang.

Whatever it was that Master Du was practicing, Wu Baolin wanted to learn it as he felt its power undulating within. When Master Du thought the boy had seen enough, he opened his eyes and stared from what Wu Baolin thought was a safe distance and undetectable position. The bright flash from his teacher's eyes gave him a start. He went running back to his dormitory, leaped and shimmied into his round polo basket bed made of tree branches and pretended to be asleep. As he laid there in anticipation of a scolding, he wandered off to sleep pondering everything witnessed that night.

"What form of exercise did you practice last night, Shifu?" Wu Baolin asked over breakfast the very next day.

"I was practicing Zhang Sanfeng Taijiquan," he answered.

"Master, why do you practice so slowly?"

"There are many reasons. I practice to slow down my heart, the place where my spirit rest also called the Blood Palace, the emperor's seat within the body. By doing so my blood and spirit are actively nourished. It also insures that my body's *qi* circulates smoothly the necessary fifty rounds per day without fail. If this can be achieved the emotions remain still, promoting peace of mind, clarity, virility and well-being, qualities useful for attaining longevity and reaching enlightenment."

Wu Baolin did not know the first thing about enlightenment despite his position in the temple. In his earliest estimation, the subject of heavenly ascension was hyperbole, his feet firmly planted on the ground. What mattered was fighting his way out, a realization that sunk in like the pungent taste of Chinese herbal medicine. Wu Baolin asked his teacher, "Is taijiquan useful as a martial art or is it solely used for meditation and health, harmonizing the body and self-preservation?"

This question pleased Master Du to no end. It was exactly the sort of response he had hoped to evoke when he allowed Wu Baolin to watch him play taijiquan. "It is the highest form of pugilism in the Daoist Canon and because of its potential elevations it makes it the most difficult path to climb successfully. There are no guarantees you will make it. While some forms of fighting can be mastered in as little as six months, taijiquan might take decades, certainly a minimum of ten years with razor sharp focus. Although enlightenment seems irrelevant to you it is a prerequisite to understanding the adaptive interchanges of taijiquan, which combine heaven, humanity, and earth as one; in the ether and on the ground. Taijiquan differs greatly from other fighting forms since it is based upon Laozi's yin and yang theories as outlined in the eighty-one chapters of the ancient classic *Daode jing* (Book of Dao and Its Virtue), using softness in overcoming hardness, and the use of soft water to penetrate hard stone.

The moment Wu Baolin asked to be taught taijiquan, Master Du questioned him. "Why do you want to learn? Is it to fight? Do you want to take revenge on someone? Build a healthy body? Perform virtuous acts? Live long? Are you looking to be a movie star to show off your skills in front of the camera? Do you want popularity and attention and for others to tell you how great you've become? Maybe you want to be a bodyguard for a prominent person after you have learned? I hear it's lucrative. You must have an adequate motive to practice and learn otherwise my time will inevitably be wasted."

These carefully crafted questions, each resonating with distinct intonations, chimed the boy internally. They were intended to elicit a spontaneous and formed response. Master Du waited patiently for his student to answer. The air became still. Wu Baolin knew he was serious about this question and did not consider all the complicated possibilities. He knew what he wanted to say but he did not want to disrespect his teacher, especially after he had resuscitated his life, so Wu Baolin answered in a serious tone, "To see how far I can go." Master Du gave him a nod as if to say his answer was satisfactory.

"I will teach you but to reach the pinnacle and understand fully the nature of taijiquan as a fighting art, you will contemporaneously work in the stables and wildlife facilities looking after the needs and care of the many animals we raise and shelter. It's a serious station with great responsibility and dangerous if you're not to the hilt focused. Can you handle the extra work? It's not a glamorous position but you can learn much through practical application. When I begin to teach you taijiquan, I expect you to be responsive and in the moment. Enthusiastic! Not here today and gone tomorrow. Once we begin, you must see it through to the end. Are we understood?"

"Yes, Master." Wu Baolin replied.

It was precisely when Master Du decided to lead Wu Baolin on a retreat to his childhood home, "The land of fairies and immortals," he called it. To seal their pact, they scheduled a lineage initiation. Wu Baolin journeyed to the Wudang mountains with his teacher in the early years following his ordainment as a monk.

One spring, after the ice broke on the stone roads of Beijing, master and disciple packed their travel gear and started south toward Hubei. Wu Baolin had never been out of his comfort zone as much as during the two months of wandering. The Wudang mountains were still one of few destinations not easily accessible by automobile. Car service was extremely expensive, and so was train fare. Monks lived on modest stipends, earning much of their food and money begging for alms, an age-old custom that was in fact losing social acceptance.

They rode on horse-drawn carriages and rickshaws. Other times they walked, especially when arriving at temples and historical sites, there to study historical architecture. Pristine landscapes, nature-made cathedrals, energy vortexes, and the purest drinking waters—things Daoists considered as real treasures—held Wu Baolin's imagination. Master and student climbed trees together eating fruit straight off the vine, siphoning *qi* from the roots to maximize energy absorption. Other stops included well-respected herbal emporiums specific to region, and the vegetarian cuisines of those places. As a strict health habit, Daoist normally stop eating when half full, however, Master Du allowed Wu Baolin to eat until stuffed, explaining that when on the road, you never know when the next meal might be. The learning was endless.

As they neared the Wudang mountains, Master Du hired a horse and cart to get them through a long stretch of farmland. It was a strategy to rest and pace themselves for the steep climb ahead. The range is difficult to access, the region traditionally a stronghold and military training center. Geographically impervious to attack, it is a perfect location for fallback and retreat. In China's long history, these mountains were invaded just once by a foreign force because of the ruggedness of the landscape, its great distance from the eastern seaboard, and harsh mountainous passes, the process not worth the end result.

As if waiting for their arrival, local Daoists received master and disciple at the main gate. The brothers escorted them up the mountain to the Purple Cloud Temple. It was a momentous event and a homecoming for Master Du, and a warm welcome for their newest family member. Wu Baolin found the hike fascinating. He was enthralled by the vibrant lush greenery of the forest alive with utterly symphonic birds and a growing number of best dressed smiles that joined the welcoming party along the way. They were moths to a flame. Master Du had not been forgotten in the twenty plus years he'd been away. He was already a living legend.

As they passed through the distinctive front doors bearing the monumental Taiji symbol, and passing through the Hall of Light, the two travelers climbed the temple's central staircase and entered the main hall to worship the Perfect Warrior (Zhenwu), Zhang Sanfeng, and the great swordsman Lü Dongbin—the three main deities protecting the mountain. The wafting scent of incense and burning embers signaled their arrival and intentions to the heavens.

Master Du's immortal teacher, the founder of the Heavenly Dragon lineage (Tianlong pai), waited in his quarters to welcome his finest student and his new protégé. A quiet symposium and confirmation followed. The two ancient masters worked together on qigong and meditation to accelerate the young apprentice's cultivation. It was the first of several mysterious closed-door sessions initiating Wu Baolin into the Nine Palaces and Zhang Sanfeng Taijiquan lineages. Eventually, they returned to Beijing but Wu Baolin did not return to the Wudang mountains for forty-five years.

Education and Growth

Master Du had long term plans for his apprentice and as his legal guardian, took the matter to heart. He was also a person of interest and not without enemies, tolerating antagonisms that potentially put Wu Baolin at risk, since the boy was his soft spot. Master Du worried when his student was away, which was often. Wu Baolin was attending school outside the temple during weekdays, an insistence of his parents, who were not totally convinced that a purely monastic education could insure a place setting in New China. Neither could Master Du ignore their family's legacy.

Wu Baolin's family in Beijing honored the system of Confucian education and classical pugilism. They also contributed greatly to traditional Chinese medicine, serving as physicians for over two hundred years and seven generations.

They were responsible for developing some well-known medicines, donated several family recipes to Guan'anmen Hospital, and were indispensable in establishing Tongrentang Pharmaceuticals.

Under the Qing dynasty, the Wu family produced an herbal compendium, the *Yizhong Jinjian* (Golden Mirror of the Orthodox Lineage of Medicine), published by the Imperial Printing Office and honored by the Qianlong Emperor (r. 1735-1796). At the time, Baolin's ancestor Wu Qian led a team of doctors and researchers in the compilation, examining everything known in the realm of Chinese medicine to consolidate, refine, and expand medical knowledge. Vast libraries of information scattered throughout the provinces of China were collected under official auspices. The team's task was to highlight the best, most practicable, and dependable clinical practices. They surveyed and tested antidotes and examined each case with equal attention, from the common cold to life threatening ailments while also going back to the classics of antiquity. In addition, they interviewed many doctors and requested their personal notes, cases, and opinions. The project took the better part of a decade, to be completed in 1742. Groundbreaking and extensive, it has since occupied a worthy place in the annals of Chinese medical history.

Moreover, Wu Baolin's paternal grandfather, Wu Xizhi, served as the personal physician to Puyi (r. 1908-1912), the last emperor. He was the one to mentor Baolin in the family's medicine tradition. In the 1950s, traditional medicine was still strong, but methods of Western science made rapid inroads, and in many cases steamrolled the traditional. As part of this, Wu Baolin's father was sent to medical school in Germany, an increasing example of China's future.

Baolin himself received access to both central and marginal allegiances, receiving a dual education and scholar-warrior training. These were very special circumstances because Daoist monks were not generally allowed to exit the monastery and immerse in secular study. Wu Baolin's before and after school activities, and the weekends, however, were entirely directed by the monastery without outside interference.

It was an ideal arrangement one might presume, but for Wu Baolin there was sometimes the remorse of lost youth passing over him. He could not help but notice his schoolmates after classes playing unsupervised in the afternoon sun while he was returning to the monastery to study more subjects only partially related to his mainstream schooling. He trained and studied every single day, gaining the distinctions of Daoist rational, but he admired his schoolmate's small freedoms and they reciprocated although he did not understand why.

In the Chinese schools, the most popular students are the academically gifted. This certainly described Wu Baolin who regularly finished at the top of his class. His mother was a school teacher in Beijing, and her influence channeled into the classroom, but it was actually his entourage that made him a real stand out.

Wu Baolin was distinguished in many ways. He wore Daoist blue or black monk clothing. His traditional long hair, a symbol of Confucian filial piety, was fashioned in a topknot, but this hairstyle was no longer a trend in China. The 'liberation hairdo', a very short sidewall hair style for men, and a short bob for women, had taken over and was yet another signpost leaning toward western inclinations. Aside from his appearance he was always escorted to and from school by highly skilled warrior monks, who were sworn never to let him out of their sight. Wu Baolin's two bodyguards carried swords. They possessed an obvious martial demeanor, which served as a powerful deterrent toward anything unwarranted.

Walking together with the three monks, and this is where things became fantastically interesting, were a pair of rowdy taijiquan monkeys from the Wudang mountains. They were fun-loving, aggressive, and constantly making their fighting acumen known, in keeping the perimeter clear. The Daoist relied on these animals for their instincts, which proved absolutely accurate in the assessment of danger. During regular school hours however, the monk bodyguards had their own duties to attend to back at the monastery, leaving just one other sentry behind to watch over Wu Baolin during school hours.

The white eagle was nearly as tall as a man when standing on the ground. This stealthy bird of prey stayed in flight high above the entourage, undetected, whenever they were in transit, maintaining the element of surprise. The eagle perched itself either in a tall tree or on the school's rooftop the entire day until class dismissal. He was there to protect Wu Baolin from the dangers of being Master Du's student, from taking uncalled-for risks, and generally steering him clear of any curious wanderings.

The two acolytes were under exceedingly strict orders to return Wu Baolin to the monastery on time, where Master Du would be waiting almost impatiently. Every afternoon for three full hours, Wu Baolin learned and practiced qigong and taijiquan directly in front of his teacher. Once immersed in the training routine, his thoughts of regret dissolved and his heart was free. In these moments, he was totally committed because the ideas being taught to him were ironically the true secrets of protecting childhood innocence and remaining youthful, healthy and happy all of one's life, and maybe for time eternal. All the attention he received did nothing to boost the ego. There were enough surrounding influences to keep the boy humbled in that respect. It did however awaken his heart to the responsibility he was inheriting, by blood and by water. It was neither a luxury nor a burden but a duty he began to embrace.

The Jump

The valley floor drew closer. Meter after meter, the mountain's embedded seams revealed the world's history to Wu Baolin as he took measure of his own life, which was passing before him at lightning speed. He had finally proven himself to be fearless but what good that would do him now? He was thrown off the mountain, and his ambitions were to blame. He knew Master Du could fly but he was not sure about himself. On that steep descent, he came to accept death on his own terms.

Halfway into the jump, he heard a cutting wind move above his position, the ambient sound coming from his blind spot. A last hope perhaps? Only he thought the wind burbled in his ears. The downdraft prevented him from turning around to confirm. He continued to fall at great speed when suddenly— *Snatch!* Like a parachutist pulling on a ripcord, Wu Baolin was harnessed, stretched, and pulled upward from his jacket's shoulder beams, putting him into backslide. His fall rate was nearly at a stop when he craned his head up and around to catch a glimpse of the miracle.

He expected to see the magical appearance of a Buddhist parasol, the auspicious jellyfish like canopy umbrella, used by ancient eastern royalty, but it was not. It was more familiar. It was one of his best friends from the White Cloud Temple and someone he had not seen for almost a year. The talons of the great white eagle, a knight in shining plumage, held his life firmly in the balance. Wu Baolin was exhilarated. The eagle's grip was ten times that of a human hand with twice the wingspan. The white eagle worked its massive wings, fanning and flying him back to the cliff's edge where he had hurled himself off not twenty seconds earlier. His blood surged. He had never felt so alive, so open, so free and so grateful. He was newly minted in that breakthrough moment.

Equally thrilled and impressed, his teacher and fellow monks were there to greet him when his feet touched down. The white eagle stood over him during the celebration. Wu Baolin's stunt had demonstrated courage and utter craziness and craziness is what Daoist cherish most. It was an unrehearsed exam that can only be administered once, and he aced it!

The event took place in the Tianshan mountain range of Xinjiang, which boasts one of the highest elevations in all of China, reaching upward of 24,000 feet. Because of this unique feature, it is home to one of the rarest birds of prey in the world, the great *diao* eagle. Few species can survive at this altitude because of the thinning air and scarcity of wildlife, however, it's a safe haven for the eagles, who belong to a rare ecosystem.

Master Du leaned hard on his young acolyte. All the way up the steep and arduous mountain trail, he hammered in his teaching points. "Every single day when you wake, you should be mentally and physically prepared to practice taijiquan one-thousand times a day. At the park. In the courtyard. In your mind. Anything less is underachieving based on the standard set by the immortal Zhang Sanfeng."

Wu Baolin had already grown accustomed to the pressurized teachings of Master Du. He knew the expectations placed on him by the monastery as well as his own family, were sky-high. Wu Baolin thought the trip to Xinjiang was to be more of a vacation away from the routine chores in Beijing, but the persistent erudition continued right up until the jump. No part of the trip was ever random.

Master Du masterminded the test prearranged with the white sky-general. The only danger Wu Baolin was ever exposed to was not rushing headlong and taking the plunge. That literal leap of faith is what prevented stunting his taijiquan growth. According to the Daoist martial arts code, to achieve true greatness in fighting, one cannot be afraid to die, or live fully. Laozi's words, "Butanzai, bushimi," is a mantra learned by every monk of the White Cloud Temple: "do not fear death, and nothing can harm you!"

Many northern hunters capture eaglets from the nest within the first three months after hatching. The brief period before they learn to fly is critical because once an eagle has flown from the nest it becomes extremely difficult to capture and train. Eagle hunters release their eagles back into the wild after seven years. The White Cloud Temple holds onto their eagles for life.

The purpose of the trip to Xinjiang was to show Wu Baolin how to recapture the eagles. While on holiday, the eagles are given to natural selection, hatching their offspring in the wild. After reproduction is fulfilled they are returned to the monastery, a pact centuries old. What Wu Baolin had succeeded in doing was twofold, passing the test of Zhang Sanfeng Taijiquan and recapturing one of the monastery's precious eagles.

The eagles preferred to stay in their natural habitat yet tend to be torn between freedom and duty. They loved the monks dearly and would miss them if they remained behind; at the same time, they loved their unalloyed freedom. However, as demonstrated in Wu Baolin's jump, the eagles never let their Daoist brothers dive to their death. Jumping is the only surefire way to recapture an adult eagle, compelling them to save you based on the strength of their bond, a mutual affinity mandated by heaven.

The eagle experienced their fair share of pain and sorrow, but these generals of military heritage, when called upon by the temple, ward off tenacious enemies. After Master Du explained these rules to Wu Baolin, some of the other monks began to jump off the mountain and it began raining eagles.

天師聖像

Chapter Two

Zhang Sanfeng

May all who cultivate virtue under heaven,
Obtain good health and longevity.
—Zhang Sanfeng

The Forbidden City in Beijing is an architectural masterpiece designed to preserve, store, and conceal the long history of China. The palace's subterranean infrastructure, the roots of the tree that one cannot see, hold scores and scores of books highlighting the history of Chinese civilization and its many cultural endeavors. As part of an effort to dismiss portions of dynastic antiquity in the 20th century, or at least minimize access to the broader narrative, the vaults were sealed after liberation, but have since been reopened.

The basements of the Forbidden City contain tall cabinets, set up side by side in fifty-yard rows, storage bins where the ancient books are kept. The tomes, about a foot thick and wide as well as three feet high, are stacked horizontally on sturdy cabinet shelves. The cool dark dry conditions prevent them from mildewing and eliminate the risk of excess exposure to heat, dampness, and caustic substances from human handling.

For centuries, archival custodians and historians ordered to preserve these works, have memorized and copied or digitized each volume in order to ensure that the materials survive. Back-up copies are distributed for safekeeping and preserved in much the same way to become the reflective pools for future generations to lament, rediscover, remember, and celebrate their heritage. This is all to say that what has not been revealed, shared, found, or stumbled upon is not proof of nonexistence.

The history of taijiquan goes back to Zhang Sanfeng, a sagely Daoist who spent the better part of his life cultivating himself among the seventy-two known peaks of the Wudang mountains. The mountains house the headquarters of the Southern School of Complete Reality, the Wudang Sect, as well as the [Zhang] Sanfeng lineage subsect, going back to the Song (960-1280) and Yuan (1270-1368) dynasties, when also gunpowder, porcelain, the compass, and paper money were invented. The mountains are covered with monuments erected under the imperial aegis of the Ming dynasty (1368-1644), honoring

Zhang Sanfeng, including named temples, etched steles, ornate statues, and brilliant frescoes. In the *Wang Zhengnan xianchuan* (Epitaph of Wang Zhengnan) by the Qing scholar Huang Zongxi and his son Huang Baijia, mentions Zhang Sanfeng as the progenitor of taijiquan. The standard lineage tree gives Wang Zhengnan as his direct disciple, while others have him a generation removed. Wang taught martial arts to Huang Baijia and also gave his history lessons of taijiquan and Daoist culture. The Huang family lived in Zhejiang, neighboring Hubei. Their capitals, Hangzhou and Wuhan, are less than 350 miles apart. The inscription found on Wang Zhengnan's tomb, moreover, summarizes Zhang Sanfeng's attainments, mentioning his groundbreaking boxing philosophy, prominent students, and extraordinary ability to overcome tremendous odds, such as being greatly outnumbered.

Some works are attributed to Zhang Sanfeng himself. They include the *Jindan zhizhi* (Direct Guide to the Golden Elixir) and the *Jindan mijue* (Secret Formula for the Golden Elixir) as well as six other volumes on personal cultivation and internal alchemy. They emphasize cultivating mood and character to gain a healthy and strong life. All eight volumes were later compiled into one volume, the *Zhang Sanfeng quanji* (Complete Collection of Zhang Sanfeng). Many important taijiquan enthusiasts received them and on their basis expanded and propagated the practice. In addition, there are also secret codices attributed to Zhang Sanfeng, not meant for public consumption.

Despite various efforts at verification, Zhang Sanfeng's historical authenticity and contributions to taijiquan have been put into question. Was he a man, a myth, an immortal, a political pawn, or someone of mistaken identity? Did taijiquan originate before his lifetime? Or much later? Practitioners inheriting oral traditions, academics undertaking strict research, and the general populace all have different perspectives. Sometimes conjecture is taken as fact, sometimes foreign materials are interjected, old and new mindsets clash. Proximity to the taijiquan root—geographical, generational, educational, or political—often results in differences of opinion and perspective. Overall, the issue of the exact dates and personages associated with the origin and early history of taijiquan is complex, discrepancies leading many to give up on Zhang Sanfeng's actual existence and see him as the fabrication of the martial arts novelists.

Part of the reason why he is dismissed as the founder of taijiquan has to do with the fact that serious hermits did not seek limelight or fortune, but made their students take an oath to keep the master's identity secret to minimize their exposures. They focused greatly on devoted spirituality and the cultivation of virtue (*de*), that is, kindness, integrity, and heavenly fervor. Endeavors would just be graced anonymously with unexpected mystery. In his *Dadao lun* (On the Great Way), Zhang Sanfeng notes, "The pure of heart, the filial

minded, the incorruptible, those doing deeds without reward or ulterior motive—they will one day become immortal."

Much confusion also has to do with his great longevity. Zhang Sanfeng is
recorded to have lived for over 200 years, a figure not unusually long for hermits at the time, but inconceivable in modern societies. Records of the White
Cloud Temple show an average age of 110 for their monks going back well
over a millennium, so for Daoist communities, the high numbers are acceptable.
Adding to the speculation are the many reports of his random appearances
over the years. Anyone who has ever attended a high school or family reunion
after many years apart can attest to the dramatic changes people undergo. In
each sighting, Zhang looks different. First noted to be a fledgling government
official and a lithesome Shaolin monk, he is later seen as a robust Daoist mountain man in his eighties, dressed in blue garb with jet-black hair and a full beard,
slapping the outside of thick pottery barrels filled with water which he shatters
with bare hands. Eventually he is spotted as a thin, tight-skinned 200-year-old
forest-dweller, smiling with a single tooth, wearing a straw hat, and gliding up
the shafts of bamboo trees. These anecdotal sightings either add to his legend
or detract from it.

Still, he remains at the heart of taijiquan history, other figures being inter-
changeable. He was, moreover influenced by his predecessors, such as the
monks of the Shaolin Temple, and Daoist internal masters such as Wang
Chongyang and Qiu Chuji. This is hardly a critique and should not deter from
his legacy. What child is born without parents? Of course, without an original
taijiquan template as conclusive evidence, i.e. a system or style of taijiquan that
bears the name Zhang Sanfeng, it stands to reason that the many existing styles
of taijiquan in circulation would serve as the identifying fingerprints and main
representation of the art. This now stands to change. The impractical deletion
of Zhang Sanfeng's absolute participation, the opinion of some, relegates the
prime mover to a conveniently labeled figurehead to augment the art in "Cigar
Store Indian" fashion. Although unintentional, is improper.

The Daoist Canon contains only one practice called taijiquan, with Zhang
Sanfeng as its founder—a title accorded to no other taijiquan master. Also, in
its original form and context, the practice known as Zhang Sanfeng Taijiquan
was never taught outside of the Daoist lineages of the White Cloud Temple and
the Purple Cloud Temple until today. But as fate would have it, China's higher
courts drastically shifted for the first time in a thousand years, opening the
gates and sending out massive amounts of information, thus providing the
chance to share the practice with the whole world. This has happened just as
the art is reaching the four corners, a completely natural and timely occurrence.
Furthermore, this volume is to establish the direct lineage of Zhang Sanfeng
Taijiquan and not any other branch or ancestral system of taijiquan or other
internal boxing schools. It is written for all succeeding taijiquan practitioners
anywhere and of any style. It is the fulfillment of a promise Wu Baolin made to
Master Du and the founder Zhang Sanfeng.

Early Years

As noted in the dynastic history of the Ming, Zhang Sanfeng was born at midnight on April, 9, 1247 in Yizhou City on the northeastern Liaodong peninsula, what is today Liaoning. His given name was Zhang Tong and his courtesy name was Zhang Junbao, the same character ("treasure") as in Wu Baolin. He received the name Sanfeng ("three peaks") only after he was inducted into the Daoist lineage.

His family was originally from the Daoist heritage site of Longhu shan (Dragon Tiger Mountain) in the southwestern portion of Jiangxi, one of the key sacred places of Daoism, along with the Wudang, Qingcheng, and Qiyun mountains. From there his paternal grandfather resettled in Jinzhou, Liaoning. His father, using methods of Daoist fortune-telling, surveyed the stars and constellations in order to locate a prosperous township where he could raise his family and continue his own education and spiritual endeavors. Based on the findings, he decided on Liaodong. There are other stories that mention Shaowu or Nanping in Fujian as his birthplace, connecting him to other local lineages.

The community in Liaodong was well educated in the Chinese classics and the full spectrum of Daoist culture. Young Junbao benefited from this early on. When five years of age, he was struck with an illness that caused the loss of his eyesight. His father was quick to seek medical attention and followed a recommendation that led them to a local Daoist priest with an exceptional healing reputation. The Daoist was able to cure the root cause of the illness, restoring Junbao's vision to normal after seven days. This introduction sparked a fast friendship that led to an affectionate tutorship of classical writing and martial arts instruction, with the Daoist priest teaching him from the works of Daoism, Buddhism, and Confucianism. This was precisely the kind of lucky break his father had hoped for his son on the new grounds.

It is said that Junbao had a photographic memory that allowed him to retain everything he ever read. Daoists are known to develop unique learning tools and techniques to enhance intellectual comprehensions and various other abilities. When Wu Baolin was a young boy, Master Du would open the spines of seven books at once, place them neatly, side-by-side in an overlapping arrangement. Wu Baolin had to read one page from each book going from right to left, and turn to the next seven pages and begin again. It was difficult, but comprehending seven different subjects instantaneously was the standard. Whenever there was a mental block, Master Du would pick up and play the *erhu*, a classical two stringed bowed fiddle. Suddenly, as if by magic, the Chinese characters would float off the pages in three dimensions into Wu Baolin's cerebral cortex and heart, in a type of branding.

Junbao's father, Zhang Juren, had high hopes for his son. Himself a much-admired scholar, he passed the imperial examination at his first attempt, then was offered various good positions with generous salary and benefits.

However, he declined government commissions, opting instead for a life of self-reflection. Because knowledge was his utmost reward, he was looked up to for his certitude. He maintained an open-door policy as a consultant, but he was never again considered for public office.

Junbao's brightness was evident at birth. By the age of twelve, he had studied and memorized the classics, mining their wisdom in ways beyond his years. It was presumed that when he came of age, he would take the imperial examinations and indeed, he passed them with ease, then obtained a government post in Yanjing (Beijing). After several years, however, he found the work unfulfilling. Since his childhood he had been raised as a scholar-warrior, receiving above average instruction in both Chinese philosophy and pugilism, the necessary skills to stand firm.

Following the death of his parents, Junbao resigned from office and returned to Liaodong to settle his parent's estate, giving away their possessions to extended family. At this time, he began to train in an abandoned temple, recovering the passion of his youth. Realizing that this training was just a beginning, he left Liaodong and wandered through the country for thirty years (from Korea to Vietnam), seeking martial edification. He visited, prayed, and inquired at every temple along the way, a reverent custom Master Du passed onto Wu Baolin. There were many celebrated schools of Chinese martial arts in those days, each representing some unique aspect, concept, or philosophy of Chinese culture. Having something of a martial pedigree and with roots deeply entrenched in Longhu shan, he was invited into the Shaolin Temple as a Buddhist monk when the school had an abundant following, exceptional teachers, and government support.

At Shaolin

Zhang Junbao thus became an active warrior monk at Shaolin in Henan for fifteen years. He trained in their martial arts while mastering the Buddhist Canon, also known as the *Tripitaka*. He was drawn to the Shaolin fighting system after receiving a fair amount of instruction from various private teachers of the widespread style.

Established in 495, the Shaolin Temple had standardized Chinese martial arts, reaching prominence under the Tang dynasty. The second emperor of this dynasty, Li Shiming (598-649) particularly appreciated thirteen Shaolin monks who successfully protected his life from assassins and hired many warrior monks as palace guardians and as instructors of the imperial guards and military cadres. He also decreed that the monks could eat meat and drink spirits due to their rigorous training schedules.

Buddhism was also favored under the Yuan dynasty who selected the Shaolin abbot Fuyu as the Grand Preceptor of the royal court. This helped carry on the traditions of the temple without interruption through the Ming when Shaolin methods of hard martial arts were endorsed and started to spread beyond the temple, spreading self-defense techniques among ordinary people along with Buddhist wisdom.

The temple was (and still is) run much like a military institution: rigidly disciplined, highly regimented, with a strict chain-of-command and onerous, never ending training. This was necessary since the warrior monks were also training soldiers in hand-to-hand combat and weapons techniques. Thus, the founder of the Song dynasty, Emperor Taizu (927-976), again instituted a martial arts exchange program, posting military troops at the temple, leaving the temple well-guarded and in good standing. Three of Shaolin's greatest fighting monks—Huiguang, Sengchou, and Huike—may have joined the monastic path following military service.

During Junbao's residency, Shaolin was considered the best martial arts school in the world. It was not unusual for challengers to arrive at the gates. The constant readiness of a strike force was an effective solution to the compulsory rules of engagement associated with the profession of warrior monks. This atmosphere nurtured him; a hard playground, it toughened the body while softening the heart in peace-seeking contemplation. "In times of peace prepare for war. In times of war prepare for peace," as Sunzi has it.

Three significant events occurred at Shaolin to lead him to end his training there and embark on the Daoist path. The first was an encounter with a powerful cook, a rather mysterious figure. The second was a serious bout with invading monks that he and the Shaolin monks lost. And the third was his off-chance discovery of an energy-based training manual.

Wu Baolin learned of these from his teacher. They describe the earliest transformations of Zhang Junbao and his first exposure to internal martial power (*neigong*). The early forms of Daoist internal boxing (*neijia*) were essentially secret daoyin exercise techniques known to few and were rarely ever put on display, mostly kept hidden, masking the invisible force inside other martial styles or as tricks. The application of invisible force was not quite identifiable even by those bearing witness. Although following the established sequence, Junbao began thinking outside the parameters of conventional martial wisdom. There have been many references to his transition from Buddhism to Daoism, from external to internal. However, the popular versions found in literature, film, and television, differ slightly from the Daoist story.

Shaolin monks, using the mountains and forest, train their bodies in all conditions of terrain and weather, outdoor elements burnishing the color of their skin. Partnering with trees in combat training, crawling over rugged mountains, or standing under ice-cold water falls, they consistently exercise the mind like steel. They also meditate in tranquil settings to contemplate the peaceful teachings of Buddhism and review the wild animals associated with their signature movements and styles, looking to unlock their deeper secrets. In addition, the forms, movements, and imagery of Shaolin martial arts are understood as the expression of Buddhist scriptures, combining meditation with martial prowess.

One afternoon, after a long training session, Junbao went strolling through the woods, and caught sight of a warm steam billowing through the opening of a cave. It was in an area he went to occasionally for quiet meditation and to take a breather from the rigors of training. As he stepped in and walked through the cavernous limestone hallway, he was struck to see an elderly man standing over a large wooden tub grasping a large flat spoon that resembled a canoe paddle or a monk's spade weapon. The man smoothly stirred round and round through the heavy thickening rice porridge, moving in a circular pattern. The fire beneath was low and consistent.

Since Junbao practiced Buddhist compassion, and because he was taught to always provide assistance to the elderly and small children, he stepped in and volunteered to relieve him. Based on the amount of porridge, he assumed there was a large family to feed. The man graciously stepped aside, thanking the young monk for his kindness as he wiped light beads of sweat and steam from his brows.

He tried to imitate the elder's technique but was soon humbled, finding the task impossible. Stuck from the start, he tried again and again, believing that once he produced enough momentum the spoon would glide like his broadsword cutting through a bamboo tree. He hit all his stances, anchored his elbows, and leveraged every angle, but nothing moved except his heart, pounding in his chest. He curiously inquired as to how it was possible for the elder to be so proficient in such a strenuous exercise, but he modestly passed it off as years of refined practice. Giving up, Junbao left the cave in wonder, thinking perhaps it was really that simple, that he needed more practice.

During the Tang dynasty, the Shaolin monks made significant innovations to their fighting system, greatly bolstering its reputation. Although a private institution, Shaolin was public in its representation of Buddhism and its well-known martial-arts style. The world was a fighting stage and unquestionably run by martial law. The act of making any martial arts public suggested an invitation to all and created a setting where young men could learn from others. Thus it earned the plaque hanging over the temple gate: "Best Martial Arts in the World." This achievement garnered attention from far and wide, and because of the exalted title, the Shaolin monks were obligated to defend the plaque, playing host to anyone who stepped forward. Shaolin monks were both an inspiration and a target.

Several days after Junbao met the elder in the cave, a group of esoteric northern monks came crashing the gates of the temple, requesting a friendly competition. Although friendly in intent soon the adrenaline began to push, reputations were on the line, and serious injuries common. Hard knocks were often necessary to force surrender, and applied without apologies. Although dangerous, it was the only measure to test levels of cultivation.

Junbao and his fellow fighters decisively lost their match with the monks in a major skirmish. Following defeat, the plaque was pried off the gate frame and discarded to the ground, adding insult to injury. The title now belonged to the northern school—until an uninvited guest joined the warring parties: the elder from the cave. He was alien and enigmatic, with no place in the scenario, but that did not stop him. He boldly strode into the action, picked the discarded plaque off the ground, and proclaimed it his own, saying he had good use for the wood. But the northern monks needed it as proof that they had won the fight and refused to surrender it. Unintimidated, the elder claimed that his current possession of the sign was proof of ownership, daring them to prove otherwise.

The monks stormed at the elder, ripping back at the plaque, which he held firmly under his arm. Monk after monk was either swatted, fanned, or punted away with the easy turn of the elder's waist, failing to grab the plaque. When it became apparent that their efforts were an exercise in futility, and injuries piling up, the elder walked away undisturbed, carrying the plaque across his back and leaving back toward his cave. The monks also left, but they made it perfectly clear that martial arts in China were evolving in unforeseen ways.

The elder had restored Shaolin's face by taking away the gloating and the bragging rights of the invaders. Junbao felt distinguished for having played a part in every stage of the day's events and for witnessing the ascetic's powers,

not once but twice in the same week. He determined that the elder was a Daoist hermit but kept his new insights to himself. It was the secret of the wooden
spoon, he thought. He felt a strong pull to follow the elder through this new
door, intuitively ready to leave Shaolin, having found a new dream.

Running away or quitting the school before reaching the required goals
would result in embarrassment to the family name. Shaolin was an institution,
that held on to its assets, investing heavily in people to secure its future. The
only dignified way to leave was to fight one's way out against the best of the
best. Although a remarkable monk, Junbao at that point was not among the top
fighters of his generation. Inspired by the elder, he began to train harder.

Beyond the cave, he had other secret hiding places near the temple. One
afternoon, ready for a nap, he strolled into another part of the complex known
as the Forest of Pagodas at the foot of the mountain. A field of Nepalese-
inspired pagodas, it is a cemetery containing the ashes of many enlightened
Shaolin masters. Although a place of yin, warrior monks entered it frequently,
offering their respects and gaining the protection of the ancestral spirits.

When he entered that day, something came over him. The pace of his
walk quickened, and he was pushed in a direction not of his own choosing. He
weaved in and out of the stone trees for several minutes, until he was brought
to a standstill, facing a tall pagoda. Pushed forward by unknown encourage-
ment, he began climbing step by step until he passed through an open window
at the topmost layer. He found himself in a cubic room with a low ceiling and
settled down to rest. Spreading his arms and legs across the floor, his fingers
touched an object heavily caked in dirt.

He brushed off the outer layer and found it was a book on energy practice.
He opened the cover to sounds of fracturing stitch bindings, and began to look
at the interior. Although devoid of words, it contained instructions he followed
through his *qi*. The more he stared onto the blank pages, the more he deci-
phered secret wisdom like evanescent images made by rolling clouds. As if he
had a past-life connection to the material, Junbao absorbed the contents of the
book and began to grow inside. The sensations were warming and energizing.

Taking the book with him, he continued to work with it. The more he
studied its instructions, the faster he transformed. His dreams became more
vivid and the need for sleep evaporated. His martial forms were more dynamic
and purposeful. His attitude intensified, and newfound power deepened his

voice. The changes were borderline reckless and even threatening. He was suddenly game for anything.

As the opportunity presented itself, Junbao fought his way through the ranks of the warrior monks—poised, possessed and unstoppable. Afterward, he was given the choice to pursue a life of Buddhism outside of the temple, or to be promoted to higher ranks of the priesthood. But he had long ago made up his mind, thinking of the mysterious cook who surprised everyone, and decided to pursue his destiny outside society. When he thus disappeared from the martial-arts community, he was already a legend.

Wudang

After leaving Shaolin, Zhang Junbao wandered widely through the country, visiting many mountains of China and settling for a time near Baoji in Shaanxi. The three major peaks of this region are where he acquired his Daoist title, Master Sanfeng, and a monument commemorating this is still found in the Jintai Temple of Baoji City.

Zhang Sanfeng knew that true immortals lived in the serenity of the mountains. Studying all sorts of works and scriptures, he hoped to increase his understanding with proper edification provided by an elevated teacher. At the age of 67 (an *Yijing* number, representing the dragon), he met a Daoist recluse known as Perfected Fire Dragon (Huolong) with a lineage going all the way back to Laozi. He taught Sanfeng various techniques of immortality, nurturing his seeds of Dao, then left. His farewell letter runs, "My Daoist name is Firedragon. I live unnoticed in the Great Void. After imparting immortal teachings to Zhang Sanfeng, I now head east to the isle of Penglai in the sea."

After receiving the transmission, Sanfeng worked hard, but four years into his cultivation, he found his progress too slow and decided to move on, turning to the Wudang mountains where he built himself a hut on the north face of Flag Stretching Peak. Every day, he offered incense to the main deity god of the range, the Perfect Warrior and practiced assiduously. After nine years, he finally realized the mysteries of Dao and their unlimited potential. A few years after this, at the age of 81, he created taijiquan.

Chinese culture originated at the banks of the Yellow River, and many architects of its civilization were born near there, drawing profound knowledge from the spirit of its dragon. The deepest secrets eventually made their way to the Wudang mountains, high peaks rich with magical spring waters, naturally growing medicines, and many divine energies. Heavenly and earthly *qi* mingle in the cloudy mist as mortals and immortals live together. The Wudang mountains, close to the geographical center of China, harbor a life of unique opportunity to practice and celebrate Dao.

Presiding over the mountains is the Perfect Warrior with his powerful symbol of a black tortoise entwined with a snake. The creatures represent the two major generals that serve under the god's command. The Perfect Warrior, is a senior protector of Daoism and the guardian spirit of the northern sky, aligned with water, the most fundamental of the five phases of Chinese cosmology. In addition, the Perfect Warrior is venerated as a founding father figure of Chinese civilization and regarded as a magician capable of controlling the elements and enforcing karmic law. Many movements in Daoist martial arts are based on the tortoise defending itself against the snake; the combat arrangement of the eight trigrams, moreover, originally appeared on the shell of a tortoise rising from the Yellow River, in the so-called *Hetu* (River Chart). In his human form, the Perfect Warrior similarly carries an armored shell under his robes.

The Wudang mountains are called "martial" in close connection to the deity and understood as the country's main stronghold against any violation of physical or spiritual law. In this effort, they stand for the staunch preservation of yin and yang and all Daoist thought. Like the White Cloud Temple, they are a place of knights that guard the teachings and the power of the religion, keeping order and balance throughout the cosmos.

The Perfect Warrior
attained the highest state
of spiritual enlightenment
and immortality by refin-
ing his entire being into
pure spirit-light after a
lifetime of cultivation. A
fresco telling the story of
his triumphant success
survives on a wall of the
Mozhen Jing (Grinding
Needle Temple) on the
mountain, while his main

sanctuary is on the Golden Summit (Jinding) on the very top. The temple is
flanked by two cranes on Heavenly Pillar (Tianzhu) Peak, while the other sev-
enty-one peaks show their reverence. In its halls the fire of pure-yang energy
burns brightly, especially during the mid-autumn festival, when the gods visit
the earthly realm.

The Wudang mountains, well protected geographically by narrow gorges,
have always been a powerful stronghold. Traditionally, its area was used for
soldiers to come and regroup, restore, and develop new strategic ideas in a safe,
protected environment, and even today it is still the home of important military
installations. However, just about when internal martial arts came to the fore,
northern armies were invading, gaining much Han Chinese territory. Upon the
unseating of the Song dynasty, the Mongols ruled under the title of Yuan—the
only foreign invaders ever to reach Wudang. The northern nomads tended to
be larger in physical stature than the Chinese, giving them an obvious physical
advantage on the battlefield and leading to many victories. These were pro-
foundly stressful times, when the threat to Chinese civilization became reality,
echoing earlier times, such as when the Great Wall was first built under the
First Emperor, Qin Shihuang (260-210 BCE).

All this culminated into a major challenge. In order to prevail and move
out from under the knife, something new, original, and undecipherable was
needed, a flexible antibody to cast aside the immutable. These were ideal conditions for developing new strategies, anything that could depose the foreign
masters. Necessity became the mother of invention, inspiring the creation of
taijiquan.

Many layers of informed instruction provided the impetus for the development of taijiquan. The most widespread story is that Zhang Sanfeng received
a transmission from a snake and a magpie locked in battle. People have retold
this tale for centuries: the visceral descriptions of the battle are some of the
best examples of taijiquan theory in action. This experience was the precursor
to a much larger event, when the teachings of the Perfect Warrior appeared to
Zhang in a dream. But the actual transmission—the main download that would

define a new breed of Chinese fighter—happened inside the main hall of a Wudang temple during the mid-autumn festival.

One afternoon, a crowd of birds alerted Zhang Sanfeng of an event taking place outside the window of his study. As he peered out onto the ground, he was surprised to see a magpie and a snake pitted against each other. This, of course, was unusual—not the everyday predator-and-prey face-off one would typically find in the wild. The two were not natural enemies but more like antagonists. The theatrics were perfectly staged, and the fighting techniques they displayed gave Zhang valuable insights into new fighting concepts. He watched curiously.

The wise snake patiently harnessed intrinsic energy, remaining still. When it retracted and coiled its body upon itself, it became a spring-loaded, explosive organism that could unfurl and attack at lightning speed. The magpie, on the other hand, was not intimidated but calmly opened and crossed its wings forward, pinning the snake down. At other times, it lightly floated off the floor prior to impact, anticipating the strike and absorbing the deadly force across an opened and curved wingspan. This allowed it to redistribute and diffuse the concentration of venomous power through its soft feathers, offering a widened flat surface that gave the snake nowhere to sink its fangs. It was all very impressive—meeting the hardness with softness. Zhang Sanfeng saw a need for both.

The magpie, however, was not just on the defensive; it was also loud and aggressive during the provocation. It levitated off the ground, adding to its list of advantages a fourth dimension, so to speak. It stayed light on its feet to create new angles of attack. The hardened beak of the magpie was strong enough to break through the tough scales of the snake, when given the chance. Its attitude gave it the upper hand. To the magpie, the snake was nothing more than an oversize earthworm. But the snake's defense was noteworthy and admirable nonetheless.

Zhang Sanfeng noticed its body, in the form of a helix, constantly coiling—much like a wooden top or a barber pole perpetually spinning. When rocks are thrown at a spinning top, for instance, they carom and the tossed rocks careen off. The circular patterns, gliding movements, and shifting positions, when put into service, kept the snake from losing the offensive. In addition, the snake used its tail to whip over the top and strike the magpie's head and body, or sweep around to the magpie's blind spots, thus disrupting its footing and concentration as well as drawing energy in from its opponent to use for its next movement. It's no surprise, then, that both animals are considered to be gods by Daoists.

He duly categorized the two creatures and their unique individual styles into yin and yang. The snake was yin. It lived underground, was coldblooded, and slept in hibernation for half the seasons. It had a hardened exterior and, when attacking, was almost fully extended in a straight line, although the recoil was extremely swift. It traveled horizontally on its belly or sat still when meditating or sleeping.

The magpie, on the other hand, was yang. It lived in the trees above the ground, was warm-blooded, and was active for most of the seasons. It had a soft exterior and traveled by air, stood in a vertical posture on two legs when awake or asleep, and was always ready to escape danger. It used its opened wings in a rounded half-domed shape and its beak when attacking; its wings were akin to shields and its beak a sword. In his mind, Zhang Sanfeng began to combine the two, light and grounded, floating yet rooted, evasive while present and engaged. His motto became, "Float like a magpie and ground like a snake."

The Mid-Autumn Festival

Soon after it was the time of the mid-autumn festival, a thanksgiving holiday in observance of the harvest moon during the eighth lunar month (late September), when the full moon is biggest and brightest, closer to earth than at other times, its effects on the ocean's tides and the earth's magnetic fields peaking. It is honored by the symbolic eating of moon cakes, delicious round, pie-like pastries filled with lotus-seed or red-bean paste, often containing a golden salted duck egg-yolk to symbolize the moon.

Daoists in addition believe that the moon is the original mother of all and honor the festival as a period of holy purification. The monks begin their religious duties 49 days before with various measures of purification and intense meditation. Their daily routine turns into an almost exclusive yin-based regimen in order to take full advantage of the moon's qi at its zenith. Wu Baolin, when young, was locked in a room for the full 49 days, left to practice round the clock. The moon's energy field is so palpable during this time that a practitioner of Five Centers Facing Heaven Qigong may absorb a year's worth of lunar essence in a short time.

Also, the mid-autumn festival is when the immortals and fairies who live in the heavens choose to come to earth. A grand procession streams down from the stars as the celestial beings make their way into the human realm. They arrive to give messages and spread teachings, correct misunderstandings, perform healing, bless fated relationships, and help clean the slate for fresh starts. Almost all of this is done with an anonymous, invisible touch. If human beings are fully immersed in *qi* cultivation during this time, they may stumble upon a course of extraordinary happenings and worth. It is a time to "count one's lucky stars."

The most literal soul-searching happens at this time, during a ceremony called *jiangling*. It is a limited window of opportunity to connect with one's spirit guide, heavenly teacher, or higher astral self. Receptivity usually occurs on the earthly plane, although not exclusively. This is an edification period for monks as well as all seekers of profound wisdom. By practicing cultivation under these conditions, practitioners openly call their higher self from heaven for an exchange of ethereal information, spiritual evolution, and physical healing.

In this context, the ritual component of Zhang Sanfeng Taijiquan ensures that the secret star above and the original self in the body align completely. At

the moment of birth, these two are separated, the accompanying trauma leaving most people longing to rejoin with the other half of their essence. This feeling of lack or vacancy sends many on a spiritual journey: some choose to fill it through the marriage of souls; others find it in career or friendship; yet others attempt to go directly to the source. Because the secret star is always in line with one's personal destiny, it can and does guide the original self by optimizing life's choices. It is like an original GPS of destiny. This fully connected alignment is how Zhang Sanfeng came to realize the new dimension of taijiquan. It happened through a dreamed communication with the god.

During the mid-autumn festival of 1328, after making himself presentable, lighting incense, and setting out offerings of fresh fruit and flowers on the altar, Zhang Sanfeng stood solemnly before the Perfect Warrior and the other deities high in the wings. It was his habit to call on the heavens for knowledge, guidance, and healing during this time. He still worked on improving his range of skills to stay current in the martial world, evolve the forms, overcome and undo aging, and maintain a sharp mind. But these were not his only motivations. He sincerely wanted to leave a legacy that would benefit humanity. He made his wish and, at midnight, began to prepare for the Five Centers Facing Heaven Qigong and the *jiangling* ceremony. The full moon had already risen above the horizon.

He quieted his monkey mind by addressing the random thoughts that spun round his head, quickly and concisely answering any mental questions until they slowed and became inactive. It was important to him to empty his mind methodically by acknowledging any incessant thoughts and providing

closure to ongoing situations. Then he worked through the practice from beginning to end and stood perfectly still with his eyes closed and called upon the
heavenly teacher to appear. He was patient.

After some time, he felt a presence in the room. He relaxed his body and
let go of any fixed ideas. Once he settled into this frame of mind, he began to
move inexplicably in anomalous patterns. Eventually he stopped moving and
opened his eyes to face the altar, seeing the statues came to life, turning like on
a carousel, revolving faster and faster until vortexes of *qi* surrounded them.
Images of snake and magpie appeared before him, right next to the Perfect
Warrior.

Spontaneously, Zhang began to move in rotary fashion, faster and faster,
his body ebbing and flowing, pushed and pulled in the process like by currents
in a whirlpool. His feet remained strongly connected below, and his steps low
and fluid. His mind was nothingness, centered and calm like the eye of the
storm. Explosive bursts of balanced power came crashing down in waves, the
riptides hidden internally below the calm demeanor of his body. It was the start
of a new fighting style not even he could recognize, combining the totality of
his own life events with an extraordinary cohesion. He had somehow been re-
arranged and made whole again.

He moved along with the ceremony, then engaged in a vision quest each
night of the festival, working for many hours until the festival's end. By then he
had formed a working basis for Zhang Sanfeng Taijiquan. He would continue
to develop these new discoveries and techniques for decades to come, increasingly synthesizing all kinds of Daoist tenets into the practice. He married the
best of Daoist principles with the best of Chinese martial arts, the metaphysical
with the fist, giving that which is latent an incredible potentiality.

Wudang Revival

Prior to the modern development of the Wudang mountain's spiritual community—the elaborate construction of the various temples and monasteries—no
emperor had shown genuine interest in the alpine refuge. When word of Zhang
Sanfeng's discovery of taijiquan began to spread, interest surged. He was by
then already a living legend and reportedly could defeat the best warriors with a
single move, using a mysterious imperceptible force. Taijiquan heralded a revolutionary change.

Thus, in 1413, three years before the construction of the Forbidden City
in Beijing, the third Ming Emperor, Zhu Di (r. 1402-1424), ordered the construction of an elaborate Daoist temple on the Wudang mountains, the Palace
of Great Harmony (Taihe gong). This followed the traditional model of dynasties strategically aligning themselves with a geographic power-point, a center
that represented one of the five phases and symbolized the core of power. It
was activated particularly during wars, conquests, and other events where the

emperor wanted to secure victory or ensure the protection of his people, integrating the theory of the five phases with imperial decision-making and the peace of the nation.

The Palace of Great Harmony was designed as one such strategic power-point. Although over 600 miles from Beijing, it became the focal point of dynastic power, considered as important as the Forbidden City. It took ten years to complete the construction, requiring massive strategy, deployment, and allocation of resources—the cost over a million taels of silver.

It was now clear that there were very specific motivations involved in the construction of the temples and palaces on the Wudang mountains—the emperors often did this as a way to place them in some sort of good favor. If well received, perhaps these gestures could gain them a consistent audience with the legendary Daoist immortals. Their magical resources and direct connections with the heavenly realms were well-known and sought out by imperial families for centuries to help them navigate and dominate the entire Asian continent.

Part of this motivation was to lure the enlightened Daoist Zhang Sanfeng out of hiding, in the hope of making him a master adviser and alchemical teacher to enhance and prolong the dynasty. There is a traditional belief, articulated in the *Yijing*, that the accretion of wealth is limited to three generations. In other words, success reaches its zenith during the third generation, after decline sets in. This also means that dynastic rule is limited: opinions turn rigid, outlooks become narrow, and corruption and stagnation ensue. Just as different crops flourish in different seasons, leadership must be infused with youth, change, and creative spirit. For decades and decades, government officials searched for Zhang Sanfeng in the hope that he could provide all that, but his whereabouts remained unknown. Despite the government's attempt to solicit his presence through imperial edicts delivered to Wudang, he remained unresponsive, reclusive, and elusive.

This is not unusual behavior for a Daoist. When Mao Zedong came personally calling on the White Cloud Temple, Master Du similarly refused to leave his seclusion. However, upon the chairman's third visit, Wu Baolin's Daoist uncle managed to persuade Master Du, to answer just two questions: "How long will I live?" and "How long will I be in power?" Master Du was extremely reluctant to answer these questions, as he did not want to get involved in politics, but eventually he answered "eighty-three" to the first question and "forty-one" to the second, based on *Yijing* calculations. These same numbers (8341) would later surface on the uniforms of the Central Security Bureau of the Communist Party, the private security detail assigned to high-ranking leaders. Mao had become chairman of the politburo and *de facto* leader in 1935. He died in 1976, 41 years later, at the age of 83.

Emperor Zhu Di, too, was persistent and undertook several trips to the Wudang mountains in search of Zhang Sanfeng, but without success. In his travel log he notes that while searching the mountains for Zhang, he met an old Daoist monk sitting on the side of a footpath, idly passing the day. He ques-

tioned the old monk on the whereabouts of Zhang Sanfeng. He replied, "Do not even attempt to locate this sage and even if you are so lucky to find him you still may not recognize him sitting before you. And if he catches wind that you seek his audience, he will hide where you will not look." Not willing to accept defeat, the emperor ignored the monk, dismissing him as crazy, and marched on.

When he still could not find Zhang Sanfeng, the emperor retreated to his camp. Some days later, he began to think about that apparently insignificant meeting with the crazy old Daoist. For no apparent reason, he could not shake the image of the old monk. Suddenly, it dawned on him that the old unkempt man was none other than Zhang himself. Realizing that his only meeting with the famed sage had already come to pass, he ordered the construction of a new temple called Temple of Meeting the Perfected (Yuzhen gong), thereby to commemorate this fortunate encounter. The temple was original in that it did

not follow the same architectural blueprints as imperial palace layouts and its site was where Zhang Sanfeng practiced his austerities, once built becoming his true home temple. Later destroyed by fire, today only brick walls and other building materials remain, such as his hand carved stone bed, old steles, and the raised one-piece stone platforms that supported the enormous bronze statues of Zhang Sanfeng, now protected at the Wudang Museum of China. Highlighting its significance, Yuzhen gong is the first temple encountered astride the original gate, Xuanyue Archway, a masterpiece stone carving, the imagery linking generations of the Complete Reality School, through the Tang, Yuan, and Ming dynasties. The temple is currently under full renovation.

From Zhu Yuanzhang, the founder of the Ming dynasty, to Emperor Zhu Di, many leaders made concerted efforts to find the legendary Daoist, without success. Each tried to lure him to court, but Zhang Sanfeng enjoyed the peace of the natural world in the Wudang mountains too much to leave. His demeanor toward the emperors and lack of cooperation with the imperial court earned him great respect from the Ming dynasty, who bestowed upon him the title

Great Daoist Master. A bronze tortoise and towering stele standing at the Purple Cloud Temple bear an inscription to describe the special envoy that traveled to the Wudang mountains in the earnest hope of entreating Zhang Sanfeng to visit the capital. It says, "Your virtue is of the highest order. None measure up to you. Your endeavors are in perfect harmony with nature, imaginative and mysterious. My skills and wisdom are insufficient, and underdeveloped virtue. I write these characters to you in the earnest hope that we may one day come face to face."

It was precisely this type of dedication, unwavering focus, and resistance to worldly indulgences that helped Zhang Sanfeng break through level after level of self-cultivation. It was this broad but single-minded simplicity and the absence of distraction that also kept him relevant. Though the emperors of the Ming dynasty never found him, his legacy grew out of the dense forest of the Wudang mountains, forever cementing him as the founder of internal martial arts.

Fighting Fit

By all accounts, Zhang Sanfeng was a mountain man and a martial genius. The two characters for "man" and "mountain" joined form the word for "immortal." Zhang Sanfeng was a naturalist whose appearance reflected his surroundings in addition to the many transformations that take place when one practices in the wilderness. Aside from anecdotal sightings, descriptions suggest that his body was built like that of a turtle and his bones like that of a crane. He had intensely bold eyes and large ears, a beard with whiskers as sharply honed as spears, and a large bamboo hat otherwise described as a percussion symbol, most of the time draped behind him to shield his strength while inadvertently augmenting his already turtle-like body.

His everyday attire was predictable and never reflected the fashions of the day. Instead, he wore the same shirt year-round. Perhaps a more thoughtful wardrobe would have been a distraction from his training and meditation, which were often spontaneous and strongly moved by the spirit. Then again, perhaps the light vest and plain shirt he wore were his camouflage, the lack of sophistication a  way to remain ambiguous. He could eat vast amounts of food in one sitting or abstain entirely for months at a time. The horsetail whisk was another distinctive part of Zhang Sanfeng's appearance and aura. "Extra-ordinary is the person who holds the horsetail whisk," as the ancient saying goes.

Only a few trusted disciples knew Zhang Sanfeng's whereabouts at any given time, if he decided to disclose his location to them. They include Song Yuanqiao, Yu Lianzhou, Yu Daiyan, Zhang Songxi, Zhang Cuishan, Yin Liting, and Mo Shenggu, also known as the Seven Heroes of Wudang. While many consider them fictional, because their names are found in unsubstantiated martial arts novels, Zhang used them in a chain-of-command to help train the over 600 students the Ming government sent to the mountains to spread the benefits of taijiquan in the country. Of course, there were other students who were not affiliated with the government and made it to the mountain on their own. Wang Zongyue, who wrote on behalf of Zhang Sanfeng, was one of them. His comprehensive discussion of taijiquan came to be widely reproduced and distributed. Another student, Sun Biyun, although not an accomplished practitioner, managed the infrastructure and development of the Wudang temples across the range.

Not mentioned in the popular history books is the standout, Zhang Daishan. He was the top-rated student of Zhang Sanfeng, achieving the highest levels in taijiquan. Three more generations came after him, before reaching Master Du Xinling.

Zhang Sanfeng himself taught many of these trainees, able to work even in advanced age because of an important training secret. After each practice session, he would sit on a wooden peach-tree chair at the edge of the court—peach being the wood of longevity, able to remove fatigue, aches, and soreness. After sitting on this chair, he would spring back to his feet with renewed vitality and practice even more. Several of his disciples eventually started their own lineages both on and off the mountains, but always under his guidance. These many streams of knowledge poured off the mountain and eventually made their way into mainstream Chinese culture.

Zhang Sanfeng diligently kept up with other routines to stay fit. Whenever possible, he drank water from two fresh coconuts, but only after exercising with them first: after all, the water that sloshes inside a coconut mimics the water that moves inside of a human being. This allowed him to understand and sense the internal motions of an opponent—their action and inaction, alike.

He also practiced swordplay under moonlight to recharge his body, the sword becoming a figurative lightning rod that attracted *qi* and passed it into his meridian system. Short of teaching formal classes, he was rarely seen practicing taijiquan alone because he preferred working at night under the cover of darkness, thereby to lose himself in a meditative state. To deepen his breathing, he would climb the Golden Summit on windy nights; to deepen his understanding, he would spend rainy days catching up on his studies of the classics. All of this kept him young and energetic, free of stress, bright of mind, and healthy on all fronts.

Some of his special gifts eventually became the markers of achievement in taijiquan. After a heavy snow, he would walk along the paths in and around the temple without leaving a single footprint behind. This skill became known as "walking upon snow and leaving no tracks." And when he descended upon the snowy courtyard during practice, the snow would melt around his every step, leaving the stone ground covered in clear water in his wake.

When all was said and done, Zhang Sanfeng preferred the solace of the mountains and rivers and the curious activities of animals to the company of human beings. After all, nature had more to teach him about the mysteries of the cosmos. He studied it deeply so that he could reclaim what had been lost by those living in modern societies. To counter humanity's diminishing drive and sixth sense, he would disappear into nature with his family of monkeys and entrusted cranes.

His monkeys would gather fruit from the trees and pull various grubs for him to eat. There was one in particular—a legendary white male ape which he named Xueding, "Learning Stability." The beast was exceptionally intelligent compared to other primates, quite able to learn taijiquan by simply observing Zhang Sanfeng. Teaching primates to calm their heart and spirit is often a futile act; primates are unpredictable and rambunctious by nature. Daoists call the heart the monkey-mind, the seat of concentration, because a wandering mind makes spiritual cultivation impossible. Miraculously, after scores of training sessions, Zhang Sanfeng was able to train Xueding far beyond the others. Xueding was not simply a parlor trick. He was a loyal subject and a true talent, and living proof that taijiquan was spiritually evolutionary. Just as in the Legend of the White Snake, where the white snake spirit living in the waters of West Lake of Hangzhou, aspires to become an immortal, Xueding was also the beneficiary of practicing Daoist arts. His body became humanistic, possessing a relaxed balanced upright posture and calm demeanor, and compassionate eyes, despite the full body of white hair. Whenever Zhang walked through the forest, he would execute various fighting techniques on the trees, using different parts of his body, breaking off dead branches. Then Xueding and the monkeys would pick up and carry the broken pieces to use as firewood. Xueding was a master in taiji long staff.

The cranes, on the other hand, served as Zhang Sanfeng's air force. They kept him safe by warning him of any intruders even several miles away, giving him and his entourage ample time to execute any contingency measures. They deterred wild tigers and pythons from entering into the restricted areas. Often unnervingly close due to their confidence and tactical shrewdness, they rerouted predators and protected the perimeter around the monks. However, when the deflective tactics failed—and when retreat was no longer a choice—Zhang Sanfeng would stand his ground.

Even if the attacker happened to be a snake, he was unfazed. He knew the secret of defeating snakes, and could slip through its fast strike, using one hand to grab the serpent by the neck just behind the head and the other to grab its central body. He would slide his grip down to the lower portion of the snake. By using the "opposing forces" principle of yin and yang, he would straighten the snake's body, his arms moving apart and diagonally in order to defuse the snake's greatest strength: its ability to coil. This technique, known as "Parting the Wild Horse's Mane", was done with a swift moving stance, a concentrated turning of the waist. Zhang Sanfeng would throw the snake's rigid body against a mountain wall, easily bursting and breaking its body into several pieces, later dried and turned into medicine.

Similarly, when mountain tigers came to compete, he knew precisely how to attack their weakness. Martial masters have always revered and studied tigers, a mountain's most dangerous hunter, fearless and ruthless. When a wild tiger challenged Zhang Sanfeng, he had to defeat it then and there—giving it a second chance to come around would be dangerous. (Familiarity breeds confidence, as they say.) Thus, whenever a tiger lunged at him, looking to draw first blood, he would evade the attack by turning and angling his body, minimizing his width, so that the tiger would miss their mark. Taking advantage of the tiger while it was in midair, he would apply the "Bend the Bow-Shoot the Tiger" technique of capturing the tiger's hind legs and pulling them apart, tearing the groin and tendons. Indeed, he had so much admiration for the tiger's fighting prowess that he paid extensive homage to the tiger in his taijiquan form, high-lighting both the tiger's strengths and weaknesses.

Both of these techniques illustrate a key fighting principle in Daoist martial arts: a quick and precise elimination of the opponent. The world of nature predicates itself on survival. Both of these techniques, "Parting the Wild Horse's Mane" and "Bend the Bow-Shoot the Tiger", take a no-nonsense approach to fighting. As observed through the centuries, natural hunters and fighters instinctually attack in only two areas when going in for the kill: the throat and the groin. Daoist martial arts are derived directly from wild animals. According to Daoists, if you do not directly attack the throat or the groin, you do not really understand the essence of natural combat. If you try and run away from a tiger, its first instinct is to impair your ability to flee by attacking the tendons, loins, and groin. However, when a tiger is confronted head-on, it will immediately move in for the throat—which Zhang Sanfeng would anticipate and avoid by attacking the tiger's groin. This is why he would grab the throat of the snake first before gaining control of the rest of the body.

Chapter Three

Animal Prowess

Daoism, with some roots in shamanism, is deeply connected to nature. Long before the West inspired Beijing to undergo accelerated modernization, the law required monks to be assigned a companion upon entering the society of the White Cloud Temple. This companion, usually some kind of a thought-provoking pet, would act and serve as the initiate's teacher. The assigned companion was not necessarily of the newcomer's own choosing but had to match on the initiate's characteristics as observed by senior masters. There were no restrictions on the nature of the companion—it could come from the animal kingdom, wild or domesticated, or the realm of plants (flowers, trees, and so on). Even precious metals or stones such as granite, crystals, jade, gold, and iron could become an initiate's new companion. The idea behind this pairing was to match the personal *qi* of the initiate with an appropriate enhancer and model. There could be more than one affinity depending on the complexity of the initiate's incarnation and the precise data from the priests' evaluation.

This evaluation or examination took into account the natural characteristics and tendencies of the subject and, if necessary, in a thousand-and-one ways. They applied the science of Chinese physiognomy to form ideas based on clues, which were combined like pieces of a puzzle. These observations were culled from the body's surface as well as its interior; any veils of secrecy were lifted under special pretense. The priests asked many carefully crafted questions. What does this person resemble in the world (monkey, snake, elephant, kangaroo, eagle, fish, etc.)? What is his or her body type? What are signature behaviors and mannerisms we can glean? What is the extent of his or her physical abilities? Does this person have any special eating habits, cravings, or dietary preferences? Does he or she produce any innate sounds or primeval corporeal movements without forethought? They also analyzed the initiate's sleeping habits and sleeping-and-sitting positions. They reasoned that the easiest times to catch sight of the animal soul was when the subject was totally relaxed and let his or her guard down, which happened most often during sleep, acupuncture, massage, intoxication, or enjoyment of a delicious meal.

Initiates to the White Cloud Temple were not the only individuals to experience this nuanced process of discovering a person's animal soul. Elizabeth

Taylor, goddess of the American silver screen, once consulted Wu Baolin because she was curious about her original nature and animal soul. Master Wu invited her for a meal to discuss it in more detail. When they sat down at the restaurant, he insisted on choosing the food from the menu. She agreed. Even before the food arrived, Master Wu, chatting with her, had already begun the process of close observation and gathering clues about her soul.

There were seven dishes laid out on the table that day, and of those seven Elizabeth Taylor seemed only interested in one: the chicken. Master Wu gently enticed her with the other well-prepared dishes, but she could not be bothered, even though there were no frog legs, grasshoppers, or anything excessively exotic that might curb an American appetite. For the duration of the meal, only the chicken appealed to her. As the meeting drew to a close, she waited for Master Wu make his calculations and give his assessment, but the pieces of the puzzle had already been arranged: Elizabeth Taylor was a fox. It was clear to see from the surface—the foxy resemblance accented by the signature beauty-mark on the side of her face. However, what concluded the inquest was the affectionate and almost obsessive way in which she ate the chicken. Chicken, as it turns out, is the preferred delicacy of the fox, which regularly risks life and limb to raid well-guarded chicken coops.

Animal Vitality

But how can all of this be explained? What were the priests at White Cloud Temple looking for, exactly? From what part or parts of the body was this presumably distinct immaterial piece of information emanating? To explore this, we might take a closer look at the Daoist concept of *ling*, often rendered "numen" in English but perhaps best described as the life force. The word indicates the supernatural or divine dimension of spirit and intelligence. *Lingqi* consists of cosmic particles that float freely throughout the universe, boundlessly permeating everything and allowing individuals to experience an uninhibited, inseparable sense of self and reality. Neither having form nor tied to the body, ling (or numinous particles) remain unattached until they are assigned a destination in the physical world. Humans, animals, trees, plants, rocks, minerals, and all other life forms contain a unique pattern of numinous qi, some more evolved than others. These patterns are much like highly sophisticated DNA strands that store generations of information and history, perhaps all the way back to the beginning of time.

Each numinous particle can be broken down into three sub-divisions: spirit (*shen*), spirit soul (*hun*), and material soul (*po*). In human beings, spirit exists in the heart and is anchored by the blood; the spirit soul is stored in the liver; and the material or animal soul dwells in the lungs. Together, they form the quintessence of nature. Moreover, they are perfectly synchronized, arriving jointly with the first breath or cry of a newborn baby.

You may be wondering about the animal soul of Wu Baolin himself. When it came time to measure Wu's companion, Master Du crowned him a tiger and placed a tiger cub in his ward. Wu and his tiger spent a fair amount of time together growing up, especially when public school was out of session. It was not just fun and games for them. They needed to learn essential lessons from one another during this timely window of young development—they needed to take advantage of the neural malleability of youth so that they could establish a foundation for future wisdom and growth.

Wu Baolin was required to lift his tiger for two full minutes, three times a day. One day lost was equal to ten days of practice, so it was critical that they maintained a strict schedule. This was a strength-building exercise as well as a bonding exercise—a kind of marriage, if you will. Theoretically, if they missed no days of training, Wu would be able to lift the tiger up when it was fully grown or until they outgrew each other's dimensions. If too many days were missed and the momentum was lost, he would need to start the exercise over with another cub. Wu Baolin spent seven years with the same tiger before they parted ways. Until then, however, they both enjoyed an exhilarating set of fighting and wrestling matches. Wu's forearms and skin were marked by teeth indentations and etched claw-marks.

Another exercise Wu Baolin had to practice with his tiger involved holding on to its tail. While he did this, Master Du would guide his meditation toward the correct feelings and attitude one must have while holding an acupuncture needle during insertion.

"When you insert a needle into a patient," Master Du explained, "it must be done with the same caution, care, and sensitivity as grasping the tiger's tail. The tiger's tail should neither be held too firmly nor too loosely. If held too firmly the tiger might blow back and scatter his power onto you, and if the tail is held too loosely the tiger's power will escape, thus losing the healing initiative. You are the director of this forceful *qi*. This is a very sensitive area for tigers since the tail fills with yang energy just before engaging in the explosive pursuit of their prey. In other words, there is a degree of unpredictability that you must always account for and be ready to adapt yourself to. This is also applicable to taijiquan, when you sense your opponent's next move."

This method was the perfect Daoist exercise and metaphor for treating disease with acupuncture. Other schools relate the feeling of holding the needles to that of holding a calligraphy brush, and this technique is a practical substitution. Students of this method are tested by surprise when a teacher unexpectedly pulls their brushes away from behind their shoulder during writing practice. If they were holding on too softly, their brushes would be snatched away; if they were holding on too tightly, the heavier ink strokes would be stalled in some way. Keeping the angle of the needle steady at insertion and allowing the fingertips to guide and push the needles through the epidermis without the patient feeling the puncture is the sign of a master-hand, though sometimes deliberate painful stimulation is required for treating certain diseases.

As the tiger cub grew in size, it served as a bodyguard to Wu. Its presence alone was the ultimate deterrent. In Beijing, it was not the least bit unusual for large animals to walk in public places with their keepers. There were few with the wherewithal to challenge his companion. The tiger was a godsend.

The harsh cold seasons of the north did little to discourage the monks of the White Cloud Temple from carrying out their duties. These monks would take solace in the fact that they did not need to use blankets to stay warm most nights of the winter, which could reach glacially cold temperatures. Throughout the year, they wore just one or two layers of clothing. In January and February, during the coldest months, they added insulation, stuffing either raw wool or quilted cotton and sometimes newspapers between the two layers, though they more frequently generated their warmth by practicing taijiquan and qigong exercises. More *qi*, more heat. Methods also included the intake of seasonal foods and herbal concoctions. The training and diet were enough to keep their body temperatures perfectly regulated and their immune systems optimized. The old-fashioned brick oven beds were always on standby and used whenever called for.

At night, during rest, the defensive *qi* that guards the body from the six external invasions (wind, cold, heat, summer heat, dryness, and dampness) naturally retreats inward from the body's surface area, fortifying and regenerating the internal organs in an organized effort to consolidate. This retraction of the defensive *qi* during rest is precisely why blankets and insulated shelters are necessary for living beings, even those who live in warmer climates. Otherwise, the unguarded pores, dermis, and subcutaneous layers (including the meridians and other channels) become susceptible to disease. Wu Baolin had not quite developed the gold-steel body resistance to the cold that some of his fellow longstanding monks had. He was still rather young when he came to ingratiate himself with his tiger; his yin and yang energies needed protection from the formidable elements. Thus, at night, when the temperatures dropped, Wu Baolin lay with his tiger cheek to cheek, his body shielded by this living breathing comforter, his spirit animal in the flesh, absorbing the internal force of the tiger's *qi* and thereby enhancing its already-present nature in himself.

Daoist Zoology

In his early years at White Cloud Temple, Wu Baolin spent a large portion of his time learning about wildlife farming and animal husbandry. After all, the monastery was home to an interactive zoo that needed tending to on a daily basis.

Wu's duties included cleaning up animal scat, watering and grooming the horses in the livery stable, and sweeping up all the winter coats that the animals had shed. Indeed, these animals were his earliest patients and kept him busy. He administered medical treatment in the first-stage infirmary, kept all the animals' bodies in fine fettle, wrote medicinal herbal prescriptions, monitored the prenatal condition of any pregnant animals, and assisted in the birthing processes. He fed animals according to specific feeding schedules that varied based on species: nocturnal or diurnal, herbivore or carnivore. He also checked these animals in and out of any temple community projects and work orders where they were included, such as training exercises and temple security.

For many years, Master Wu manned the stables found in the wildlife post at the temple. Although there was a fair share of domesticated animals kept—including pigs, chickens, oxen, and sheep—the majority were still, by nature, wild. The temple also kept many exotic pets gathered from around the world: tigers and snakes, wolves and coyotes, mules and horses, fighting monkeys from the Wudang mountains. Prized and exclusive to the temple were the famed eagles, which Genghis Khan had gifted to a great emissary of the White Cloud Temple many centuries before. The eagle were so magnificent that Genghis Khan took his own son's life after he was found to have killed one of the Khan Empire's eagles. "One good General is worth 10,000 infantrymen," as the saying goes. The eagles dominated reconnaissance in the sky and are suspected to have been the unknown key secret to the martial prowess and success of the Mongol Empire. They were treasured, invaluable, and off-limits to almost everyone. At the temple, the animal keeper was tasked with singing to the eagles; a kind of language evolved between the monks and this amazing bird.

Detailed records of all of Wu Baolin's duties and observations were logged during and after shifts to grow the temple's knowledge base. Each of Wu's new and unique insights into the taxonomy of things either supplemented or provided a foundation for patterns, which could evolve into theories over time. These logs also allowed Master Du, who was in charge of Wu's curriculum, to assess Wu's comprehension of materials and monitor his progress.

In addition to his responsibility to tend the animals, Wu Baolin was tasked with emulating the behaviors and patterns of his new friends. He respectfully imitated their facial expressions, vocalizations, breathing rhythms, resting patterns, and spoken languages. He learned how to interpret their emotions so he could respond appropriately, developing the ability to discern if they were hungry, sick, uncomfortable, constipated, homesick, lonely, in estrus, in need of proper exercise, and so on. He needed to know, for instance, that pigs have a tendency to lay around on their sides if not encouraged to move and walk, a dangerous habit of the species that could lead to congestive heart disease and digestive disorders due to lack of exercise. (The likelihood of internal ruptures and hemorrhaging in older larger boars might prove fatal in these domesticated environments.)

Many years later, the San Diego Zoo invited Master Wu to visit a sick tiger who had lost its appetite. The zoo's veterinarians had run many diagnostics but could not reach a diagnosis. Master Wu entered the cage and sat with the tiger, brushing its fur with his hands. After several quiet minutes, Master Wu said goodbye to his new friend and walked out of the cage. He explained to the zookeepers that the tiger had conveyed that it was tired of eating chicken and needed to consume some red meat. The zookeepers ordered red meat immediately, which the tiger ate without hesitation. It made a speedy recovery.

Wu Baolin's observations about the animals that surrounded him provided deep insight into the ways in which humans had domesticated them or harnessed their abilities. For example, warhorses—which were used as early as 5,000 years ago on Eurasian continents according to the earliest written Chinese records—demonstrated great acumen and the ability to quickly adapt to the unknown in life-or-death circumstances. Wu, through consistent shadowing of horses, noticed that they would lick their lips when they were acquiring knowledge. He realized that their humanistic nature and intelligence allowed them to preview hazards in such a way that they could anticipate coming challenges, making them fearless and formidable even when outnumbered by predators.

Wu was able to corroborate his observations with the extensive records memorialized at the White Cloud Temple. For instance, the temple had texts (dating back to the Tang and Song dynasties) which documented the aptitude and fighting maneuvers of the legendary warhorse steeds of the northern nomadic tribes. For centuries, these horses were bred with a perfect balance of size, strength, and endurance. They were skilled enough to knock down enemy horses and their riders, sideswiping their adversaries with their adroit shoulders and remarkably agile hips—key contact points that practitioners of taijiquan use to unbalance and destabilize their opponents. Due to these horses' hyper-flexible lower vertebral spine, they were able to launch enemy foot soldiers into the air with their long, stout necks, and trample them underfoot with their hooves. They were also renowned for their on-the-ground endurance, which was unmatched. Certain Mongolian breeds, for instance, could run all the way to the citadel in Moscow from Mongolia without stopping, aided by a desert variety of the ginseng root known as *suoyang or* "locking up yang," which grows in the arid regions of northern Asia, mainly at high altitudes within Tibet, internal Mongolia, Qinghai, and Gansu.

Not only did Wu Baolin learn a great deal about the animals he was surrounded by—he also learned how these animals taught each other. For example, Wu watched with surprise as oxen took their cues from sheep. He surmised that if a big-hearted creature like the supportive ox could take direction from a sheep, a young boy should be able to humble himself and listen intently to the sheep as well (not to mention, of course, all the other animal teachers who encircled him at the monastery). Wu placed himself directly below his animal mentors, reasoning that it resembled the way in which water and wisdom, a unified pair, flowed downstream to fill the lowest hollows. Since the animal's skills and survival tactics hinge on natural instincts, the understudy must be sensitive to the inherent sensory stimuli and projections they emit, especially if those stimuli and projections have not yet fully been awakened in the student. The teachers all had precious wisdom to share. Whether it was the cat or the tiger, the understudy's respect for the teacher must be the same. In the same way, the taijiquan mind must always be prepared and alert to the subtlety of intentions, even when the focus is on martial arts combat.

Wu Baolin's days at the monastery were long and the learning endless. Wu routinely conducted experiments with the animals to learn about their relationships with each other. He once placed the playful but roughhousing cats in the same hutch with the timid and diplomatic rabbits and watched as the cats attacked, swiped, and pounced with absolute impunity. One day, a single rabbit retaliated and chased down a cat, biting it down with its long and sharp incisors. This spontaneous retribution from the rabbits effectively ended their constant harassment. It was a lesson in behavioral science and martial arts attack timing, indicative of the way a single action rooted in patience and tolerance can create a major shift.

The relationship that really challenged Wu Baolin's preconceived notions, however, was the unusual friendship between a wolf and lamb inside the monastery zoo. The two creatures had both been born in captivity and were raised together since birth. They were the best of friends, breaking every rule of nature even when faced with the envy and contempt of their respective animal families. They never disagreed and genuinely enjoyed each other's company; sometimes, Wu would find them snuggling in the grass. One day, the lamb died. Following a brief bereavement, the wolf fell into a deep depression, losing its appetite and dying soon after. Wu took the lesson to heart—friendships could form even between presupposed enemies, given ideal circumstances. Even once in a while, people could rise above the age-old rules of astrological incompatibility.

The animals that Wu Baolin kept company and tended to taught him that death—and death ceremonies—were both celebrated and mourned among animals. Wolves, as Wu Baolin learned, have a rank-and-file hierarchy that defines their social system. Alphas maintain order in the pack with their leadership, decision-making, and delegation skills. Betas and omegas, who are defenders and often persistently vie for positions nearer to the top of the pack, are less frequently observed outside of captivity—in the wild, wolves depend on each other equally for survival. When inevitable changes in leadership occur, the alphas retreat to the back of the pack and eventually disappear into the landscape to find a dignified death. The pack stops and turns back to pay its respects to the dying.

The eagles, on the other hand, had a vastly different approach to death. Whereas the wolves ran just before dying—as if to take that momentum into the spirit world—the eagle flew straight up into the sky as high as possible, their bodies falling weightlessly to the ground after they took their last breath. It was a beautiful representation of the ideological separation between yin and yang—though the eagles' bodies fell, their spirits continued to soar. Eagles with young still in the nest would often sacrifice themselves to their children, carving themselves open and feeding their own innards to their fledgling—necessary for their young to take first flight. In this way, the eagle embodied and became an emblem for the mentality among the monks: unconditional compassion and love, even if it meant making the ultimate sacrifice.

Snakes

Due to their personalities—which ranged from docile to aggressive, compassionate to indifferent—snakes were a more complex creature to raise. Snakes prefer to be in solitude; in fact, most of them hibernate six months out of the year. In Chinese culture, snakes are regarded as little dragons and their intrinsic energies play a major role in spiritual transformation. Some people believe that snakes are the predecessor of the dragon, the template that gives it its form. Although the rat is generally listed as the first animal on the twelve-animal zodiac, riding in on the oxen's back in the first pairing, the true number one position belongs to the dragon, followed closely by the snake.

In Chinese culture, the snake is associated with medicine. Inside the Yuan Chen Celestial Hall at the White Cloud Temple is the Chinese Sexagerny Cycle found in the physical form of sixty individual deities, representatives of a sixty-year birth cycle (jiazi) of astrological designations. The sixty are a combination of the twelve animals and the five phases. In this pantheon, five deities are identified with those born in the year of the snake. One in particular holds a staff in the right hand with a serpent coiled around it. This deity is associated with the practice of medicine.

The snake is a recognized symbol of medicine across many other cultures, its signature passed down from antiquity. Modern medical associations throughout the world continue to use the crest of snake and staff, an embodiment harking back to ancient civilizations. In Greek mythology, the god Hermes is often found depicted with a caduceus, a winged staff wrapped by two serpents. In Hermes' case, the symbol represents not only medical healing but also the practice of alchemical sciences. Echoing this, China's premiere herbal pharmaceutical company, Tong Ren Tang, emboss two anciently drawn dragons as their company's insignia across the product line.

In fact, the relationship between snakes and medicine has even worked its way into the Chinese lexicon. When Chinese medical physicians examine a person's internal organs, they tend to first study the tongue. The tongue, in a way, acts as the external reflection of the heart; its surface helps doctors determine the cause and condition of disease within the body. Not coincidentally, the

Chinese word for snake is pronounced shé, and the word for "tongue" in Chinese is also pronounced shé (with the same tone). Indeed, when one thinks about it, the form and movement of the tongue holds a strange resemblance to those of a snake. Even the texture—the papillae of a tongue comparable to the scales of a snake—strike an uncanny parallel.

At the White Cloud Temple, snakes are believed to fully embody medicine and are even considered natural-born physicians. They can either be dispensed for consumption as herbal medicine—an important ingredient in the Chinese pharmacopeia—or kept alive and administered in a clinic.

Tong Ren Tang pharmacy manufactures an excellent herbal mud pill called da huo luo dan. The formula is primarily used to treat various heart-related conditions. Although the ingredients and processing are still mostly kept a secret, its chief ingredient—baihuashe—is public knowledge. Baihuashe is the white flower snake, aptly named for its floral snakeskin pattern. Every part of the animal is specially dried and used in the pills.

The use and power of snakes in medicine have a long history on the Asian continent. Their importance and continued development in Chinese medicine cannot be undervalued. The role of snakes in healing was not, however, limited to internal medicine. At the White Cloud Temple, snakes of a particular disposition were used in physical therapy practices, to treat weakened limbs due to paralysis from stroke, and to rehabilitate the body from other injuries (in particular, the different healing stages of bone breaks).

Doctors would often allow live snakes to slither on the limbs and torsos of physically impaired patients. Depending on the patient's physical symptoms (such as extreme flexion or extension of the limbs and joints as well as pronation or supination), the snakes would position themselves according to an innate instinct, wrapping themselves around the affected areas in either clockwise or counterclockwise directions in order to counter-rotate the disturbances. Using torsional forces, they could pull, straighten, and/or bend and reshape the limbs, muscles, bones, and sinews. Snakes are masters of using pressure control to restore anatomical balance. These methods also helped to reduce or eliminate tremors, a consequence of neural damage from a stroke.

The squeezing and contraction of the blood vessels help improve any limitations of oxygen and blood flow to and from the heart, brain, and extremities. Inadequate blood supply to the heart or other organs is sometimes an underlying cause of stroke. In this way, snakes were used to squeeze and pump blood through the vascular system, increasing arterial pressure and possibly preventing the incidence of future strokes. Well-trained Chinese medical massage therapists emulate these snake maneuver theories to deliver a similar result, a technique that the Zhang Sanfeng Taijiquan practice has developed. These kinds of treatments are generally administered in conjunction with acupuncture and a Chinese herbal medicine prescription, and should only be done under the care of an experienced physician.

Unfortunately, snakes are not always known for their benevolent actions and talents; in fact, it is often associated with duplicitous and amoral behaviors. Synonyms of snake include "seduction" and "crimes of passion" in the *Baishe zhuan* (Legend of White Snake), and in Western cultures common expressions such as "snake in the grass" and "cold-blooded" abound. Indeed, there are certainly two sides to the snake: lethal and nonlethal. On September 9th of the Chinese lunar calendar, known as the Double Nine Festival, Daoist pour realgar wine around the perimeters of their abodes to ward off all poisonous creatures—particularly snakes—for a full year.

Yet still, snakes are intelligent, charming, and attractive, three characteristics that make them formidable and shrewd. There are caveats to this interpretation of the snake. According to Daoists, there is no creature more loyal than the snake—not even the dog, despite its unanimous acceptance as "man's best friend." The royal families of dynastic China did not leave the security of their family to the canines; they believed that a dog's natural tendencies were better suited for the outdoors: protecting the perimeter and guarding the family fortune at the rear gate. Nor did they leave the responsibilities to a nanny. Instead, the royals placed their most prized possessions, their children, under the watchful eyes of snakes. Snakes, as it turns out, have a great affection for children, thus making them excellent caretakers and vicious deterrents. In addition to their protective natures, snakes were said to supply high levels of energy to the room. This aided in the child's development by stimulating both physical and intellectual growth.

Beyond medicine and protection, snakes also branched into Snake Boxing and the martial arts arena. Entire defense systems were created around the snake's special talents and concoctions made from its venom. Its ability to circumvent attacks, punch and jab (with its head), leap, as well as stand and run on its tail-end without having arms and legs is actually an impressive display of power. Combat challenges between humans and snakes at the monastery were measured and calculated, and an excellent way to gauge a fighter's speed. It was akin to rodeo riding in America, where only the biggest and strongest broncs and steers were selected for competitions.

Wolves

Aside from protecting the monastery after hours, wolves were also fengshui conductors. Fengshui is the traditional Chinese way of siting graves, houses, and furniture in the most *qi*-efficient way. Widely used in Daoism, today it is practiced in a do-it-yourself fashion by many people and widely available instruction manuals and videos. Masters use strategies and calculations involving physical additions and subtractions to a home or a business or a final resting site in order to create harmony and prosperity between heaven and earth for the inhabitants of these structures and places. It's similar to what an agriculturist can do with irrigation systems when there is a lack of rain. The agriculturist will draw in, channel, and distribute measured amounts of water from a greater source, such as a river or a lake, in order to irrigate their crops and spur robust growth. Naturally, sunlight from the sky and rich soil are integral to these successes.

In the original teachings of this unique Chinese field, wolves have a high sensitivity to energy currents. In fengshui, these are known as dragon veins, the bio-electric earth flow that moves above and below ground, making up part of the earth's magnetic field. In nature, certain creatures use prevailing earth currents to move across long distances, similar to train-hopping. These ley lines are invisible streams of yang energy located on the earth, in the sky, underground, and underwater, and have been given names such as the Trade Winds, East Australian Current, the Silk Road, Route 66, the Milky Way, and so on. On the ground, wolves have an exceptional understanding of these currents and strategically use them for fast-moving long-distance travel. Wolf exploration is a mission fundamentally related to guarding lookout posts along territorial borders and the reconnaissance of the territories falling beyond those borders. In modern times, these currents could now be called freeways or highways, and because of this updated translation by Daoists, automobiles have become symbolic of wolves.

Wolves also use their understanding of these currents to efficiently stalk, flank, redirect, and trap their prey, forcing it to fall into those unnatural currents, which tires it out more quickly. Wolves generally stay very close to these powerful sources to internally absorb the qi, especially during the lean months when hunting is scarce (either due to limited breeding or reduced numbers due to hibernation and inclement weather). Though some wolves can consume as much as twenty-two pounds of flesh in one sitting, they may go many days or weeks without any successful hunts. They spend the rest of their time engaging in a high level of practice, with the moon and earth's magnetic fields to bolster them.

In the old days, whenever Master Du was called upon to perform fengshui outside of the monastery, he always tried to bring children below the age of nine years with him. The younger the children, the more accurate the assessment of the readings, and a boy's feedback was usually more accurate than a girl's. When young children are introduced to a foreign environment, they may remain calm and comfortable and explore the new space, engaging in laughter and constructive play. This is a good indication of a positive reading of that environment. However, if the children begin to cry or appear frightened, become destructive, or are immediately moved to urinate or fearfully cling to an adult, the space is deemed negative and not seen as a solid starting point for the proposed endeavors. In the future, such sites will most likely present limitations on the return investment, or, in the worst-case scenario, result in the death of the new occupant(s).

When children were not available for fengshui readings, Master Du and Master Wu would instead take with them a small pack of wolves from the monastery, with the purpose of using them to barometrically assess the *qi* of the land or home in question. The wolves were not transported in a cart and cage, but held on a leash despite their powerful impulses to snap without warning and bolt.

When the wolves arrived at the new construction grounds, they were unleashed and left free to roam. If they eventually came to lay and rest, that area was deemed a prosperous and blessed zone by the heavens. But if the wolves did not come to lay down and instead continued to roam and hesitate, perhaps even restlessly, Master Du and Master Wu would advise against the project area and recommend that the developers search for a new location.

It is interesting to note that wolves, even when born in captivity for several generations and raised by humans, resist domestication. This in spite of the fact that some of the most dangerous animals in the world—such as lions, tigers, bears, and elephants—have been successfully tamed by man or used for work and entertainment. Not even optimal living conditions with abundant food can bend a wolf's will. Under the surface of their intelligent demeanor is the opportunist, survivalist, and free spirit, waiting to attack or escape and return to independence. Though wolves have never been convinced by the illusion of freedom, the Daoist monks of the White Cloud Temple were somehow able to manage these animals and harness their exceptional talents with minimal risk.

To protect themselves against the dangers of the wild (humans and animals alike), the Daoist monks developed their own voluntary immunization system. Monks participating in this program routinely ingested the five poisons (snake, scorpion, toad, spider, and centipede), gradually increasing their dosages over time until they built an immunity to the poisons, while also developing a sensitive palette to toxins, in turn making them excellent tasters. The five poisons eventually created a responsive immune booster against many lethal toxins. This considerably lowered the risk and vulnerability of contracting disease and effectively thwarted assassination attempts by food or drink. After several years of preparation, the monks who were inoculated in this practice were able to handle the wolf packs with minimal threat of harm and backlash from the animals, who would never attempt to draw such toxic blood. The natural instinct of most animals, even in a hardship as dire as starvation, is never to consume a rotted carcass or any poisonous flesh. The exception to this rule is some of the scavenger species whose gastrointestinal system has the enzymes required to digest expired carrion.

Wolves are generally nocturnal and worship the moon. Their act of howling at the moon is a call to the heavens and sometimes a call-to-arms. Because of their deep-seated connection to the dark side of moon, wolves are acutely sensitive to both negative and positive qi, which makes them masters of psychological warfare and of the subconscious. For that reason, they can act as ushers for the dead, repossessing souls and crossing them over first through the mountains and beyond into the realms of the next world. This role may explain the instinctive reverence and apprehension that humans have for the wolf. There is a mutual respect among the two species, a parity specially designed by nature that keeps them in accordance with the laws of nature and the cosmos. Neither man nor wolf, in this arrangement of checks and balances, is able to overthrow nature in any ill-advised pursuits of supremacy. In Daoist cosmology, the wolf is man's equal.

The Art of War by Sunzi is a well-documented treatise on the fastidious craft of warfare conservation and is required reading at the White Cloud Temple. Not only is the book a masterwork that provides startling insights on diplomacy, social customs, and the appropriate behaviors and actions necessary to maintain harmony between men and nature; on a deeper level, *The Art of War* is about fengshui science, which intends to combine the three tiers of the universe—Heaven, Human, and Earth—in hopes of keeping the Middle Kingdom in a perpetually progressive cultural growth cycle that strives for virtue rather than bloodshed. Sunzi, the author of the book, was notably a prized student of Laozi, who has been a great inspiration for many Daoist achievements, including Zhang Sanfeng Taijiquan. But it was from Sunzi's intimate relationship with the wolves that he drew his deepest insights regarding the craft of warfare. The transmission of knowledge between them was so vast that he was able to develop an entire branch of Daoist philosophy and a complete exercise system—the practice of the wolves—which remains one of three great rivers of Chinese austerity.

Sunzi genuinely sought peace, not strife. With the best of intentions, he publicly released the information he'd culled and developed in order to reduce the aggression and alarming casualty rates of many warring states at the time. Despite his good-hearted motives, many have since taken advantage of his wisdom and advice, exploiting them exclusively for the purposes of physical and psychological control.

Birds

Daoists believe that birds have a special relationship with nature and serve as messengers of heaven. In fact, they have the ability to reveal heaven's secrets by setting forth changes in the world, and thus play a key role in *Yijing* divination. For this reason, initiates of the Dragon Gate lineage do not cook or consume birds. The White Cloud Temple was, by design, named in honor of the birds. In particular, its name pays homage to the immortal cranes, which loom inside the patches of water above the monastery.

Birds, like wolves, are gifted fengshui barometers. While Master Du and Wu Baolin would walk outside the monastery, a flock of birds would fly overhead along with them. Daoism suggests that birds are winged fairies which carry precise edicts from heaven. The *qi* that birds generate through their shifting flight patterns act as a kind of information service and make them particularly useful in isolating energetic vortexes. This gives them the ability to identify where positive charges are most concentrated.

On one occasion, the owner of a vineyard invited Master Wu Baolin to Northern California wine country to do a reading of a vineyard. A budding winemaker was interested in purchasing the vineyard. As soon as Master Wu stepped foot onto the land, a multitude of birds—hawks, vultures, and other birds of all sizes and colors—seemed to explode from the sky and canopy, encircling him. Master Wu spotted a night owl perched in the shadows of a cubbyhole of one of the structures before taking flight to a quieter sanctum. The assorted flock eventually drifted away from Master Wu's position to circle over a small plot of the land, indicating that the best grapes would grow there. Regrettably, these birds flew nowhere else on the vineyard, and so the search continued. It would be several months before the next viable vineyard would appear on the market when Master Wu got the call.

When Master Wu got off the plane that particular day, it was raining hard and storm clouds filled the sky—not the most ideal conditions for reading qi. The client, nervous, had tried to postpone the meeting days in advance; he wanted "ideal" weather conditions. Before he got on the plane at Los Angeles International Airport, Master Wu assuaged his worries and convinced him to remain confident.

Sitting in the passenger seat during the ride from the airport to the vineyard, Master Wu meditated, making hand mudras and chanting Daoist scriptures under his breath. It was still raining. The escort vehicle pulled over along
the prospective new vineyard, its tires sledging through the mud. Master Wu
popped out of the vehicle and promptly gazed up into the sky (the first step of
any fengshui reading). The sky was mostly overcast with the exception of a
perfectly rotund opening over the center of the prospective vineyard. In that
moment, sunlight shone through, a vision of blue firmament and silver-lined
clouds. When Master Wu looked more closely, he saw a white crane span directly above the small aperture of clear sky just before it collapsed and blurred.
He had seen enough. He reentered the vehicle and said, "Acquire the property.
You will definitely succeed here."

At the monastery, birds played significant roles in the management and
engineering of day-to-day temple life. The roosters, for instance, rose first,
starting each day with raucous crowing. In Chinese mysticism, the rooster is
considered the "king of all birds" and a talented singer and communicator. Its
incredible voice had, once upon a time, won the rooster this distinguished
honor above all other birds (including the eagle) in a contest. Yet roosters are
not great fliers; their power is somewhat earthbound, as if they surrendered
their ability to fly well in order to possess great courage. This courage is ex-
pressed every morning at daybreak. A rooster's alarm is not only intended to
wake, but also to ward off the ghosts and demons right before the sun rises. In
this way, the rooster is a delegate for the sun, symbolic of the pure yang force.
Certain lama monks of Tibet wear a yellow hat, which resembles the comb atop
the rooster's head, and begin reading scriptures between the hours of three and
five in the morning, before the sun rises. In the same fashion as the roosters,
these monks also play the Tibetan longhorn, which ward off any evil spirits.

The great eagles also played a vital role as sentries at the temple. Whenever the monks opened their services to the public, the eagles would stand up,
patrolling the temple perimeters. If someone tried to steal anything from the
monastery (such as a relic atop an altar), the eagles would intercept and detain
the thief until the monks could arrive to reclaim the pilfered property.

Geese, too, were trained to defend the gates of the monastery, especially
at night. Geese have a special vocation: They can easily fend off or consume
snakes whole without any danger to themselves. Any time patients of the monastery suffered from skin conditions such as a rash or hives (whose appearance
on the skin resembles snake scales), the physicians would prescribe goose meat,
since these types of skin conditions are usually related to misaligned snake energies. By this logic, people born in the year of the snake are advised to avoid
the consumption of goose meat altogether. In the broader pharmacopeia of
Chinese medicine, goose eggs were also used in treating bone spurs in the heels
of the feet.

Geese are fearless birds and use their powerful bite and honk to fend off predators, trespassers, and attackers. A goose can even pose a significant threat to humans; in numbers, geese can be even more dangerous. A single goose can use its weight and the aerodynamics of its oblong figure to knock a person to the ground from behind. It can use its head and beak to rabbit punch the back of the person's head and the base of the skull, causing dizziness or a loss of consciousness.

Geese also have a part to play in the analysis of the *qi* of an indoor or outdoor space. A Daoist will use a goose feather and hold it higher than his or her head before dropping it into the air. If it floats down at a 45-degree angle all the way to the ground, there is a proper balance of qi.

Perhaps one of the most interesting examples of the age-old working relationship between man and bird is cormorant fishing on the Li River in Guilin City, China. Fishermen raise these seafaring birds from hatch and train them to retrieve fish from the river. Out on the river, a fisherman will tie a loose collar around the lower throat of the cormorant in order to prevent it from swallowing the fish it catches. The fisherman will use his legs to rock the flat-standing boat, plunging its edges into the water and churning it. He will also sing to the cormorant to encourage it to dive in and pluck fish from the agitated depths of the river. After its work is done, the fisherman will remove its throat collar and feed the cormorant.

Monkeys

In Beijing in the old days, there were many groves, fields, and small gardens scattered throughout the city. People cultivated many indigenous trees and plants for purposes of food and medicine. They often focused on specific warming fruits and vegetables (such as gourds, squash, jujube, etc.) to survive the harsh seasons. The White Cloud Temple was no exception to this tradition. There was once a large field behind the temple that sported groves of trees and a plethora of vegetation. One could sometimes see monks standing on branches of trees, eating fruit off the vine—this practice, learned from the monastery's monkeys, allowed the monks to siphon the *qi* from the roots of the tree.

Because monkeys are highly intelligent animals, the monks—and other human beings—have been able to learn a great deal from them. Monkeys are notorious pranksters and find amusement in turning the world on its head. They can also be incredibly fearless, outwitting even a tiger in a friendly but annoying game of tag. Their opposing thumbs give them the ability to throw stones and even excrement to defend themselves from an attack, all the while issuing a shriek at the top of their lungs. Their agility on the ground and in the trees gives them a range of ways to attack, including jumping, swinging, bouncing, tumbling, etc. They are also one of the most functionally adaptable species due to both their quick intelligence and the fact that they are not limited to a single living environment (such as mountains, grass, trees, or water). According to the science of fengshui, people born in the year of the monkey are virtually immune to favorable settings and layouts, and allowed, even encouraged, to be impulsive.

When Master Du became Head Abbott at the monastery in the early twentieth century, he brought a troop of the Wudang mountains fighting monkeys with him to Beijing. Master Du's monkeys were a part of the very same primate lineage which Zhang Sanfeng introduced to the Wudang mountains during the Ming dynasty. Prior to Zhang Sanfeng's arrival, there were no monkeys of this kind in the central mountain region. Zhang Sanfeng himself trained these creatures in taijiquan; they were his adopted youth and some of his first students of the art, and today continue the fighting tradition internally among their own species at the mountain.

Both the fighting monkeys and the great eagles acted as Master Du's personal bodyguards for the 40-plus years he spent at the White Cloud Temple. No one dared enter his quarters unannounced for fear of their rude and unforgiving "clash first, talk later" approach. The eagles would scream ear-piercingly in variable decibels at every passerby and the monkeys would grunt or squeak loudly. It was easier to leave security to these animals rather than other humans because of their extrasensory abilities and undying loyalty.

The animal bodyguards protected Wu Baolin in much the same manner as they did for Master Du. The truth remained clear to everyone: Wu Baolin was the only one Master Du trusted enough to keep close. After all, Master Du had raised Wu Baolin since he was four-years old. The bodyguards understood this connection and thus did not repel his private company; they allowed Wu Baolin to go in and out of Master Du's company freely.

Apart from their role as his protectors, the monkeys were also Master Du's personal physicians and massage therapists. Even though Master Du was always in great health because of his exercise and clean dietary habits, he still required some maintenance here and now. Monkeys, conveniently enough, are natural-born doctors. They have developed their own system of natural medicines, which they use to treat fellow monkeys, and their hand dexterity has been known to rival that of human practitioners. They locate the painful spots on a person's body—either acupuncture or trigger points, which surface randomly on the body.

Once monkeys find the trigger points, they use their thumbs, fingers, or knuckles to press repeatedly and vigorously on these points while periodically checking the expressions on the faces of their patients. If the patient shows expressions of pain and anguish, the monkeys will press even harder, grinning and laughing until the areas are finally relieved of their pain.

In addition to the lessons he learned while observing the adroit and intelligent monkeys, Wu Baolin was privately trained in Traditional Chinese Massage by Master Du. The training included the full spectrum of tuina, bone setting, qigong massage therapy, neural regulation, taiji massage, and other specialties. Wu Baolin had to practice regularly on his teacher, but he did so reluctantly because Master Du was extremely lean and dense. After decades of continuous martial arts training, Master Du's physical body was like rock. As a youngster, Wu Baolin found it nearly impossible to practice on Master Du, but with practice he became quite proficient. By emulating the monkeys' techniques and spending three solid years under their tutelage, Wu Baolin was able to sharpen his skills.

When Dr. Wu attended Kyoto University in Japan, he had a vast array of scientific resources at his disposal, including state-of-the-art medical devices from Germany and the United States. However, he still preferred to spend his time in the animal labs, testing the ancient techniques he'd honed over the years on subjects—his favorite of which were the monkeys, since their behaviors and anatomies were most like those of the humans treated as patients. Using CT scanners, Dr. Wu inserted needles into delicate areas of the body close to the heart as well as the nerve centers in the brain, looking to verify why monkey intelligence was higher than in other animals. Daoists consider the monkey to be the cleverest of all the animals. And though it is common belief that a larger brain has greater learning capacity, monkeys have comparatively small brains. When Wu Baolin was learning qigong in the monastery, Master Du taught him ways to keep the brain healthy and young. One such way was to comb the fingertips through the hair and head from front to back. Master Du told him this was not only to keep the brain sulcus from filling with plaque, but also to deepen the sulcus grooves for greater intelligence and learning capacity. What Dr. Wu discovered in the scans and the live inspections of other animal brains immediately after slaughter was that monkeys do in fact have naturally deeper sulci. In the Daoist classic, *Journey to the West*, the monkey protagonist, Sun Wukong (the Monkey King), is trained to a high level of proficiencies and spiritual cultivation by a Daoist master.

In the early 2000s, when China was on the rise, Dr. Wu Baolin was approached by government officials regarding a Chinese relic that was being prepared for an international auction. The larger than life monkey head, cast of pure gold, was expected to come in at several million dollars. This treasure had once been an important part of a dynastic collection of Chinese zodiacal animals. In the twentieth century, the monkey head was removed from the Old Summer Palace in Beijing and taken outside Chinese borders. These officials had come to ask Dr. Wu's opinion on the value of this piece, its importance to Chinese culture as a whole, and where they should draw the line so they could set the preapproved budget. Dr. Wu's advice was simple. "At all cost outbid everyone else!" he said. "If not, there will always be a breach in the wall of China's education and finance." His advice was not based on the combined appraisal of gold and art alone, but also on the cultural essence and *qi* of the Chinese monkey spirit, which some believe actually resides inside the golden head. Since then, other pieces of the collection have been relocated and brought back to China, but to date the set remains incomplete.

The Tibetan Mountain Dog

One of the most amazing creatures Master Wu Baolin ever met was the Tibetan mountain dog known as *zang'ao*, a canine of almost mythical proportion—Marco Polo described it in his travel writings as comparable in size to donkeys. Tibetan monks have traditionally bred these thickly-maned dogs to help protect the monasteries and temples from intruders, bandits, and wild beasts. They were ordinarily kept on the ground floor and along the perimeter of the structures to patrol the walkways and open bridges of the larger monasteries together with palace guards. Smaller Tibetan spaniels stood as lookout sentries on the upper floors. Using their sharp vision, the spaniels gave prompt warnings when they saw incoming visitors. The mountain dogs also helped local tribes and nomadic herders of Nepal, Mongolia, China, and India by protecting their livestock from wolves, bears, leopards, and tigers.

Because of their reputation as brutal defenders, the mountain dogs have grown in popularity. These days, they have been bred down in size by commercial breeders from the guardian-size variety of 200 to 300 pounds down to 75 to 160 pounds in an effort to make them more manageable and affordable for purchasing and maintenance (one can imagine how large of an appetite a guardian-size mountain dog has!). Because of the guardian breed's girth and thickness of fur, they have a tendency to do poorly in warmer climates, developing very serious lung conditions, shallow breathing, and even death from overheating. Considering that the White Cloud Temple (which is located in Beijing) could get particularly warm in the summertime, there were no mountain dogs at the temple.

The mountain dogs' inability to tolerate warmer climates is not necessarily a weakness. If anything, it highlights their remarkable evolutionary adaptation to extreme cold. In fact, the mountain dogs acclimatizes to the frigid weather conditions of the Tibetan Plateau much better and faster than other animals of the same region, including the wild boar, Tibetan antelope, snow leopard, and yak. The mountain dogs' ability to resist altitude sickness, a condition that occurs when the body, or a region of the body, is deprived of adequate oxygen supply at the tissue level, in these high-altitude conditions is due to their lower hemoglobin levels. This is a trait that the mountain dogs share with their wolf ancestors.

While on pilgrimage at a monastery in Tibet with his teacher, Master Wu Baolin briefly shared a room with a full-grown guardian breed mountain dog and the monk who was paired with this magical creature. Although the dog was resting on the floor, its presence, heavy breathing, and low-pitched moan—a sound of contentment for the species—kept him hypervigilant; he could feel the internal vibrations of the dog from all the way across the room. And although the mountain dogs are considered a domesticated breed, the Tibetan monk explained to Wu Baolin that his mountain dog could hold its own against wild animals.

Indeed, one of the most distinguishing characteristics of the mountain dogs is its ability to fearlessly engage in battle. The original guardian type is able to firmly hold its ground against a tiger or lion, in what usually ends in a draw. Their full mane protects the vulnerable respiratory areas of their throat from being slashed by attackers, and their incredible neck strength makes them a force to be reckoned with. Against wolves, which hunt in large packs, the mountain dogs display an even greater courage. Over the centuries, they have developed an extraordinary vertical leaping ability. When the mountain dogs become surrounded by a pack of wolves, they wait until the wolves are just close enough before springing high into the air and repositioning themselves mid-leap to the outer ring of the wolf formation, so that they land precisely onto the spine of a wolf with their full weight, breaking its back, and ravaging the wolf's neck and crushing its larynx with their strong jaws. If the mountain dog wounds or kills the leader of the wolf pack, it has dissolved the cohesion of the group and already won.

Guardians of Dao

Over the millennium of its existence, the White Cloud Temple has amassed a great many treasures. The traditions and artifacts passed down over the generations include books on myriad subjects (medical, religious, martial, talismanic, etc.); fine gifts and great works of art from emperors, Dalai Lamas, and other important supporters; spiritually powerful artifacts that aid in self-cultivation; and even a collection of the shrunken burnt bodies of purified monks who fell marginally short of achieving the ultimate rainbow body ascension but nonetheless achieved immortality for their hardships.

It would be no understatement to say that these treasured artifacts were all worth dying to protect. When the monks of the monastery would go to sleep, the night watchmen—tigers, wolves, and geese—were allowed to roam the temple grounds. No one in their right mind would dare trespass unless they were skilled enough or desperate enough to risk their lives. The guardian animals evoked the symbol of the Four Buddha Attendants, the fierce guardians of the Dharma, who stand at attention in the entrance hall of all Buddhist temples.

At one point, the White Cloud Temple housed a progressive training system made up of 36 chambers. Each chamber contained a unique fighting trial that a Daoist fighter would need to complete successfully before graduating on to the next stage.

The chambers were first made popular by the Hong Kong film *The 36th Chamber of Shaolin* (1978). Each chamber in the film's story is designed to teach the Shaolin monks a particular skill set and philosophical lesson, such as balance, dexterity, strength, reflexes, visual acuity, and tranquility. In the film, the monks repeat each set of chamber exercises over and over again, day in and day out, until they fully master it. This was, of course, the "Hollywood" version. Similar exercises were obviously a part of the daily training curriculum of the White Cloud Temple, but these were just the preparatory work a monk needed to finish before entering into the thirty-six chambers themselves.

The real chambers at the White Cloud Temple contained living, breathing adversaries. Module one, the starting point, contained nature's weakest fighter: man. Module thirty-six, the final stage, contained nature's strongest fighter: the tiger. In between the first and last were other very clever adversaries: wolves, coyotes, birds of prey, giant serpents, big cats, monkeys, and so on. If you failed a level, you had to repeat it, reviewing and refining the knowledge and techniques needed to outwit that particular opponent, after which you would take the exam again. Monks who entered into the chambers needed to deeply understand the esoteric laws, physical strengths and weaknesses, and points of attack of their adversaries long before taking them on as challengers. As if the chambers were not already grueling, the animal challengers were often deliberately left hungry to amplify their fierceness and will to survive. To make matters even more complex, certain chambers put the monks face-to-face with multiple entities: a pack, flock, convocation, troop, or other collective noun of an animal adversary.

To navigate the difficulties of the chambers and incapacitate an opponent, monks relied on thoughtful analysis and planning, spontaneous wisdom, sheer accidental luck, or painful trial-and-error. Often, teachers would not disclose to their students the Achilles heel, the mortal vulnerability, of the different animals.

It is difficult to attain the highest level of mastery in Zhang Sanfeng Taijiquan, but the practice itself is still a fantastic fighting system for any learning stage; in fact, its methods are sound and relevant even for complete beginners. In particular, a significant part of its efficacy derives from the fact that it works both the body and the mind. Before stepping into the thirty-six chambers, a monk needed a strong *qi* presence to give them a psychological edge that could, if harnessed, force the opposition to involuntarily lose their nerve and get smaller. In the same way that the growl of a mountain lion in the distance can make a person curl up in fear in his or her sleeping bag, or the loud barking of a dog can startle and intimidate onlookers, the monks needed to develop strategies to deliver an effective "first strike" against their opponents. In the more difficult modules, a monk would apply such techniques. If he were facing a snake, for instance, he would imagine himself as a goose to give him the power of a goose; if he were facing a deer, he would draw upon the energy of a tiger.

Covering

Covering involves the manipulation and transformation of internal energy in order to effectively manipulate the *qi* in another—their animal soul. This is exactly the area where the external systems and the internal systems of Chinese martial arts conceptually diverge, and where the power of the mind and *qi* take the lead.

Covering involves the use of mind-directed *qi* to preemptively alter a situation and energetically manage, ground, or cut down a difficulty. At its core is the foundational understanding that every living organism has its resistances and its vulnerabilities. The Chinese 12-animal zodiac is a perfect example of relationships in nature that either generate or control one another. The twelve animals have best-case and harmonious compatibilities: rat-dragon-monkey, ox-snake-rooster, tiger-horse-dog, and rabbit-sheep-pig. Of course, these are ideal matchings but not the hard-and-fast rule. There are other pairings around the wheel that make for healthy relationships in various dimensions of life: marriage, business, family, friendships, etc. With that said, there are some matchings that should typically be avoided at all costs, such as the dragon and tiger; snake and rat; and the trio of monkey, rooster, and dog. These combinations generate conflict when intimately crossed. Additionally, the animal which holds the position directly opposite (180 degrees) of another animal on the zodiac wheel is, as a rule of thumb, counterproductive to the other (e.g., rabbit-rooster, snake-pig, dragon-dog).

Because each and every person is born to one of the twelve animal signs, all the signs holistically fulfill a role in predator-and-prey food chain. Sometimes, the natural enemies we encounter in life are not rooted entirely in an astrological incompatibility and instead indicate a more deep-seated rivalry based on a past-life regression, age-old family feud, rival school of philosophy or training, etc. Circumstances can also drive competition, such as class examination scores, a heated race for valedictorian honors, athletic achievement, or any of the important distinctions that determine, in this case, future placement in higher education or the job market. It should be noted that individuals can rise above much of this conflict by choosing to live by Confucian ethical concepts and naturally occurring societal placement, within family and extended relationships outside the home. Without this wisdom, we continue to ricochet within a dichotomy of enemies and allies.

To transfer the ideas of covering on to combat, a person must employ the active imagination of the two eyes as well as the third eye (in those who have cultivated and awakened it). A Daoist fighter must be able to quickly ascertain exactly what he is up against in the ring. Using discernment to uncover deeply shielded secrets of an opponent—and allowing the fighter to recognize his opponent's true nature, powers, and behaviors—allows him to form and shape a solution in the form of the opponent's antithesis. Lifting the mask, so to speak, exposes any susceptibilities. After the fighter identifies the solution, he must summon the antithesis. This requires the capacity to transform the spirit's energy.

Examples abound in both nature and Chinese mythology. Cats, for example, cover mice. Introduce a cat into an environment with a dense rodent population and the cat's presence instantly changes the energy field enough to cause the mice to decamp. Dogs cover cats. Despite the cat's extraordinary acrobatic talents, it finds it difficult to escape a less dexterous—and, in close quarters, less speed—dog, despite the dogs' innate lack of lateral movement stabilization. The cat's sudden panic and loss of breath and strength is triggered by the dog's loud bark. Tigers cover dogs. Lions cover tigers. Yet despite the lion's strength, it cannot take down the true king of the jungle, the elephant, who can easily punt lions away with its powerful legs or take them head on with their powerful necks and tusks. Who can control and cover the elephant?

Elephants, as it turns out, have a great fear of mice. Elephants instinctively sleep on raised bedding surfaces and tightly roll their trunks under their chin (which is the same position it assumes before charging toward an enemy) to ensure that a mouse cannot crawl up inside the shaft of its trunk and reach its skull and bite the brain. Other examples are the goose swallowing the snake. Roosters pecking centipedes and eating stones. Foxes eating chickens. Chickens eating worms. Spiders fear wind and so naturally build their webs into corners most of the time, where the wind cannot reach. Dolphins are courageous against sharks. In the mystical realms of fengshui theory, the qilin, or Chinese unicorn, can help control the heavenly lions that stand guard at the gates of palaces and strongholds. In short, covering is the use of wisdom to protect life.

In Daoist medicine, the martial theories of covering have tremendous advantages in overpowering disease, providing damage control, and minimalizing the growth and progression of foreign cellular activity in the body. This covering technique is applied in the same fashion as the combat preparatory activity and with a deeper meditative appliance, thus marrying martial and medical theory. Here is an example of the holistic, systemic application. The five phases correspond to the five yin organs and the five animals. Therefore, if the lungs are diseased this is an attack of the tiger. If the patient is born in the year of the ox, the tiger has the upper hand because they are the natural predator of the ox; i.e., the tiger controls and covers the ox. Therefore, a Daoist physician will assume the role of the lion, because the lion is the controller and extinguisher of the tiger. Also mounting this fight are acupuncture needles (which one can think of as micro-swords) and medicinal herbs (think: soldiers under the command of the physician).

Eagle Day

"Why are you fastening pieces of meat to my clothes, Master?" asked Wu Baolin, on an otherwise typical day. "Are not we still vegetarians?"

"They are not for us to eat," said Master Du. "Your skills will be tested today. They will be tested over and over again if necessary until you have proven yourself invincible. In fact, you can expect to be challenged and tested throughout your whole life in more ways than one."

Wu Baolin, still confused by Master Du's comments and the meat now dangling from his clothes, tried to piece together the strange situation. Master Du escorted Wu Baolin to the towering cages that housed the eagles, and Wu Baolin suddenly understood. He remembered Master Du's order from a few days prior to put the eagles on a fast for "health reasons" and to keep them enclosed, no exceptions. They had remained somewhat quiet in their habitat, conserving their energy during those past few days. But when they saw and smelled the fresh meat dangling off of Wu Baolin's shirt and pants, they produced ear-piercing shrills. They began shifting their positions in anticipation. These giant birds of prey loved Wu Baolin, who had cared for them over the years. Master Du had even forced him to sleep with the great eagle (not, of course, Wu Baolin's voluntary choice). Their razor-sharp talons and beaks screeching against metal sent chills up Wu Baolin's spine, as he had gotten very little sleep those nights. They were intimidating, more so than Wu Baolin's tiger—not to mention there were more than one of them.

"Climb in the cage," Master Du ordered. Wu Baolin knew very well that this exercise was not up for debate. As soon as he entered the barred enclosure, the eagles began swooping down in succession so as not to crash into one another, each flyby punctuated with one or two talons and as many as four, attempting to snatch the dangling meat from Wu Baolin's clothing. The talons of the great eagle were known to exert as much as four-hundred pounds per square inch of bone-crushing force. They made unorthodox inflight maneuvers from every angle, including rolling inversions. Master Du had not just randomly tied the eagle food anywhere, either. Indeed, he had placed the pieces of meat over vital acupuncture points, the points that, if struck, would result in death. Wu Baolin could not just cower into the fetal or turtle position because the pieces were also tied to his back and arms. Instead, Wu had to shift, evade, block, counter, and mirror the multiple attackers, becoming more aware of his totality and presence than ever before. He found himself crouched and inverted, coiling and twisting his spine to adapt to the all-encompassing feeding frenzy. He maintained this heightened awareness as he fought for his life against the squadron of screaming eagles. They were determined to eat, and he was wearing lunch. His parasympathetic nervous system was at full capacity. His *qi* surged, unblocking every channel and pressure point in his bioelectrical system, from the soles of his feet—yongquan—to the baihui at the apex of his head.

Master Du voiced a command (not in Mandarin) and all the eagles rose to the heights of the enclosure and perched quietly. They had also been adrenalized by the nature of the vigorous exercise. "Feed them well today and thank them for teaching you," Master Du instructed Wu Baolin, who was still trying to catch his breath.

The principles derived from animal play and Daoist zoology bred confidence in Daoist warrior monks. The modules of the 36 chambers taught basic fighting principles in real time. Daoism, like Zen Buddhism, attempts to bring the whole being into focus all at once, to awaken and enliven the spirit, and in a flash, bring the present moment into a pure awakened state. A monk who could complete the 36 chambers was considered to be at a level high enough to safely defend against twenty men at once. They sought absolute autonomy, the underlying stimulus of true enlightenment.

Chapter Four

Theories and Concepts

Zhang Sanfeng derived much of the theoretical basis for his style of boxing from the *Daode jing*, an ancient philosophical treatise attributed to Laozi, as well as from the *Taiji tushuo* (Explanation of the Diagram of the Great Ultimate), the interpretation of a systematic chart of the cosmos. Both elucidate the unfolding of the universe and the process of life. They place the origins of the great ultimate of yin and yang, the Taiji, in Wuji, the non-ultimate or nonbeing, represented by an empty circle. The mother of all things, it is also the great void of supreme stillness and Dao itself.

A seed is planted therein and when sprung in the elemental birth, it stirs the emptiness like the Dragon that moves about in the fog unseen, nevertheless sensed ubiquitously. This is the yang born of the yin. Afterward, the Taiji appears, as yin and yang grow to fullness and balance. The Taiji symbol is the one core representation of the Daoist universe, now formed in the circle, and composed of the two halves, yin (black) and yang (white), with the two bordered on the inside by the swirled Dragon essence. Yin and yang are the negative and positive energies of all material and relationships in the universe. At this stage, while in motion, the two may begin to act independently but always remain complimentary in their functions and tasks. This is the one becoming the two. Produced from their social intercourse are the three treasures of essence, energy and spirit. Together the three produce the myriad being as they circulate through the five phases.

Taiji is the core concept of Chinese civilization and a key model of the culture. Yin-yang thought informs everything—sciences, spirituality, medicine, politics, social norms, exercises, philosophies, cuisine, and more. With its adaptability and changing forms and directions, much like the meandering course of a river, Taiji philosophy is a pure expression of the primordial Dao. It is called the "way of nature" and the supreme path. Daoists believe that to follow the way of nature is to retrace the steps back to the mysterious source of life, as if one were following the path of a river back to the ocean. Laozi called this source "Dao." Zhang Sanfeng said that "humanity and heaven are one," and his profound comment speaks volumes to humanity's point of origination in this cosmology. Because the beginning of the circle is the end (and, as follows, the end of the circle is the beginning), followers of Dao work their entire lives to cultivate their way around that circle in what is known as a complete turning, the circle itself drawing open the portal of all marvelous things. Laozi said, "We work our whole life to undo death. The reward is immortality."

Taiji philosophy is inherent to Chinese culture and has survived through every invasion and change in regime. For thousands of years, Daoists have used Taiji philosophy to build upon every known observation. Through unique guidelines of analysis, experimentation, and meditative study, they have managed to arrive at the pure and sublime truth. For example, they studied the Chinese silkworm and observed that the insect spun silk in two directions: clockwise nine times and counterclockwise six times. Because these numbers draw a parallel to yin (6) and yang (9), early Daoists emulated the pattern into their forms of self-cultivation.

As this base of knowledge grew, an increasing number of centers of Daoist study and thought emerged. These centers are some of the oldest-known universities of Eastern thought, long out-shadowing the multiplicity of modern-era Daoist monasteries. And while many modern-day monasteries have taken on the responsibility of spreading this knowledge beyond the Asiatic continent and enriching the lives of individuals everywhere, the more abstract ancient beliefs and discoveries have been historically guarded by the temple monks and nuns as secrets. Among those guarded secrets of the physical and spiritual masteries is the practice of Zhang Sanfeng Taijiquan and Daoist qigong, two systems that are capable of helping humans attain longevity and idiosyncratic skills.

Practice Principles

Taijiquan combines the arts of pugilism, meditation, and restorative health, a first-of-its-kind approach to fitness and self-preservation in China's rich and ancient martial history. But what exactly does taijiquan even mean? Taijiquan is translated "Great Ultimate Boxing," a reference to the source of all creation, and the fluid forms of the practice are the physical expression and orderly manifestation of this Daoist concept. As Master Wu Baolin often explains, Taiji means "the supreme state of spiritual being." As individual words, "tai" speaks of something extraordinary or of somebody par excellence, and "ji" indicates "an aim or pole in the distance," indicating the Dao.

These very specific and baseline principles of Taiji are always kept in the periphery when practicing Daoist self-cultivation, with the true aim of achieving human perfection and ultimately merging with Dao. The third character, *quan*, means "fist" and denotes "struggle": a reminder that one must suffer hardships ("eat bitter") in order to attain their goals. The forms of taijiquan reproduce and manifest Taiji philosophy through a continuous sequence of slow, graceful postures that sync with and mirror the pulse and motions of nature. One of the guiding precepts of this stand-alone martial art is that, during practice, the player is able to consciously rediscover (through sensitivity and reflection) a metaphysical awareness of other life surrounding him, the oneness that individuals often experience in youth and forget later in life. If practiced well, the player can develop a harmonious alignment with the life forces around him instead of being in opposition or discord with them. In this way, the player of taijiquan learns from nature how to fine-tune, calibrate, and eventually drift along the preordained laws of change, reconnecting to the path that leads back to the primordial source. Colloquially, this is called "going with the flow."

For example, when the winds blow through a bamboo forest, the bamboo trees dance about, swaying in any direction the wind goes while their leaves rustle. When the even more forceful monsoon winds blow, the bamboo still does not resist but rather conserves its energy and bends with every node all the way down to the ground when necessary. At the same time, it uses its natural hollow characteristics of emptiness (kong) to either absorb and store the wind or let pass through. After the winds have exerted and exhausted their measure, the bamboo stands up unscathed, no worse for wear. If one allows oneself to become soft, small, and insignificant, like a blade of grass, one can withstand and survive almost anything.

Wu Baolin says, "I stick to you whether you are weak or strong. If you are soft, I am soft too. If you are hard, I am still soft. We melt away hardness. The teeth are hard; the tongue is soft. When you are a hundred years old, your teeth will likely be gone, but your tongue will have survived. This is the subtle power of taijiquan."

This principle of yielding and softness has applications far beyond taijiquan—in fact, it permeates the activities of daily life. Whether we are absorbed in important negotiations, dealing with personal struggles, or even caught in the weeds of a stressful and hectic day at work, we tend to be most successful when we "go with the flow" and take such events in stride. Although humans are enlivened by conscientious effort, the path of least resistance often leads us to the outcome we desire with minimal exertion and maximal learning. The saying that we should be like water is now a trite, but still holds true. In a physical altercation, like a fist fight, taijiquan theory teaches us not to meet force with force, but instead to meet force with softness by giving way, borrowing the incoming energy, and using it later in a countering movement. Therefore, in taijiquan we bend like the bamboo tree, but only to whip back—redirecting the wind's own force back in the direction from where it came, oftentimes multiplied in force. If you have ever been hiking in the woods and pushed aside a soft springy tree branch to clear the way, only to have that branch whip back ten times stronger, you already understand the gist of this principle very well.

In combat, this strategy may be misconstrued as coward and perhaps insidious to those who are not familiar with it, but bending and yielding are, in fact, embodiments of self-discipline and resilience, and evoke the peaceful and harmonious nature of the bamboo tree. However, because of human folly and the inventory of uncontrolled and misunderstood emotions that we carry, we often find ourselves in difficult positions where we do not know when exactly to back away gracefully or save face. For instance, most all of us found ourselves in at least one conflict with our parents when we were teenagers. Shouting at the top of our lungs and disrespecting them was always a losing strategy; despite our youthful, fiery vigor, our parents outgunned us with simple authority. Though most of the conflicts we had with our parents probably blew over, certain ones might have caused hurt feelings, regret, or even lifelong discord. All in all, not a particularly wise or productive way to handle sensitive issues.

In the natural law of the wild, these situations usually play out quite differently. During mating season, if two tigers find themselves vying for the same mate or perhaps competing and clashing for the hunting rights to a mountain or cave, they will inevitably come face to face with one another in a showdown. This does not always lead to a fight. Often the weaker tiger will sense and acknowledge that it is already a losing match and yield. But if the tigers are comparable in strength, a fight will be the only way to determine who can claim the mate or hunting grounds. At some point during the fight, one of the tigers will recognize the other's superior strength and back off before it's too late, choosing to lick its wounds and live to fight another day rather than pursue the contest further—even to death. In taijiquan theory, this is known as "using force to overcome force," and is believed to be an inferior approach to resolving disputes. The will to survive supersedes all else.

According to Yijing theory, much of what is understood in the world as ideal, is flawed. People desire the most beautiful mate with the smoothest skin, or wish for the largest home, or the most expensive highly technical car. From the exterior, all of these things look perfect, but Daoists do not see the world in this way. For example, they believe that someone who is too beautiful will attract too many suitors; chasing a true beauty often leads to lasting disappointment or a broken heart. Conversely, it is very confusing and difficult for the beautiful person to choose the correct caller when there are so many, and this can lead to misstep. Daoists also believe that a man's skin should be smooth and a woman's rough, which goes contrary to what many cultures perceive as being appropriate. There's the question of posture. The "perfect" straight posture rarely breeds longevity while the person with a curved posture may see more decades pass in their lifetime. Whenever Master Wu Baolin shops for vegetables and fruit at the marketplace, he is looking for the best qi. Most people will choose the brightest examples, perfect and without flaws, but Master Wu was taught by his teacher not to overlook the less attractive produce, especially those which have been bitten into by the insects. Why? Because insects do well to avoid tasting anything that has been sprayed with pesticides. This explains why people who witness taijiquan and have no history or background of the art often find it strange that such a slow and peaceful series of movements are regarded as the supreme martial art in principle.

Again, taijiquan does not use domineering power in the traditional sense. It refuses to use force against force. If the body and mind are soft and relaxed, both maintain the capability to adapt and change positions to varying degrees, thereby leaving unlimited options for self-defense and control of the directive. This should not be interpreted as a full retreat, although there is a time and place for that particular tactic. As the Yijing says, "We are not surrendering the chessboard to the opponent, but rather making it next to impossible for them to advance, and while in that process, setting up the counteraction to the opponents advancing tactics." When a person yields, the attacker's force and power, over time, become overextended, absorbed, or depleted, and their initiative taken away. The taijiquan fighter can reenter the field and harness all the "borrowed" energy, redirecting it in the correct ratio necessary to neutralize the struggle and diametrically reflect the intent of the attacker. In this way, taijiquan teaches an inimitable way of channeling internal energies (one's own energy reserves and the borrowed energy from an opponent's own reserves) that are cultivated through softness, deep concentration, and patient, relaxed physical techniques.

In taijiquan, one must possess a focused mind and be physically receptively in order to control an adversary's movements. During training, a person's bodily reflexes are tuned to react to spontaneous movements. Practicing, of course, is non-negotiable. When Master Wu learned taijiquan, he was required to practice a new movement 1,000 times before learning the next move or sequence. This instilled in him the confidence to relax the body and mind even while under pressure to perform and defend during real-time training exercises.

What is it that confidently strengthens the internal stylist enough to approach combat situations in a near peaceful state? We know of the plan to bend and yield and deflect, but what is the hidden secret, the actual resolve that lies in wait until it becomes necessary to use it? That determination is qi, and it is the prime focus of neijia boxing. *Qi* provides an invisible advantage that is difficult to detect, not unlike the air stored inside the bamboo tree.

The Subtle Power of Qi

Before all else, it must be iterated that the most basic role, function, and purpose of Daoists is to harvest *qi* from nature. *Qi* is the central force of the universe and material power of Dao. It is the "formless form" and path of eternal Dao, the vital energy connecting all existence to the source of creation, the essential substance that makes all beings come to life. *Qi* is an all-pervading biomagnetic force coursing through the atmosphere and all that exists; it is responsible for nourishing and animating the infinite multitude of living entities, present both high and low, as well as in the past, present, and future. *Qi* is the life breath of the universe, allowing it to expand and contract as a single organism without bounds. Words cannot begin to define the intricacies and scope of qi. Its manifestations are ever-changing, never subject to the limits of time and space. Realizing its subtle vibrations and their purposeful differences is the internalization of the way of nature, the Dao. Living beings receive the unique powers of *qi* and its perceptible sensations through their five senses and the mind. While it is present, there is life; without it, there is death. "No qi, no life," as a saying goes. For this reason, Daoists earnestly pursue the conservation and enhancement of *qi* in multiple ways.

Human beings are imbued with three heavenly forms of *qi* from birth: primordial essence (jing), a crude energy stored in the sexual glands; primordial energy (yuanqi), which accumulates in the lower elixir field, located in the abdomen one-and-a-half inches below the naval, and primordial spirit (shen), the most refined form of *qi* that resides in the heart. They are called the Three Treasures of the body, matching the prenatal *qi* inherent in all beings. According to Daoist teachings, the three must be carefully safeguarded and unified through cultivation, which allows one not only to achieve longevity but also begin to realize the plethora of ancestral information stored deep within oneself. Without working with these resources, a human being has enough raw fuel to live for approximately 120 years. Their preservation and cultivation, on the other hand, greatly enhance a person's intellectual and creative development by igniting dormant neurons of the brain as well as supporting his or her spiritual evolution. Cultivation of the Three Treasures makes it possible to avoid disease and degeneration—the pitfalls of the aging process—and keeps the immune system in sound condition. Still, as long as people are alive, even the most basic activities—eating, walking, reading, breathing, having sex, and sleeping—burn off, to some extent, the original fuel provided by the Three Treasures. This reality prompted ancient longevity seekers to wonder: "What other sources of *qi* can we access and how can we best use them?" Their queries led them to certain discoveries.

As it turns out, there are timeless reservoirs of *qi* located outside the body (in the heavens and on the earth) which never age or lose their rhythm. They are the sun, moon, and stars (the Three Treasures of the heavens), as well as fire, water, and wind (the Three Treasures of the earth). All life is thus connected to a great living body—the cosmos—which maintains itself incessantly processing *qi* on all levels. Biologists have classified human beings, plants, and minerals—everything that exists on land and in the oceans—in a vast and dense taxonomy. However, in the end, they are still all part of a massive, interlocking continuum, reliably linked by *qi* in its many different forms.

In addition to being active, conscious participants in this system, Daoists also conducted observational experiments with the hopes of discovering the most powerful forms of qi. They ascertained that without ingesting *qi* from food, a person could sustain life for about a month. Without water, the survival rate was still about two weeks. But without breathing, it was a matter of minutes. Thus, they determined that breathing was both indispensable and the most readily accessible type of qi. It was life's essence at its purest. In addition, breathing is a major common denominator shared by all life forms living both in and out of water, thus marking them as sharing a similar energetic nature. Daoists thus came to value accessing *qi* through breathing as more important than eating, drinking, or sleeping—though they never ignored these other important sources of qi, of course. Based on this realization, they focused their exercises on breathing and developing techniques in conjunction with biodynamics.

Longevity is a primary goal of Daoist cultivation. The monks at White Cloud Temple enhance their longevity by capturing and borrowing *qi* from the treasures of heaven and earth with the help of specialized breathing techniques and precise movements and visualizations that accompany the breathwork. The combined activities guide the *qi* through the body's passageways and refine it in designated areas of a person's internal landscape, where it is stored. The body acts as a refinery in this process, replenishing and energizing itself down to the cellular level—similar to the way that plants use photosynthesis. As a result, primordial energy is preserved and alchemically refined to reinforce and grow the immortal embryo, the accumulation of spirit energy developed internally. The results are increased health, vitality, and longevity.

Daoyin as Foundation

Daoyin, the traditional basis of the modern practice of qigong, is the mother of taijiquan, the ground of the Daoist internal boxing systems and each of the other internal schools. Historically, daoyin can be traced back to the Warring States period, when it served in medicine—preventative and life-extension—and spirituality. The latter involved a way to actively integrate the wisdom of the *Yijing* into human affairs, to encourage mystic inquiry into self-discovery, and expedite change and maturation in the human organism in relation to nature, society, and personal destiny. The purpose of daoyin was to merge and harmonize the oracle and the organism, and become a necessary tool to combine Heaven-Human-Earth into one. This internal system of exercise uses stillness of the mind, specialized breathing, gentle motion, and visualization to absorb nature's qi, which strengthens the body from the inside-out to virtually limitless shares, if pursued diligently.

Since the central essence of Zhang Sanfeng Taijiquan is predicated on daoyin practice and theory, it is different from the other mainstream martial arts predating neijia boxing. This is why taijiquan is sometimes referred to as "moving practice." The importance of daoyin in relation to Chinese culture and taijiquan cannot be underscored enough. Arguably, daoyin is China's greatest treasure. "Reap the wind and reap its benefits." Taijiquan is the benefactor of these ancient roots and ultimately its formidable nature arise there.

It is important to note that pure, undiluted daoyin practice is still 100 times more powerful than taijiquan, even though it lies at the heart of taijiquan practice. Daoist exercises can harvest and synthesize raw forms of *qi* into pure spirit essence better than other forms of practice, including hard-style martiial systems. But, because of taijiquan's versatility and multi-functional benefits as a self-defense system, first-class physical therapy exercise, and spiritual medita-tion, it remains a highly regarded practice in the Daoist canon.

Daoyin focuses mostly on *qi* cultivation, since *qi* drives spiritual transfor-mation, physical vigor, and longevity. Zhang Sanfeng took advantage of such practices on the Wudang mountains, where he had the opportunity to meet with iconic and famous figures that inspired him over decades until, at the age of eighty-one, taijiquan was born. It was the culmination of a lifetime of study and determination to set apart his legacy.

But Zhang Sanfeng did not stop there. In the decades after forming and bringing the taijiquan set into a fully ripened state, he sought to accomplish even more. The apotheosis of his system came to be when he assembled three masterwork practices into one set, collectively known as Zhang Sanfeng Taiji Qigong. These practices became the hidden bedrock of his legendary mystique and is also what fueled his second century of life. He was 120 years old, com-pleting his second 60-year cycle. Zhang Sanfeng's contributions were inspired and corroborated by a romantic love interest, a talented Buddhist nun from neighboring Mount Emei in Sichuan. She gifted him the vision.

Zhou Zhiruo was the fourth-generation abbess of the Emei lineage of Buddhism and the student of Miejue Shitai, the third-generation predecessor. Mount Emei is a holy place and one of the four sacred Buddhist mountains in China. It is the home mountain of the bodhisattva Puxian, one of the four main disciples of Shakyamuni Buddha. Emei is still a community famous for its martial arts code, and at the time, allied with and exchanged cultivation secrets with practitioners on the Wudang mountains.

Zhang Sanfeng's relationships with Buddhist lineages went back over half a century, to his Shaolin days. He and Zhou Zhiruo shared many ideas together as well as a mutual fondness for one another. Her contributions were critical in helping him to spiritually pierce the next ethereal amnion, which he faced courageously. She was also the love of his life. The three qigong forms he developed surpassed even his own earlier taijiquan practice in terms of developing *qi*, the promotion of health and longevity, and of building serious martial power, along with the mind's ability to manipulate *qi* at will.

In his youth, Master Wu Baolin was especially drawn to martial arts practices, using up any spare moments to indulge perfection in the forms and techniques. Whenever Master Du found his student's fist clenched, he reminded Young Wu that his time was better spent practicing qigong in order to have the meaningful edge and clarity in life as well as in combat tests. He explained, "Taijiquan theory and technique has its own golden ratio, use only four ounces of energy to move 1,000 pounds." However, after trying tenaciously, Wu Baolin discovered that to truly apply this ratio, one must first possess 1,000 pounds of energy to be able to efficiently move 1,000 pounds with only four ounces. "This can only be done with qigong as groundwork," Master Du concluded. Only after many years of training did Wu Baolin finally come to realize Master Du's wisdom clearly. He also came to realize that Laozi, the master of masters and a key architect to Zhang Sanfeng's taijiquan, did not routinely practice taijiquan methods, but rather focused his efforts on daoyin, Taiji philosophy, and the *Yijing*.

Daoist exercise has two classifications of energy cultivation: yin and yang. Yang *qi* is the fire, the sun, the masculine. Yin *qi* is water, the moon, the feminine. When cultivating yang *qi*, we practice during daylight hours; when working on yin *qi*, we practice at night. Taijiquan finds itself again in a very unique category because it cultivates both essential forces of yin and yang, through postures of emptiness and fullness. To fully grasp this concept of taijiquan, the characteristics of yin and yang must be explored.

Yin and Yang

When every type of light in the universe combines, the result is pure white (yang); when every color in the universe is mixed together, the result is deep black (yin). This encompasses the full spectrum of all light and color. Together, yin and yang exemplify the coming to and going out of life as each reaches its zenith and the other begins. The peak transformation points continue to weave into one another in the same way that night bleeds into day and day into night. Daoist practice, thought, and cosmology are fundamentally imbued with the relationship between yin and yang, according with their cyclic processes of infinite change.

Yin and yang form the principal structure and function of creation in the manifest physical world. Their interplay coexists like the positive and negative currents of the earth's magnetic field or the polarity found in an ordinary battery. They are also reproductive energies, the masculine and feminine aspects of nature joining to perpetuate existence in daily communion. The formation of a child growing in the womb is thus a complete turning of the Great Ultimate. All organisms contain the vital forces of yin and yang, no matter their size or shape. Despite the fact that yin and yang are contingent upon one another, the two nonetheless possess extremely different qualities.

In taijiquan, three notions stand out most as they relate to the birth of action. First, movement (yang) is born of stillness (yin), and movement, in turn, produces stillness; second, yin is the foundation of yang, and the origin of motion; and third, yang is outward expression.

The values of yin and yang govern both the inherent stillness and motion of taijiquan. For instance, imagine a fish holding still in the depths of an ocean. This is the state of yin (both water and fish). When the fish begins to swim, the movement has changed its state from yin to yang. The ocean is the state of Wuji. The fish is the yin particle. The movement is the yang force. Together, all three transforming into a state of Taiji. This concept is why Zhang Sanfeng preferred practicing taijiquan when it was dark. The night was Wuji, the state of nothingness, and he was the yin particle of stillness, which gave rise to yang (movement). He followed Taiji philosophy to the letter.

When Zhang Sanfeng Taijiquan is practiced on soft ground, the footpaths and footsteps left behind form a Taiji symbol. Another manifestation of the practice is that over time the player of Zhang Sanfeng Taijiquan, literally becomes round in the shape of the Taiji symbol. Roundness symbolizes heaven; earth is the square; and man generally represents the triangle or mountain pyramid. The lesson here is that everything in taijiquan is round…

Master Wu Baolin appeared in the doorway wearing all black, an aesthetic he took after his Daoist teacher, Master Du. He placed his arms across his chest as he observed closely a new lot of taijiquan enthusiasts in practice. Many of the students were oblivious to his presence until he suddenly roared in Mandarin Chinese, "Everything in taiji is round! Wrong! Do it again!" It was his unique way of introducing himself to a class that had commenced two months earlier. Everyone quickly turned their heads to face him as he stepped out from the doorway. The venue was perfect, a private parking lot which one could enter from the Beijing Chinese Medical Center. On Sundays, when there were no cars, the spot was quiet and surrounded by walls and an old tree in the corner of the southeast quadrant—ideal for martial arts and daoyin classes.

Master Wu Baolin approached the dozen or so individuals who were there to learn taijiquan on a weekend morning in Santa Monica. All of them came from diverse walks of life. One student, who hailed from the Great White North, was singled out in particular. He was standing in front of the class and had been demonstrating his taijiquan form before he was caught by surprise by Master Wu Baolin's arrival. Understandably, the student grew increasingly more nervous as Wu Baolin circled him and said, "Wrong! Do it again!"

For the last eight weeks, this new class of Zhang Sanfeng-Wu Baolin Style taijiquan students had been led by a pair of student-teachers handpicked from Master Wu's first class of American students, years prior. Master Wu's appearance on this particular Sunday morning was his first encounter with these students—and it was clear that they still had much to learn.

With his right hand, Master Wu grabbed both of the student demonstrator's hands, which were medially joined together, palms-up. In this position, he vehemently pried the student's hands perfectly flat. That subtle adjustment set off a chain-link jolt throughout the student's skeletal apparatus. "Wrong! Do it again!" Master Wu repeated, walking around the lone demonstrator. The student failed again to grasp the lesson.

Finally, Master Wu turned his attention toward the class of weekend warriors. They were an eclectic bunch: physicians, kung fu practitioners, actors, writers, teachers, dancers, artist, waiters—what seemed to be a reflection of the total population of the then-quiet beach town. The class of students were now and rapt with attention, as if waiting to be inspired by Master Wu.

With an altogether different tone of voice, Master Wu gently began to explain that everything in nature is round and circular and constantly in motion—therefore, the movements of taijiquan are also spiraling and neither linear nor square. Whether it's the turning and twisting of the waist (along the dai mai channel), the long curves of the arms and hands and joints, the sunken hollow of the chest and armpits, the knees (which, at all times, should be bent so that the buttocks are rounded out), the lines that one draws in the air and on the ground—there's roundness.

"All things alive are round and soft," Master Wu said. "All things dead are straight and hard."

The class murmured among themselves, contemplating these simple and profound teachings and attempting to thoughtfully integrate them into their practice on that morning. Meanwhile, Master Wu gazed up at the sky and began a slow deliberate step into the personal space of the lone student demonstrator. Everyone's eyes shifted and followed. By the time the student turned to face Master Wu Baolin, it was too late. A mysterious paralysis and wave of invisible force suddenly emerged from below the lone demonstrator's feet as a rush of strong water-like current began to float the student's body as if it were a boat at high tide. As they say in taijiquan, the roots had been cut. Master Wu's palm followed closely behind, striking the middle elixir zone (heart center) by way of the solar plexus, sending the student through the air like a kite stolen by the wind. With two-to-three feet of air below his feet, the student landed over ten feet away and stumbled backward another as the invisible power of taijiquan continued to tumble inside the body. "Again!" Master Wu pointed to the warm black tar surface near his feet as if calling the student back for more punishment. At last, the student demonstrated the movements correctly.

To say that everything in taijiquan is round is in fact a deep and profound statement. When the bamboo tree is connected to the earth and rainwater, it is flexible and soft. When uprooted or disconnected from the source, the bamboo tree consequentially becomes straight, dry, and brittle, splintering into dust. Humans fair no differently. With advancing age, energies wane and the body becomes stiff; only six hours after death, rigor mortis will have set in. In order to sustain life and achieve longevity, we must observe certain principles of roundness.

The Tornado Effect

One of the teachings that makes Zhang Sanfeng Taijiquan uniquely Daoist in comparison to the other taijiquan schools is it moves in only one direction: forward, from beginning to end. Think of a tornado, which is a destructive vortex of violently rotating winds. An active tornado only spins in one direction. The longer it turns in that single direction (we will call this clockwise direction yang) the bigger and stronger it becomes, pulling in energy and building upon itself into an unstoppable destructive force. As soon as the direction changes (we will call this counterclockwise direction yin), the tornado dissipates and disappears without a trace.

If taijiquan is practiced in two directions, forward and reverse, it becomes far less fruitful as an exercise, neither mounting nor decreasing qi. One more or less stays around zero on the integer line. It is like turning the water faucet on and off, over and over again, never giving a chance for the water pressure to build up, or for the water level to rise to the rim of the basin long enough to wash one's face.

Much of this idea of the tornado effect mimics patterns in nature. For instance, a tiger has two doors (an entrance and an exit). The sun always rises in the east and sets in the west. Tree rings only grow and spiral in one direction. The earth on its axis turns in only one direction, as do the stars, and the star constellations above. And depending on the hemisphere in which one lives, downward flowing water only circles the drain in one direction, every time. In this way, the ancients ascertained that clockwise is a generating and gathering direction and that counterclockwise is a dispersing and diffusing direction. Although, at times, Zhang Sanfeng Taijiquan appears to move in reverse (stepping backward), the meridian *qi* is still directed in a generating cycle (clockwise and forward). The tornado concept applies in a Daoist's day-to-day activities, influencing the way they stir food while cooking, roll their medicine pills, or prepare the dough of their noodles and dumplings. These principles are best explained by the generating and destructive cycles of the five phases theory.

We can best examine the principle of the tornado effect through the generating and destructive cycles of the five phases. The five phases are wood, fire, earth, metal, and water: everyday materials from which the things of the world are made. Produced from yin and yang, they are connected to one another and form a paradigm which controls, creates, and facilitates the cyclical changes of life. All perceptible phenomena, known as the 10,000 things of the colorful world, are composed of the waxing and waning of the five phases.

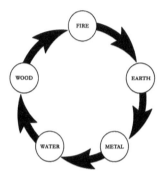

The generating aspect of the five phases begins with wood, which matches the east and the rising sun. In a circular and clockwise direction, wood gives rise to fire in the south. Fire, in turn, replenishes earth (located in the center of the four directions). Earth, in the depth of its soil, creates metal in the west. Metal transforms into water in the north, and water returns to nourish wood in the east, thus completing the generating cycle. This is the Zhang Sanfeng Taijiquan philosophical method of practice: positive influence and growth, collecting *qi* and generating energy, and making connections with your destiny and good opportunities. In fact, cultivating the five phases in this way produces an impenetrable armor from within the body—much like the invisible shell of *qi* that Zhang Sanfeng noticed when Zhen Wu appeared to him.

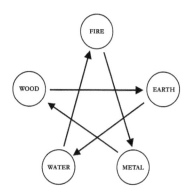

The controlling cycle also begins with wood. Instead of moving in a circular pattern, it moves in lines to reach the countering phases and looks like a five-pointed star. In this system, starting once again in the east, wood controls earth in the center, breaking the soil with its roots and drawing in its essential nutrients. Earth controls water in the north with its ability to absorb large quantities of liquid. Water flows toward fire in the south to extinguish the flames. Fire, containing immense heat, liquefies metal in the west. The controlling cycle completes itself with metal, such as an ax, chopping through wood. Although the controlling cycle is sometimes referred to as "destructive" when it exists in excess, it nonetheless serves as a positive counterbalance to the affirmative generating cycle and thus helps to maintain overall stability. However, in Taiji combat, the controlling cycle of the five phases is used to keep your opponent off balance, limiting his or her ability to generate strength against you.

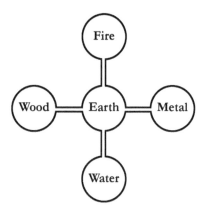

There is a third diagram of the five phases that positions the earth in the center of the four cardinal directions. On the perimeter are north, south, east, and west. The player of taijiquan stands in the earth position (center) at all times. The balance of yin and yang inside each phase enables and perpetuates each phase's driving functions and purpose to persist. In this way, these opposites are always in motion. An outward expanding action such as stepping forward with a palm strike is a movement of the yang expression. Shifting the stances toward the back while yielding or strategically pulling in force is a movement of the yin expression. As the Taiji diagram shows, yin and yang are constantly transforming into one another and always contain their counterpart. In his teachings, Zhang Sanfeng is adamant about sticking to the principles of yin and yang. Otherwise, he explains, Dao is lost. "When moving upward, think clearly of moving down. When moving downward, do not lose sight of what is above. And when moving forward, the mind's awareness should be moving back. If stepping to the left, notice the right."

Health Benefits

For thousands of years, the Chinese have recorded the health benefits of exercise. They have been able to measure and monitor, with great accuracy, the effects that different exercises, as well as medicines, diets, acupuncture point manipulations, and other various forms of treatment and lifestyle, have on the whole of body, mind, and spirit. Master Du was a skilled Daoist physician who could get a read on Wu Baolin's health and *qi* level solely by listening to the sound of the temple bell after being struck by his young student. Thus, as Wu Baolin says, "Taijiquan helps to regulate the nervous system, and balances yin and yang in the body."

Using the senses as instruments to gather data on the body and detect abnormalities were perfectly acceptable techniques in the old East. Upon rapid globalization in the Information Age, many ancient Chinese medicinal practices were quickly dismissed in the West and, for a long time, did not reach the global mainstream. In the time thereafter, many notable institutions in the West, including prestigious universities and medical research centers, have conducted and published their own studies on the health benefits of taijiquan using standardized scientific testing. To a great degree, these studies arrived at many of the same conclusions as the original data presented by early Chinese physicians.

The health benefits of taijiquan are wide-ranging and well-documented. For centuries, studies at home and abroad suggest that regular practice may have a positive effect on Alzheimer's disease, hypertension, arthritis, balance, memory loss, and cardiovascular circulation. It may also increase energy levels, boost immunity, and regulate body temperature. The increases in energy may have immediate effects on stress management and strength building. In the elderly, any or all of these benefits may appear in as little as six to seven months of regular practice; in younger people, they may appear in considerably less time. Ideally, an individual should supplement his or her taijiquan practice with a healthy lifestyle to see maximum results. This may include a balanced diet, good sleeping habits, reasonable work schedule, and limited indulgences.

Chinese medicine and health practices approach disease with the attempt to prevent, rather than treat. Acupuncture, traditional Chinese massage, herbal pharmacopeia, physical therapy exercise, and medical daoyin are all methods of treatment and maintenance. With that said, these methods have also been successful at treating a wide spectrum of disease. There are five-thousand years of reported studies and written documentation to support its successful uses.

In 2015, the Nobel Prize acknowledged research around Chinese herbal medicine—specifically, it lauded the successful isolation of the primary active antifebrile component found in sweet wormwood, an herb of Chinese pharmacopeia first recorded 1,700 years ago. According to ancient Daoists, the best ways to prevent disease are taijiquan, daoyin, high-quality water, and a clean diet. When put to use, these facts are by and large the most impressive qualities of Chinese medical teachings. As the saying goes, "An ounce of prevention is worth a pound of cure."

Over the course of several decades, Kyoto University in Japan conducted studies on the benefits of varied exercises on longevity. Daoyin was number one and taijiquan came in at number two on the list of best exercises to prolong lifespan. This more or less corroborates research at the White Cloud Temple, where daoyin, taijiquan, and high-quality spring water were the keys to a long life. Naturally, it's important to consult a qualified physician to rule out any serious health risks, but for most cases of minor health issues (such as lethargy, weak immune system, lack of stamina, etc.), Daoist exercises seem to offer great support.

Zhang Sanfeng himself was a master physician, specializing in medical massage—bone-setting, daoyin therapy, taiji massage, *tuina* (push and seize), *anmo* (rub and press), and *roujing* (gentle and quiet) massage. In this way, a key majority of the Zhang Sanfeng Taijiquan set is modeled after the praxis of Chinese medical theory. It follows the directional flow of the meridian system, matching the founder's understanding of the profound importance of having an unobstructed roadway for energy to circulate through the body's channels.

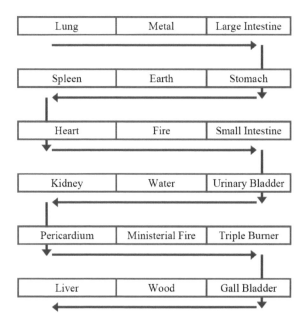

The Chinese meridian system has an exact starting point and an exact ending point. Both points meet and join on the same bridge. In a healthy body, this system remains in motion and circulates *qi* through the twelve channels a total of fifty times per day, moving in steady streams through channel after channel, with each organ given a chance to rest during their assigned hours on the biological meridian clock (except, of course, for the heart). If the meridian system becomes hyperactive or hypoactive, a person may develop excesses or deficiencies of yin and yang. If one does not address these imbalances promptly, they may lead to varying degrees of illness. Acupuncture and herbal therapy are most effective in establishing and maintaining balance in the meridian system. In taijiquan, however, the practitioner takes an active role in initiating the slow flow of *qi* throughout the body.

At a glance, the first thing one notices is that taijiquan is practiced slowly. This actually helps maximize the potential health benefits and also significantly reduces the risk of injury. But there's more to it than that. Daoists believe the heart is programmed with a finite number of heartbeats. Once that number is reached, the heart will cease to function. Many studies have shown that high-level athletes rarely attain longevity because of the increased frequency of their heartbeats. Taijiquan's slow approach to health oftentimes appears "easy" and not stimulating in comparison, a refutation of the mantra "no pain no gain." In fact, taijiquan is not, as its reputation may suggest, an exercise reserved solely for the elderly.

In our age of accelerated lives and technological noise, it takes a greater deal of effort to expand one's attention span and practice patience. But the way of Dao—that conservation is the way of nature—has not changed at all. An ancient Daoist theory, based on yin and yang, is that if you want something, you must go the opposite way. For instance, if you want to have lightning speed as a Taiji boxer, you have to practice as slowly as a cloud's drift. And if you want to travel far, do not run. Other reasons taijiquan is slowly practiced are to calm the mind and the breath.

Mind and Breath

Basic taijiquan starts with the mind. In internal boxing, the mind (*yinian*), is defined as intent, also called the will or willpower. The tranquil mind controls the movement of the qi, sending and gathering it first into the lower elixir field (the

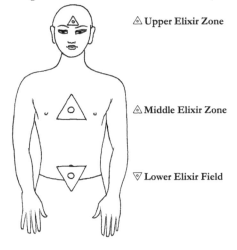

△ Upper Elixir Zone

△ Middle Elixir Zone

▽ Lower Elixir Field

point three fingers'-width below the navel), where abdominal breathing begins. After the *qi* has sunk into the lower elixir field, it begins to circulate through the meridian system and guides specific movements and postures. In other words, it's not the muscles, skeleton, or nerve impulses which do the initial work—rather, they are only engaged after the mind and *qi* have become combined. After enough practice, when the *qi* is uninhibited and active, a person can experience the sensation of being a floating cloud.

The combination of deep breathing and the spiraling movements of taijiquan gently massage the internal organs. This increases the efficacy of the digestive system, which helps keep the hollow organs clear of obstruction. Deep abdominal breathing is the perfect way to explain the kidneys' role in Chinese medical theory. According to the theory, the kidneys are in charge of inhaling and the lungs are in charge of exhaling. When a person places proper focus on this sequence, he or she can increase the capacity of air he or she can hold, thereby strengthening the respiratory and circulatory system's capacity. This, in turn, boosts metabolic function. One may help prevent or reduce cardiovascular health diseases such as arterial hardening, hypertension, and coronary plaque or thrombosis through the practice of taijiquan and its specific breathing.

Breathing is the most essential function of life. Healthy cells will die without sufficient oxygen; without air, a person can become completely brain dead in as little as four or five minutes. Recent studies suggest that cancer cells radically thrive in low-oxygen environments and, conversely, fare poorly in oxygen-rich environments. The steady pace of deep breathing found in internal exercises such as taijiquan play a crucial role in the combat and prevention of disease.

In Zhang Sanfeng Taijiquan, a practitioner either deliberately presses, lightly massages with one's knuckles, or visualizes the stimulation of the principal 365 acupuncture points (the small caves and vortexes of energy that locate themselves along the meridians) in spiraling movements. Doing this helps the practitioner reach the ideal meditative state by eliminating tensions and emotional stressors that create barricades between *qi* and the spirit (shen) points that serve as gates to an expansive consciousness. In combat, a relaxed state of the mind allows the taijiquan fighter to be adaptable. With the meridians clear and flowing smoothly like a river, a fighter is also able to move and concentrate his or her *qi* at will.

Acupuncture point manipulation in combative taijiquan can be dangerous. In fact, it was only taught to the most disciplined students. Masters of the art were extremely careful not to teach anyone that had the predisposition of becoming a "poisonous dragon." It took many years of training. In Old China, when fighting contests to the death was commonplace, the most effective way to defend one's life and neutralize an attack was by using internal force to target an opponent's acupuncture points. By striking these select points, one could inflict serious bodily injury ranging from a weakening of the nervous system to incapacitation of muscles, ruptured internal organs, internal bleeding, and even death.

These days, of course, practitioners emphasize the more meditative (and regenerative) aspects. The key movements of Zhang Sanfeng Taijiquan form as a self-administered physical therapy routine that helps one maintain the musculoskeletal and nervous systems. In the same way that a chef makes handmade Chinese noodles—carefully pulling dough open and stretching it apart in strands in repeated motions—the movements in taijiquan increase the elasticity of the nerves and sinews.

By increasing the flexibility of the sinews, one increases the mobility of the joints. According to lore surrounding Daoist daoyin and Zhang Sanfeng Taijiquan, every inch of increased tendon length is equal to ten additional years of life. Increased tendons loosen the joints, potentially reducing the risk of rheumatoid arthritis, bone spurs, degenerative disc disease, loss of articular cartilage, and overall stiffness. Exercises that grow the sinews and bolster the joints are especially important because sinew naturally loses suppleness and shortens as we age. Keeping the sinews relaxed and pliable in turn allows the joints to remain open and to store qi. This stored *qi* serves like a granary, providing needed energy to counteract fatigue during exercise, lowering perspiration, increasing the bone marrow production, and preserving synovial fluids in the joints.

In fact, these movements and principles evoke the fluid motions and abilities of the cat. According to the Daoist account, the cat is a master teacher from heaven. The cat is considered by Daoism to be the master teacher of both taijiquan and Indian yoga, as well as roushu, a Chinese health and performance art of contortionism; the cat's displays of flexibility are second to none. For most observers and enthusiasts of taijiquan, it is a common misnomer that the migratory red-crowned crane is a majority contributor to the theories and movements of the taijiquan form(s), based on the magpie and snake legend. This is most evident in a signature taijiquan move known as "White Crane Spreads its Wings." This particular standing posture with curved arms outstretched is a classical posture of the art. Zhang Sanfeng was certainly well-versed in the crane and snake style martial arts of the Shaolin Temple, but taijiquan was to be of a different origin. The technique, "White Crane Spreads its Wings" is actually derived from a cat posture. When staring from the front of this posture, imagine that the Taiji player is lying down on their back and you will see the feisty spirit of the cat outstretched and lying down on its back, taunting you to scratch their belly, but beware.

In the transition between White Crane Spreads its Wings and the Brushed Knee movement, there are two transitional movements that use the hands and arms to fan across the body. These smooth defensive blocks are better categorized as the quick hard slaps issued by the cat's padded paws. The entire feline family is extremely skilled at boxing. Their speed and agility and footwork are unparalleled. The cat's weaknesses, however, are in the shoulders and jaw, and their strengths intensified in the claws, tendons, and teeth.

How is the cat influential to taijiquan? Because of its softness, speed, balance, explosiveness, and agility. Cats know how to relax completely and are the most limber. They are the masters of releasing every tension in their bodies, dropping their shoulders (first rule of taijiquan) so that the forelimbs drape flowingly down to their sides especially when seated in recline. Try lifting a cat, asleep or awake, and they may slip from your hands like water, and although cats have a fluid nature, they are still yang fire. This mastery of relaxation, when applied in taijiquan, helps the body to elongate and stretch without forcibly stretching the body's muscles and sinews, or fold and roll into a ball. In this way, execution is done safely and with an extremely low risk of injury (pulled muscles, torn sinew, broken capillaries, and ruptured corpuscles). It is because of this relaxation ability that cats retain explosive speed even when old.

To practice taijiquan with the proper form, it is critical to keep the knees slightly bent—especially when you're transitioning from one position to the next. Bending your knees and shifting your body weight from one leg to the other by pivoting on the soles and heels of the feet exercise the calf muscles, which represent the heart in Traditional Chinese Medicine (in fact, calves are often called the "second heart.") Apart from the similarities in shape between the calf and the heart, the calves contain acupuncture points that are connected to certain heart and kidney conditions. By this logic, massaging the calves can help strengthen the heart and have other cardiovascular benefits.

The way in which taijiquan tones the muscles differs from more explosive forms of resistance exercises. In taijiquan, a practitioner holds a low center of gravity, which produces slow stretches and contractions in both the major and the minor muscle groups. This tones and builds power in the muscles as well as stimulates the nerve bundles that permeate those muscles. It's a slightly deceiving kind of work—though the slower, more deliberate movements may not appear to challenge the muscles in the same way that, say, weightlifting does, the reality is in fact the opposite: a greater number of muscles are activated. This is largely due to the constant turning and twisting from the seat of the occipital bone as well as the lateral rolling of the joints from the toes up.

In addition to stimulating an ecosystem of musculature that is typically neglected, the slowness of taijiquan essentially eliminates the risk of strains or injury—that is, if a person practices it with the correct postures. After all, a person's joints are never actually straightened into a locked position; this acts as a kind of built-in safety mechanism that ensures that the joints remain slightly bent, rounded, and protected.

In this way, the low-impact nature of taijiquan serves not only as a useful preventative exercise, but also as a remedial modality for individuals with existing joint or body pain. In taijiquan, pressure is kept steady on the hips and legs, diverting any tension away from the fragile lower back. By creating pressure in the muscle groups around the bones (as opposed to the bones themselves), taijiquan in fact strengthens the bones. This process is analogous to the way in which coal, under conditions of unyielding, incredible pressure, can turn into a diamond. And that the bones are strengthened from the outside-in, a taijiquan practitioner is directing *qi* to fill the porous bone marrow, which collects and solidifies in the bones themselves and may, over time, reduce the risk of osteoporosis. This phenomenon is succinctly captured in a taijiquan phrase that describes the bones as "steel wrapped by cotton."

Taijiquan produces different physiological results when compared to the aesthetic of the contemporary bodybuilder—which is an ideal so pervasive that it has even become the picture of health even in the East. In taijiquan, function supersedes image. Master Du, for instance, was ultra-lean and had forearms defined by deeply grooved fissures close to the bone—steel-corded sinew without any extraneous skin, muscle, or fat. Master Wu Baolin still believes that it was not Master Du's intense training or diet of tofu, cabbage, and carrots that was primarily responsible for his incredible physique. Instead, it was his quotidian routine of drinking 150-year-old undiluted black rice vinegar straight from a porcelain cup.

Spine and Qi

The lower back is a crucial and particularly notable part of the spine because it often produces problems for people who do not take care of it. Daoist physicians say that lower-back pain is often a consequence of an immobile waist due to lack of exercise.

Most white-collar workers in the modern era find themselves sitting at a desk or in front of a computer for eight-to-ten hours a day—not including the sedentary round-trip commute, which may average to an additional hour per day. Taijiquan offers relief for lower-back pain because it incorporates frequent turns of the waist, creating an image akin to an old soybean grinder, which has two wheels: the top wheel turning in perpetual motion and the bottom wheel remaining still. In fact, waist turning activates the Belt Vessel, which demarcates the upper and lower wheels and is the only horizontally positioned *qi* meridian on the body. It begins at Spirit Gateway (Shenque CV-8) point in the navel and circles around to the lower back across the Gate of Life (Mingmen GV-6) point opposite the navel on the back between lumbar vertebrae 3 and 4. The constant turning of the waist during practice keeps the area of this most important acupuncture point open and the spine mobile.

Keeping the Gate of Life open has a number of positive health ramifications, since it is a vital to kidney function. The kidneys are water, and the Gate of Life is fire. When healthy and open, water and fire can work together to produce a steady flow of steam power in the kidneys (which are the root of the body)—which becomes energy for other vital organs in the body including the brain.

While these notions are quite common knowledge in taijiquan literature and communities, Zhang Sanfeng also saw the spine as a hunter's bow, the sinews that attach to the spine as bowstrings, and the limbs as arrows. In a situation where an individual's sinews are working in harmony, he or she can muster a great deal of explosiveness during practice. The technique of "Bend the Bow-Shoot the Tiger" perfectly embodies this metaphorical understanding of the spine, sinews, and limbs, and a band-stretching and -releasing function. Another application of this image in taijiquan is when a taiji fighter, presented with a frontal attack, moves to sink and hollow the chest and abdomen so that the spine curves like a drawn bow. At the right moment, the fighter straightens his spine and allows the energy that he has harvested in his spine to project forward, throwing back the attacker's own force.

With that said, a taijiquan fighter can exercise his spine both vertically and horizontally. Twisting horizontally in one direction and releasing in the opposite direction (for instance, in the exercise "Parting the Wild Horse's Mane") produces the same effect as flexing the spine vertically.

The source of Zhang Sanfeng's legendary power was his spinal cord. And what, apart from the spine, so deeply connects the hemispheres of the body? Running all the way up to the head (which Daoists consider to be heaven), the spine is a kind of conduit that channels the heavenly energy of the brain. A person can hold and release *qi* from his spine, weaponizing both the limbs and every part of the body connected to the spine. In nature, this concept is seen in the actions of an electric eel, jolts which incapacitate prey.

Zhang Sanfeng's nightly meditations testified to the tremendous power he could harvest in his spine. Between the hours of 11 pm and 1 am, he would stand in a static posture. Throughout those two hours, his clothes would sometimes rustle even when there were no signs of wind; if he was meditating indoors, vibrations would ripple through the walls like tiny shock waves.

In taijiquan, his kind of explosive power is known as *fajin*. It is an internal martial arts technique that harmonizes qi, mental clarity, and proper Taiji form to create natural force. *Fajin* allows a Taiji fighter to focus, generate, and discharge his or her *qi* for self-defense. This *qi* comes from the deep reserves of the lower elixir field and spine, and its expulsion is often assisted by the breath.

Taijiquan is often called "mind boxing" because it is ultimately the mind that directs *qi*. When doing *fajin*, the mind plays an essential role in both expression and reach. It is the mind, after all, that enables a person to go beyond his or her physical limitations and guides the inertia of intrinsic power to explode through physical or muscular power. For example, if someone is standing before you, and you concentrate your fist onto their chest, the power you release will not travel beyond the surface of your opponent's chest. However, if you do not acknowledge your target's presence before you, and instead concentrate the force of your fist onto the wall twenty feet behind your target, you can topple your target as if he were never there.

An emperor once called upon Zhang Sanfeng to quell a rebellion of a hundred fighters. Supposedly, he defeated them all single-handed and with minimal effort. There are many legends like this in Chinese history: masters of internal arts, with otherwise unremarkable physiques, dropping the strongest stallions with the touch of their palm, rupturing their enemies' internal organs without leaving a bruise, or warding off multiple attackers by launching their bodies into midair. An uninitiated and purely rational mind may find it difficult to accept these types of martial arts accomplishments, relegating them to the stuff of comic books and superhero fantasies. For Daoists, however, superhuman strength like this is not a question of true or untrue but rather a question of accessing or tapping in to the deep reservoir of power at a universal source. This deep-seated power is precisely what Daoist monks seek to find and unlock in their daily practice.

Over the centuries, Daoist masters have found different ways to tap into this hidden reservoir. For instance, the eminent war strategist Sunzi found that placing his soldiers in life-or-death situations as well as motivating them by asking them to recall their lives beyond war—their family, friends, and loved ones—motivated them to fight on a kind of otherworldly level, even when they were outnumbered on the battlefield. This is also precisely what Master Du sought to cultivate in Wu Baolin when he asked him to leap off the mountain in Xinjiang.

Other examples include the story of the mother who lifted a car with her own strength in order to retrieve her child, who was pinned underneath it, or the mother who single-handed fought off a full-grown polar bear, emanating a larger-than-life ability in order to protect her children and her children's friends, who were playing nearby. These stories exemplify the power of the supreme Dao, which both transcends and undergirds the phenomenal and ephemeral aspects of the entire cosmos.

Water

Water is a particularly important subject in Daoism. As the *Daode jing* says "In all under heaven, nothing is softer or weaker than water. Yet for tackling the solid and powerful, it has no equal" (Chapter 78). The text further explains its inherent nature as quiet strength, humble character, nurturing heart, noncompetitive soul, patient spirit, and endurance. In this way, water is closest to the true nature of Dao. These aspects of water were inimitable to the newly developing taijiquan.

According to common lore, Zhang Sanfeng always followed a rolling brook on his way to worship his main god, the Perfect Warrior, closely associated with the north and the power of water. He also reportedly taught his students taijiquan in the waters of Taiji Lake, north of the Wudang mountains. Pilgrimages such as these have been retraced for many generations by Zhang Sanfeng followers seeking ultimate truth.

A student or practitioner of taijiquan can learn much by interacting with water. Its free-flowing nature and agility can conform to the deepest hollows and oceans as well as the highest mountains and clouds. It knows both freedom and stillness; indeed, nothing is freer than water. Its formlessness contours to shape. It slides around, rushes over, or drops under any obstacle. When necessary, it can even penetrate straight through an obstruction. Furthermore, water can capture and reflect light—not to mention it supports life.

All in all, water is Daoist thought in motion. When practicing taijiquan, a person's energy is kept in the pubic region (in the large intestine and colon), where the lower elixir field is located. This internal energy, qi, mimics water, which always collects in low places. Upon reaching this relaxed state of focus, one becomes ready for practice. In that moment of stillness—or Wuji—the practitioner should feel as water does: quiet, gentle, and balanced.

Water is categorized as a yin substance and is responsible for moisturizing the entire planet's atmosphere. This includes human beings, who are comprised mostly of water. Water partakes in all of life's activities. It carries electrolytes in and out of the body. These electrical charges, or qi, are considered a yang substance (fire) which animates life. Water and *qi* are codependent in living beings. Without water, these electrical charges would falter—they would have no medium or conduit to sustain themselves. (Lightning, for instance, strikes most strongly during rainstorms.) To have peak energy, sufficient water hydration is a prerequisite. After all, not even the resilient bamboo tree can remain flexible enough to withstand heavy storm winds during a drought.

For Daoists, not all water is created equal. The best water is taken while still flowing, either from a stream, spring, or faucet. If the water is coming from a faucet, the first cup or two must be recycled or returned to the source to avoid consumption of stagnant pipe-water. As one can imagine, this poses a major challenge to most individuals who live in the modern day, particularly in urban environments. Most source water is first bottled and shipped to cities.

Equally important—if not more important—is the quality and purity of the water. In fact, these factors are so vital to Daoist cultivation that the monks of the White Cloud Temple would travel three days on foot just to drink water from a sacred spring at West Mountain. These rich waters were so full of minerals that when you dropped a coin into the spring, the coin would stay floating on the water's surface. The monks would stay there for two or three days, drinking their fill.

For those unable to make the journey, the monastery would send special steeds to make regular runs to West Mountain and retrieve this special spring water. Monks would saddle large empty water containers to the horses and send them on their way to West Mountain. Once they arrived at the spring, an attendant, recognizing the horses of the White Cloud Temple, would feed and water them and fill their empty water containers to the brim and send them trotting back to the monastery fewer than twenty-four hours later. "The old horse knows the way home," as the Chinese idiom proclaims. The water that the horses would bring back to the White Cloud Temple was typically reserved for the elder monks; depending on the season, such journeys were sparing. Unfortunately, this special spring has since been destroyed.

The magical spring on the Wudang mountains, known as the Yellow Dragon Emperor Spring, still survives. Drinking this water can greatly lessen the symptoms of a diseased body—this includes significant reductions in pain, often in as little as twelve hours. This spring is near the top of the Wudang mountains; you can only reach it by foot along the pedestrian pathway that leads to Jinding.

Once, a prominent leader in China invited Master Du to teach him the secret of longevity. In their meeting, the leader asked Master Du the best way for him to prolong his lifespan. Master Du immediately recommended that the leader take up a daily daoyin practice. Though the leader had certainly heard of the benefits of daoyin, he argued that he faced too many distractions in his line of work, not to mention incessant family demands. Master Du suggested that the leader take up taijiquan, which would require far less time, concentration, and commitment than daoyin, but nevertheless yield comparable benefits. Still, the leader objected. In fact, by this point he felt that he had wasted Master Du's valuable time as well as his own, and suddenly became dispirited. Master Du, without a beat, said that he had one more suggestion to attain longevity. The leader's ears perked. Master Du told the leader to drink as much quality water as possible every morning, before breakfast and morning tea. "You can gain a decade of life by doing that," Master Du said. "Now that," the Chinese leader said, "is something I can do on a regular basis."

Water, again, is a yin substance. As it turns out, so is the moon. (In fact, the essence of the moon, like water, acts as a moisturizer. Pearls—whose dust is an ancient Chinese beauty secret—resemble the moon and grow in an aqueous environment.) According to Daoism, the moon is the original mother. Zhang Sanfeng's preference for practice at night under moonlight is also related to and motivated by the water-practice method. In *Yijing* numerology, the moon and water are assigned the same nomenclature (the number six). Thus, such practice conditions are ideal for meditation and finding stillness. In the case of taijiquan, this makes it significantly easier to practice slowly, which slows down the heart rate and thereby extends longevity. Yin is slow; yang is fast. Night and day enjoy independent natures, especially with regards to pace. As the saying goes: "A river is better long and narrow, than short and wide."

Chapter Five

Stories of a Martial Life

Traditionally, China's wealth made Beijing an attractive crossroads, a center of cross-cultural diversity which invited the Han and ethnic tribes from various provinces to the capital. It also welcomed foreign traders and international business tycoons. (Unsurprisingly, it also became a breeding ground for rather unscrupulous individuals.) At the place where the Silk Road met the capital, one could find an old-world marketplace full of extraordinary fabrics, fragrant spices, medicine, animals, view performance art, prize fighting, and just about anything ever produced in the Eastern hemisphere.

When Wu Baolin was a boy, he strode around the bazaar as part of a field trip. Although young, he was seriously curious about the wonders of the world. Master Du wanted him to be capable of maneuvering through society and seeing through the masquerade of human interactions. The bazaar was the perfect place to learn about such things. Dashing from booth to booth, Wu Baolin tried to take it all in before having to return to the monastery. At one stop, something immediately caught his eye and he snatched up the object to take a closer look. Instantly, the shopkeeper greeted him with a swift slap on the crown of his head. It prickled Wu Baolin's scalp, but he figured it would soon go away.

When he arrived back to the monastery, he mentioned and complained about the incident to his teacher while rubbing his head. It was clear to Master Du and Wu Baolin's Daoist uncle that he had been hit with a martial skill known as the black sand palm. It's a unique force a person can gather into the palms by slapping, striking, and submerging his hands in heated black sand every day. The *qi* cultivated by this practice could easily destroy a person's life. The Daoist uncle ordered Wu Baolin to lead him back to the marketplace and point out the man who laid hands on him. They both walked up to the vendor's table and the Daoist uncle began thanking the vendor for scolding and teaching his young friend a lesson for touching what had not belonged to him. To show his gratitude, the Daoist uncle reached out to shake hands, a very new custom adopted from Western culture around that time. After shaking hands, the two monks turned away and returned to the monastery to treat the wounds that Wu Baolin had incurred from the unpleasant incident.

Master Du asked the Daoist uncle to explain the purpose of their trip back to the marketplace. He replied, "I put him to rest. Neutralize one to caution a hundred." Master Du did not agree with his decision made to end the vendor's life, even though the vendor had used excessive and unnecessary force on Wu Baolin.

Up a Tree

Every morning, the monks of the White Cloud Temple would take a jog around the temple. This was known as the spirit of wind exercise—the monks would take two inhales for every exhale. Wu Baolin was still young at the time and frequently fell behind the rest of the group. One morning, as he struggled to keep pace, he lost sight of the others behind the bend. Though he thought he was alone, a voice startled him from behind. "Why are you so slow? Have you no *gongfu*?" Wu Baolin wondered if his brothers were already lapping him. He looked over to his left and saw no one and over to his right—still no one. He did not dare stop for fear of being lapped. The voice said, "So you are the youngest student of Master Du?" The voice scoffed. This last utterance greatly agitated Wu Baolin. He was about to confront the source of this disrespect when, out of nowhere, a horizontal palm-stroke cut through the air and landed just below Wu Baolin's mid back, launching him upward into oblivion. He was catapulted so high, in fact, that he was permanently treed—stuck in the canopy, without a means of safely climbing down. When Wu Baolin looked down, the culprit had disappeared.

When Wu Baolin failed to show up at the dining hall for breakfast that morning, a search party (including Master Du) went in search of him. They discovered him in the same tree, yelling for help. After leading him down safely, Master Du questioned Wu Baolin about the entire incident. After Wu told his teacher what had happened, the search party fanned out in search of the assailant, but he was long gone. To this day, that person's identity is still a mystery. And though Wu Baolin was a slight-figured boy, the person who catapulted him into the tree was nonetheless advanced in martial arts. From that day forward, Wu Baolin was always guarded and accompanied by the monks and animals.

"*Gongfu* is not easy nor is it exciting," Dr. Wu would often say. True *gongfu* is hardly fanciful and often lacks external beauty—but it still packs enough practicality to give somebody the ability to defend themselves. The animal-based martial arts form, with its grace and elegance, as well as modern martial arts with their gymnastic-like performance, are fantastic ways to limber the body and exercise the cardiovascular system. They train all components to morph seamlessly into the next adaptation on the envisioned battle stage. However, to develop power and invisible force—a brick-and-mortar foundation and gold-steel body that can bust stone with knees and elbows—a person must undergo a strenuous, boring, and isolated kind of training in conditions that are completely foreign to a modern twenty-first century lifestyle. There is no gold medal for such suffering, no promise of achievement. True *gongfu* is elusive. True *gongfu* is imminently painstaking. There are no daily excuses or reasons for not pouring every ounce of blood, sweat, and tears into a practice. *Gongfu* means time. Each moment is a celebration of the Dao. Each day is an occasion to practice the way of internal enlightenment. Each year is an opportunity to embrace the very best and the very worst of your experiences. Each decade is a graduation.

Many individuals conceive of *gongfu* as a spectacular display of physical or technical prowess. This could not be further from the truth. In fact, Dr. Wu Baolin has rarely seen a physical altercation between skilled fighters lasting beyond one to three strokes. Generally, fighters opt to end threats quickly to reduce the risk of mutual loss and injury. The drawn-out fights of movie magic are wonderfully choreographed and played out to emotional perfection; no one can deny the artistry. Real life, however, is much less romantic or pretty, which is why Daoists prefer to leave fighting as a last resort. Often, those one, two, or three strokes reveal the true measure of the *qi* force one possesses. When an opponent is confronted with awesome power, if outgunned, they normally concede to avoid injury and live to fight another day.

Training differs vastly depending on a person's goal. Learning practical self-defense fighting techniques varies from learning prize-fighting methods. Though a punch may still be a punch, what is measured still varies. Styles of martial arts reflect in their forms and techniques where (and in what) their ultimate purpose lies: on the street, in the ring, in front of the judges. They are all useful in their own right.

In modern wushu, as well as the ancient forms such as taijiquan, a person spends a great deal of time rehearsing the physical forms. This makes for interesting practice and refinement. The *gongfu* further acquired in Daoist methodology is far less glamorous. According to Dr. Wu, it can even be quite boring and often uncomfortable. Nonetheless, the results are practical and effective. At the White Cloud Temple, many pledges wanted to become fighting monks. Any student's underlying intentions were highly valued. The depth of their motivation would suit—and determine—the length of their path.

Lift-Punch-Jump

Once, at the White Cloud Temple, Wu Baolin met a Beijing man who came to visit the temple. Like so many others, he was a victim of a local mobster and his heavies, who persistently harassed him and demanded money. He had come to the temple that day because he wanted to know how he could stop the racketeering.

Master Du agreed to help him with his plight. He put Wu Baolin in charge of the man's training. On the first day, Young Wu walked the man over to a row of six five-foot vessels filled to the brim with water. You could tell that they were heavy simply by looking at them. Young Wu ordered the man to lift and carry each vessel across the courtyard. He lifted the urns one at a time and walked, hugging them to keep the weight close. By lunchtime on the first day, he was shuffling from fatigue and his clothes were drenched from the spillage. Wu Baolin coached him to ensure that each vessel stayed filled with water. After three months, the man was hardly breaking a sweat and he no longer needed to wrap his arms around the vessels to raise them; instead, he used the strength of his hands to press them up.

For the next exercise, Wu Baolin took the man to a wall inside the temple. Nailed onto the wall was a traditional Chinese almanac calendar. Its dated sheaves of paper were shaped like a book; there was one sheet for every day of the year. The book's spine was located on the top border, like a legal notepad. Wu Baolin ordered the man to punch the ream of paper repeatedly using his right fist only, demonstrating proper form—the vertical fist and knuckles directed at the center of the calendar, slightly above shoulder height. As the man started to punch the calendar over and over again, the skin on his knuckles broke, his blood stained the pages. Blood is thick, sticky, and dries quickly. The man's blood provided an adhesiveness that helped him pull and tear the pages away each time he rechambered his strike. After a month, the man had gone through a stack of calendars, whittling each one down to the final page.

For the final exercise, Wu Baolin told the man to dig a hole in the ground, one foot deep. It needed to be wide enough for a person to land and stand in comfortably. For two months, from dawn until dusk, the man jumped in and out of the hole repeatedly, his weight gradually deepening the cavity (with excavation) until leaping three feet, in and out of the circle, looked easy. He kept doing this for two months. To the man, of course, all this training seemed to have little to do with combat. In fact, Wu Baolin himself had no idea what the ultimate plan was—only Master Du held the answers.

Still, the man followed through with everything that Master Wu asked of him. Master Du, after training had ended, called Wu Baolin and the Beijing man into his study. He was holding a scroll stamped with red cinnabar sealed with his personal stone. He handed the scroll to Wu Baolin and said, "Escort our guest back to his village. When you arrive, go directly to the headquarters of the mobster who has been illegally taxing the people of the village. When our guest confronts him without words, break open the seal and begin to read the three points I have outlined. Let each be completed before moving on to the next. Understood?"

"Yes, Master," replied Wu Baolin. And they were off.

The two reached the village by midday and went to the known hangout of the mobster. Wu Baolin, as instructed, stood off to the side while the Beijing man stood outside the quarters defiantly. He had been a voice for his fellow villagers in the past and had paid a price. This time, however, he was silent. When the mobster came forward to put the Beijing man in his place, Wu Baolin cracked the seal of the scroll and began to read loudly, at the top of his lungs. "Lift the water vessel!"

Using his two hands the Beijing man lifted his oppressor far up off the ground in total control, as easily as he would an infant. "Punch the calendar!" Wu Baolin said. Letting go with the right hand, he chambered the fist and plunged it into the face of his foe, sending his body back so that he landed flat on his back with a loud thud. "Jump out of the hole!" Wu Baolin said. The Beijing man squatted and leaped upward and landed on the thoracic cavity of the downed man, crushing his rib cage and swiftly killing him.

The Valley of the Wolves

It began with a grievance. A man could not shake a nightmare out of his head—it played in a deranged loop in his mind's eye. The images were of his family, and they haunted him so much that he was unable to sleep. Often, individuals with unresolved issues or in an acute need of help would knock on the front gates of the White Cloud Temple, looking for a way that would get them through a darkness or to a destination point. Mostly, they sought guidance and wisdom. Sometimes, however, they sought the only sensible solution: revenge. To them, revenge was the last hope that they would ever find peace of mind again.

According to Daoism, two species exist at the top of the planet's food chain. They have counterbalancing influences in the world—not unlike a system of checks and balances in politics. The histories of the human being and the wolf (which Daoism considers equals) predate what was orally described around campfires. This relationship has almost never been based on friendship; instead, it is grounded in a kind of mutual respect, in both the physical and spiritual realms. The domestication of the wolf into the dog is a true testament to the mutual admiration—and occasional fear—between human and wolf. After all, even in domestication, dogs who are not trained or tamed will invariably express the conflict and defiance that are characteristic of the wolf spirit.

This particular man with the nightmares of his family knocked on the door of the White Cloud Temple and told his story to Master Du. Wolves had invaded his home and murdered his entire family and livestock while he was away. He emphasized this last detail—that he had been away while the ravaging occurred—because he believed it to be coward and calculated. Not surprisingly, wolves are infamous for their flawless military tactics and perfectly timed strikes. The man's voice trembled in anguish. He was incoherent and inconsolable—he vowed to destroy every wolf in the valley. Listening to the man relive this nightmare was difficult, even for Master Du, who was rarely disturbed by anything. As Master Du listened to the man spill his heart and call for blood, he found that he could not disagree with the man's urgent desire for revenge.

Master Du invited the man to stay the night. His hope was that, after a night of calm rest, he could persuade the man to go a different path. He would try and help the man see things differently. The night's rest, as it turns out, only made the man's resolve even more intractable. Master Du explained the karmic repercussions of vengeance and the probable dangers of trying to destroy a formidable opponent like the wolf, but his words fell on deaf ears. Besides, the man had no family and none of his friends or fellow villagers would dare take on the wolves. The man had nothing to lose; this quest for vengeance was the only thing he had to live for. Master Du knew that, without his help, the man was about to embark on a suicide mission.

Finally, Master Du gave another alternative to help the man move forward with his life. He offered to teach him the Five Centers Facing Heaven moon practice, a yin-based daoyin for helping souls who have passed on to reach their next destination point. It would be a useful way to take care of the future of his lost loved ones and ensure that they moved past their traumatic deaths. Master Du also explained that the wolves would have to deal with their own actions anyway, and that karma calculates all misdoings. Master Du shared many possible ways that the man could move beyond the past and into the future without retribution. But after a few more days at the monastery, the man was still hellbent on hunting down the wolves and exacting revenge. Master Du heard his story and deliberated over the course of days.

After much rumination, Master Du finally chose to help him in the way he desired. Master Du agreed to train the man but made it clear that he would not be ready for at least a year. Furthermore, the man had to accept the training method that was prescribed, or the agreement would be nullified. They were to form their own military alliance against the wolves, but the task of revenge and potential backlash of negative karma (if the heavens disagreed with this course of action) would ultimately fall on the man's head—not Master Du's. Despite the liability, the man accepted the terms.

But there was more. While Master Du wanted to help him survive the daunting task, he also wanted to teach an important lesson to the wolves. After all, they had certainly broken a contract and acted outside their strictures. Wolves are far more than wild hunting machines. They are particularly intelligent and often act admirably, purposefully, and in a disciplined manner. In this case, they had overstepped.

Master Du told the avenger that he only needed to master one exercise before he would be ready to wage his war against the wolves. This remark made the man nervous; he could not fathom how one skill could possibly help him overcome so many fierce predators. Nonetheless, he agreed to try. Master Du proceeded to hand him a sword and led him to a single-person outhouse behind the monastery. The inside of the outhouse had been intentionally plastered with fresh feces which, in turn, attracted a disproportional number of flies. "Your exercise," Master Du explained, "is to kill as many flies as you can using only the pointed tip of this straight sword. Once you have maintained a one-hundred percent kill ratio, hits and attempts, you will be ready to enter into the Valley of the Wolves alone." Master Du could do no more than that. The rest was up to the man.

The avenger woke up every day and walked into the outhouse. He stopped eating breakfast there for a while, finding it challenging to hold down the food in the rancid air of the small shack. Eventually, he became accustomed to the stench—but still he found the exercise of poking a fly frustrating. For months he recorded zero hits. He began to wonder if he would ever succeed in the task. On his breaks, he would sometimes toy with the idea of reconsidering his whole mission, but persisted in spite of the growing doubts. Part of Master Du hoped the man would have a change of heart for his own sake. But he also knew that taking no action would give the wolves a false sense of dominance that could lead to rampant blood feuds. Master Du secretly prayed that the man would persevere in the training to mitigate the risk of a war.

After six months, the avenger began to gain pinpoint accuracy. One after another, the flies would drop and collect on the floorboard. The avenger was becoming lightning quick with his sword and an unexpected change had occurred in the dark shadows of the unlit outhouse; his eyes and pupils had dilated and become more powerful. The flies no longer appeared the size of a small child's fingernail; instead, they took on the remarkable size of a walnut. After the avenger mentioned this phenomenal advancement to Master Du, he began to don a white blindfold during practice to increase his hand-to-third-eye development. The man had become so confident during the first round of training that he happily started from scratch with the blindfold, returning to the outhouse and beginning as if a novice. After several more months, his hearing became so acute that isolating the flies individually through their sound waves was no problem. He was ready.

Master Du had the duty of giving him the option, one last time, to walk another path—perhaps even to stay and join the monkhood and train his sword skill to even greater heights. The avenger, however, could only see one road—the one that led into the valley. He took the sword—which Master Du asked to be returned to the monastery if in fact he survived his battles—and walked off.

Many months later, the avenger, keeping his promise, returned to the White Cloud Temple and handed the sword over to Master Du, thanking him for his generosity and understanding of his difficult situation. The avenger also made it known that he was interested in taking Master Du up on the offer of furthering his training. But to Master Du, the man was no longer the same person who had left the monastery several months earlier. Having slain a thousand wolves in the front, he was a different man. To accept him as a student now would have special consequences—the outcomes of which were not pretty. Master Du anticipated having to put the man down, most likely because of an impulse reaction to a minor incident. He had already deeply internalized only one method for resolving his problems. It would be hard to change this tiger's newly acquired stripes.

In their background checks, Daoism has a list of unacceptable candidates. Some of these are odd while others are obvious contradictions to the monastic lifestyle. For example, for a long time no hairdressers or foreigners were allowed (foreigners, of course, posting the risk of being insurgents). Killers, bodyguards, and punishers were also not allowed.

Master Du added the sword that was now drenched with the blood and ling*qi* (spirit energy) of a thousand wolves to the collection of high-spirited talismanic relics that shielded the monastery from dark forces year-round.

Visitors

There were always visitors to the White Cloud Temple. Though the monks did their best to stay discreet in the public eye, the temple's thousand-year history was full of legends that stoked outsiders' curiosity and created an air of mystery about the temple. Contrary to the image of knight-errants in martial-arts novels and films, Daoists are not chivalrous individuals. They also do not even try to fill that role. Monks are very pragmatic people and, as a rule, mind their own business to avoid both karmic ensnarement and the trappings of vice. Minding their own business was a way to protect their autonomy.

Nonetheless, the number of people visiting the temple periodically posed challenges. Mostly, they were empty or benign threats by the ignorant but curious who hoped to see something extraordinary. In other instances, visitors were looking to set a new personal best. True men of cultivation needed to test themselves regularly, setting themselves against greater and greater challenges. For any unexpected guests, the temple consulting the oracle far in advance.

Every morning, before sunrise, the monks would toss the eight ancient *Yijing* stones onto a template to uncover a reading. Each of these rare stones had one of the eight trigrams, and no two stones were alike. The area where the stones landed in the circle allowed the monks to predict the day or week ahead. They also worked with the sixty-four hexagrams of the *Yijing*, each consisting of two trigrams. They consulted the full oracle to corroborate the messages of the stones and ensure the accuracy of their predictions. The monks' findings funneled into the collective pool of evidence and predictions, broadening the scope and creating a more comprehensive picture to form.

Consulting the stones and oracle was like checking the weather forecast. It was essential in protecting the temple. As the idiom reminds us: it's unwise to start digging a well only when one is feeling thirsty. To placate visitors who came to the monastery in search of a spectacle, the monks would use thirteen "tricks" that gave the observer a memorable, deeply felt experience—like a souvenir, in a sense, in that the visitor would take it back to the bustle of civilization as a token that lived inside of them. These tricks included bending a spoon with one's mind or launching a sword from a scabbard strapped on one's back to have it travel like a boomerang into the distance—and back into the scabbard. All done, of course, without hands. The thirteen tricks nullified the need for violent spectacle.

Still, having a preview of any visitors—especially their natures and intentions—helped plan meetings and interactions, diffuse or thwart any potential trouble, and welcome new opportunities. On one occasion, for instance, two fighters came to visit the temple, wanting to discuss martial theories with the head abbot. They even wanted to have a friendly boxing match with anyone the temple put forward. As per usual, Master Du did not allow any martial arts activity to be taught or practiced at the monastery. "We are just simple monks here reading our scriptures, meditating on the infinite, and practicing medicine and yin-yang philosophy," he told them.

The visitors themselves had so much to say about their own exploits over tea with Master Du as Wu Baolin stood nearby and studied his teacher's conversational etiquette. The two visitors filled the air with arrogant remarks and prodded at the temple's prohibition of fighting within its walls. It was clear that the visitors were looking for a good story to tell at their next stop. Though it was harmless fun, Master Du, having fulfilled his gracious duty as host, unceremoniously lifted the lid high above the teapot. In Chinese culture, to lift the lid completely off and present it to your guest authoritatively, as if holding an imperial seal, means something like "meeting adjourned" or "out." Everyone in the room stood up, but when the two fighters thanked Master Du for the good tea, they noticed that the longish wooden bench he had been sitting on was stuck to his backside. This is a taijiquan technique known as "sticking *qi*." Shocked, the two left without a word.

On another occasion, a humble visitor came knocking. He had a genuine interest in Daoism and the internal fighting arts as he'd come to know them. He showed his sincerity to Master Du by performing the correct gestures and greetings. Master Du was moved by his gestures and sensed he was looking for inspiration, something to reach for. Master Du called on two of his students to set up one of the temple's heavy sharpening stones—reserved for sharpening steel weapons—in the courtyard. He directed another student to bring over a large block of tofu from the commissary. He asked the visitor to carefully examine the solid stone sharpener for imperfections.

Once the visitor was satisfied that there were none, Master Du ordered the tofu block to be placed on the stone's surface. He took a deep inhale and with his right palm came down on the tofu and exhaled sharply with a *ha*! sound. The soft tofu was still completely intact; Master Du's smack had barely left an imprint. He asked that the visitor again examine the stone. When the visitor viewed it from another angle and surveyed the sidewalls, he was amazed to see that the stone was cracked and splintered in several places. Master Du's *qi* had traveled through the tofu, the medium, to break the hardened stone. (This was one important reason that monks eat a fair amount of tofu—it does not interrupt the flow of the internal streams of *qi* as other forms of protein do.) This was one of the thirteen tricks noted earlier.

Other Fighters

One of the earliest and better-known schools of taijiquan goes back to the Chen Village in Henan. The fast and power-driven style, named Chen-style taijiquan, goes back to the 16th century. For many years, the village kept the teachings private, training no outsiders. Beijing was always a hub of martial arts knowledge and competition and attracted a premier boxer from Chen Village, Chen Fake (1887-1957), a grandson of Chen Changxin (1771-1853). He went to Beijing to teach martial arts and taijiquan.

While there, he heard about Master Du at the White Cloud Temple and the form of taijiquan that Daoist monks practiced. He paid the temple a visit and requested an audience with the abbot to find out more. Master Du invited the boxer inside and took him into a courtyard for formal introductions.

Chen Fake inquired, "It is my understanding that you teach a very esoteric form of taijiquan and that it predates the one practiced by my family. Can you explain it in more detail?"

Master Du replied, "A test run will reveal if this is true." He lifted his arms to his sides with his palms facing forward and began with a subtle and relaxed undulation. This was a water posture borrowed from a Zhang Sanfeng Taiji Qigong set, the same position he would assume before test runs.

Master Du said, "If you can pass under my sleeve, I will concede to you here and now."

Chen Fake did not hesitate but suddenly found it quite difficult to advance even one step. His feet seemed to be nailed to the ground, and there seemed to be an invisible wall of *qi* surrounding Master Du, not letting him get any closer. The courtyard was silent for a while before Chen Fake acknowledged his defeat with a bow. He asked if he could learn Zhang Sanfeng Taiji-quan.

Master Du bowed and said, "I cannot teach you our form, especially since you have transformed the Chen-style system. You are a master in your own right with numerous students who depend on you."

But then he introduced Wu Baolin, "However, I would like you to teach Young Wu here your best form." Chen Fake agreed. Some years later, Master Du taught elements of Zhang Sanfeng Taijiquan to Chen Fake's son, Chen Zhaokui (1928-1981).

In those days, monks of the White Cloud Temple greatly admired talent. When the international film star and martial artist Li Xiaolong (known to West-ern audiences as Bruce Lee) came to the monastery, there was a bit of excite-ment and buzz, because the challenger's persona was somewhat bigger than life. The Wing Chun fighting system that he was brought up on in Hong Kong had only one or two degrees of separation from Wudang *gongfu*. On the day of the challenge, Master Du chose Wu Baolin's Daoist brother to assume the mantle; he was the perfect person to neutralize Bruce Lee's attacks, the right-sized knife for the right-sized vegetable, so to speak. They all watched Bruce Lee rush in with a barrage of attacks, punches and kicks from all angles.

This included a signature move where he ran full speed toward his oppo-nent and jumped onto the body as if scaling a wall, one-two. On the third step, he turned and twisted his body while five or six feet up in the air, converting it into a roundhouse kick to the head. He tried the maneuver three different times, but the Daoist brother had a defense strategy against all strikes that pro-tected him like a tortoise's shell. The match ended in a draw. Master Du ex-plained to Wu Baolin that, in the light of the *Yijing*, Bruce Lee was a perfect fighting specimen. He had the natural attributes of speed and quickness, perfect symmetry, a fearless attitude, and a kinesthetic learning ability, among other skills. If he were more open to guidance and traditional training, he would be an ideal student. But by the time Bruce Lee had found his way to Beijing, his career was already set on its trajectory.

Wu Baolin's relationship with Master Du was that of father and son. Their closeness had given Wu Baolin exclusive access and exposure to many extraor-dinary feats of Chinese *gongfu*. From a seated motionless position on a wooden bench, Master Du would project his body upward into a tree with jet-like pro-pulsion. This was called flying *gongfu*. He would do other things like drink a gallon of water without stopping and shoot out a forceful stream of water from his wide-open mouth and knock grapes off the vine with absolute precision. If someone were to be struck on an acupuncture point with this high-pressured water stream, that person would certainly have internal damage or even die.

Master Du had learned every skill listed in the *Longmen jing* (Dragon Gate Classic), a secret manual of Complete Reality Daoism. In other words, Wu Baolin had access to an endless amount of inspiration and knowledge through

Master Du, who wanted nothing more than to pass on his knowledge before retiring. Although he had been waiting for and expecting a student like Wu Baolin for decades, Master Du had, before Wu's arrival, trained another Daoist monk to lofty heights.

That monk's name was Li San. Master Du trained him during the early part of the 20th century. Li San was a gifted martial artist, proficient in daoyin and well-trained in flying *gongfu*. Li San was also known as Li San the Swallow because of his ability to move around like a bird. In his entire life, Master Du only trained two students in this very rare and specialized skill, Wu Baolin being the other (though Wu's training was cut short by an unfortunate incident).

This particular skill allowed Li San to walk on walls in any direction without the aid of a rope or other holds; the tops of his feet and toes were capable of folding up parallel to his shinbones, which allowed his body's axis point to shift his weight into proper balance when climbing vertical surfaces. To put his skills in perspective, Li San could easily leap off a New York financial building, over and across Wall Street, and land on rooftop on the other side. Plus, he was an unmatched escape artist. Due to a malleable bone density, he could flatten his body when pressed against a surface, helping him to squeeze between bars, gates, and other exceedingly tight quarters.

Master Du put a great deal of time and effort into training his protégé. Li San had already bested many great fighters of the day even before reaching his full potential. He was one of only a few masters of Zhang Sanfeng Taijiquan and the best of his generation so far. And because of his advanced study in light-(flying) *gongfu*, Master Du had planned to enter Li San into several track and field events of the Summer Olympic Games as a means to reenergize the country and return a sense of identity and pride to the population. They needed something to cheer. Unfortunately, during the 1920s, '30s, '40s, and '50s, China missed the majority of Olympic Games appear-ances due to political fervor and chaos. Had things gone the way Master Du had hoped, Li San would most certainly have been a national hero. Instead, Li San retired into obscurity.

The Set of Thirty-Seven

In 1976, Master Du performed the Set of Thirty-Seven, also known as the Soul of Zhang Sanfeng, separate from the main body of taijiquan and different from the Zhang Sanfeng Taijiquan practices most had learned from Master Du. No one from the monastery, not his closest students, had ever seen the one of a kind sequence before. The Set of Thirty-Seven was why Master Du had unbreakable restrictions and severe punishments for anyone entering his private training area without a proper summons. It was also why he practiced at night when most people were fast asleep. It was truthfully the once-in-a-lifetime opportunity for these Daoist monks as they all watched him like hawks.

The high alert of not knowing what progressions came next made for an intense teaching space. He performed the pattern from beginning to end in slow deliberate fashion, so that his students could see the transitions clearly. If by observing and following along with Master Du they could commit to memory the complete order of the sequence, after only one pass, the key-code was theirs to keep. There were no consolation prizes other than having witnessed the rare moment of watching an immortal molt some of the last of his earthly responsibility like the lucky chance to watch a crane spring from the tall grasses, hearing the sound of their wings commanding the wind, fly up and across a field, into the sky and across the ocean.

The Soul of Zhang Sanfeng is the secret access code for opening the astrophysical aspects of taijiquan: leading from the classroom to the Milky Way runway while garnering the attention of taijiquan masters past and present. If the memory of the heart or mind failed to absorb the transfer, that was to be the end of it. It was just weeks before Master Du planned to weigh anchor, and rainbow body toward the ninth level of the sun. He explained earnestly that these were the most critical movements of Zhang Sanfeng's body of work, and were his spiritual imprint. The Set of Thirty-Seven was never even taught to Li San before his retirement.

When finished with the sequence, Master Du walked over to a stack of written documents that expounded and illustrated fully the thirty-seven moves. They were the last proof drawn in the monastery by Master Du. He proceeded to slap the papers one time with his palm. Immediately, the pages began to disintegrate, scattering into light pieces of floating ash, and burning white fire until there was no remenance of the written teachings anywhere. If the sequence had not been learned it was lost forever to that group. Master Wu Baolin was young with nimble mind. He had learned thousands of movements in his young life and was fit to digest condensed chunks of information, memorized by heart. This demonstrative lesson showed the value of the Set of Thirty-Seven and Wu Baolin remembered an incident in which he saw Master Du use this skill.

A warrior from India had traveled far across Asia to test his level of cultivation. Along his travels he and his confidant were pointed to the White Cloud Temple as one stop. This swordsman made it clear he was there to challenge the top position. Master Du was advised of the guests and answered the call. Ambitious and impatient, the traveler wanted to get on with it, by swords or fist. This man had come so far and Master Du thought it rude to send him away, as he often did to those appearing unannounced. But this was special. It was not every day that a highly cultivated individual from a mostly different philosophical background came to Beijing. There would presumably be more hazardous stops to follow for the traveler so Master Du would try to decelerate his ambitions then and there.

Master Du suggested that instead of risking their lives to get a gauge into their ability versus one another, he thought it best to take a different reading. The guest agreed with the host. So Master Du led the group over to a very large wide mouth container in one of the temple courtyards. It was filled to the top with water. "Be my guest," Master Du offered him the first go around. The swordsman was obliged and began to channel his breathing and focus his mind. Suddenly in a flash he slapped the water's surface forcing out of the large vat eighty percent of its contents. It was very impressive. The guest liked his chances.

Master Du ordered his students to refill the water container at once and his attitude had changed slightly. As the last bucket was poured in, he asked the guest politely to borrow his sword for a moment. The request was granted. Master Du held the sword overhead horizontally, with the sword handle in his right hand and the middle of the sword's scabbard with his left hand, and eyes closed. He drew the curved sword yanking it out fully, the ringing of combat steel against the scabbards couplings making the sound as both his hands and arms fanned out to his flanks, sword and scabbard now vertically positioned. Just as quickly, he sheathed the weapon back inside the scabbard, overhead, completely transferred the sword into his right hand and submerged the weapon into the water for a few seconds. Master Du pulled the sword out of the bath and handed it over to the guest conveying that they were finished. The guest was not quite sure what had happened at first as there was not any tangible proof that he could recognize but he thought to draw his sword. As he pulled on the handle the blade was no longer attached to the flange. The shattered pieces of steel poured out from the scabbard and pinged off the stone grounds of the courtyard. It was a test of authenticity.

The Set of Thirty-Seven, according to some legends, consists of a sequence of techniques passed down to Zhang Sanfeng by the Tang hermit Xu Xuanping, a known master of healing exercises. Originally from Anhui, he lived on the Mountain of Purple Yang and lived on a special diet of uncooked wild foods. He was over seven feet tall with hair almost as long. Through his long beard, while running into town as fast as a horse, could be heard singing the following stanza: "Carrying firewood to market at dawn, returning with wine at dusk. My home? It is in the green forest in the clouds."

Art and Artifacts

Master Wu Baolin grew up surrounded by ancient relics, antiquarian books and great works of art. And with his background in *qi* cultivation he became an expert art appraiser and authenticator. His reputation in the art world, over the years, has come to be legendary. Whenever considerable purchases were offered for discussion he was invited as an interested party to ascertain the works as true or fake; usually taken into service by the buyers or friends. Art replication or art forgery is a form of mastery although some might argue. It has been a booming business in China and around other parts of the world for centuries. At the Louvre in France for instance the number of dedicated art students that sit beneath the works of great masters attempting to reproduce the technique is all one needs to imagine. The amount of phony reproductions in circulation worldwide is uncountable. Master Wu has always been able to determine either the authenticity and/or the story behind individual pieces and thereby their true selling points.

There was set to move forward a multi-million dollar deal on an exquisite painting from a very famous Chinese artist of the Tang era. Everything seemed in perfect order except for a pestering gut feeling that left the interested party uneasy and with reservations and the fear of later having buyers' remorse. It was most likely the price tag. Private art sales are generally illicit, because all sales are understood as final. There is no fraud insurance in place to protect the buyer like in a public auction. Friends of the buyer suggested they call Master Wu Baolin to help settle any apprehensions. Another already authenticated art piece from the same artist was onsite for the comparison of signatures and the brush stroke style. At first glance not even Master Wu could tell if there were any obvious differences between the brushstrokes or the signatures on the two pieces. The handmade paper surfaces, texture and fibers, shades of color, and papermaking technique all seemed to match the period. Everything looked well except the experiment must still be conducted to remove all doubt.

Most art authentications go through a series of forensic tests that may include carbon testing, x-ray diffraction, white lead dating and so on. However, there is always the risk of altering the very sensitive and delicate colorations, and for this reason sellers decline the procedure. Besides this, if it were to be a forgery that was done during the same era, much of the data would support authenticity, granted that the style was well studied. These are never simple matters.

Bodhi-tree seeds are used as prayer beads by Daoist and Buddhist monks. The larger the seed the stronger the praying power. Nowadays, even these easy to find items are introduced to market with fake reproductions made of spurious materials. In China, when shopping this item you may ask the seller if it's genuine. If he says yes then you may ask for permission to test the seeds with fire. If they agree to the test then light a flame under the seed to see if it melts or damages from burns. If it is the real thing then nothing in the shape, color or integrity of the seed will change. Master Wu Baolin asked the owners of the art piece if they were willing to allow a similar test that did not include lighting the piece on fire but could definitely put the painting at risk if it turns out to be inauthentic. They agreed.

Like his teacher, Master Wu Baolin always practices some meditation before authenticating any items, especially when the stakes are as high as this was. He does so in order to further enhance his sensitivity to objects and their qi imprints. He sat down with the paintings, both said to be originals, one confirmed. Using three fingers, thumb-index-middle, from his right hand, he held the corner of the already authenticated painting, and with the same three digits of the left hand, he held the corner of the painting that was for sale. In his mind he began to practice the thirty-seven movements of the Soul of Zhang Sanfeng. As his qi explored the two items it began to send back reflections in the form of historical information brought into focus. It was clear to him the tale of both paintings but he realized his opinion was still only subjective. He continued to meditate to see if any physical evidence might come forward. As he neared the completion of the thirty-seven movements the painting in question began to disintegrate, breaking apart into hundreds of disappearing particles, as the illusion of a truth vanished. No one in the room could dispute the results. These thirty-seven moves are the demarcation between teacher and student. Understandably, the thirty-seven omitted from this book for the inheritor of the form only.

Chapter Six

Preparation and Prerequisites

In addition to the set of the Thirty-Seven, Zhang Sanfeng transmitted the teachings of thirty-eight auxiliary or conditioning exercises to enhance proficiency in boxing skill. Seven are known as part of Chen-style taijiquan; four are practiced in the Yang-style. Auxiliary or strength exercises are fundamental to building a particular power or accuracy, a sense for combat to enhance fighting skills. Zhang Sanfeng, trained at the Shaolin Temple, which works with 72 arts or skills, was clear on the concepts of this training aspect. The exercises not only build physical prowess but also help prevent serious injury by protecting the trained parts of the body and strengthening bones, tendons, ligaments, and muscles as well as enhanced vision.

Visualization (*xianxiang*) is the activation of the third eye. It allows the practitioner to receive advance information or form a picture of events before they happen. This makes it possible to launch a preemptive strike or anticipate with great accuracy the precise action that will be taken against forces.

Taijiquan is a fluid art that moves in endless circles much like water, which tends toward rounded shapes: rain drops, pools, ponds, lakes, winding rivers, and so on. Flowing water is powerful: it can erode shore lines, flood towns, and upend even strong trees. There is something inherently powerful in the accumulation of water molecules, and three of the four auxiliary exercises utilize water to teach control and the utilization of force.

Conditioning Exercises

1. Iron Palm Water Training—Iron Palm is a primary conditioning exercise, most commonly known as iron palm training, is a prevalent Chinese *gongfu* training exercise. Iron palm is a very versatile method that conditions as well as fuses the palms and/or backs-of-the-hands with various elements. Some Chinese martial arts schools use different colored sand or iron elements such as ball bearings to train and strengthen the hands. Some are inclined to use stones in order to toughen their hands, taking on the characteristics of those strong elements. Temperatures are also crucial to the different levels of this training as heat may be placed underneath the preferred elements along with hot oil. Some

of these harsher methods require the use of Chinese herbal liniments to treat the hands and forearms afterward to reduce the risk and onset of arthritis but also to prevent the physical and visual destruction of body tissue if not treated.

Fill a vessel with water until at least 90 percent full. Step up closely standing in front of the vessel almost straddling the container with both hands by the sides of the body. Start by raising the left hand overhead and forcefully slapping the water's surface with the palm immediately followed by the right hand, each strike splashing water up and out. Alternate left and right in fluid succession until the vessel has been emptied of water. Refill the vessel with water and begin again.

The second option when slapping the water's surface is using only one hand. Place one leg back and with the lead hand alternate slapping the water's surface with the palm and back of the hand. Repeat until the vessel is empty of water.

2. Snatching Fish—Fill a vessel with water until 90 percent full. Add a live fish or eel to the water. Step up closely standing in front of the vessel almost straddling the container with both hands by the sides of the body. Close the eyes completely shut or cover the eyes with a blindfold. Relax and focus all energies and internal vision into the water filled container. Be patient. Wait for an intuitive impulse, or captured vision/eyesight, or sensitivity to the fish swimming closer and within reach; using either the left or right hands quickly reach into the water and attempt to capture the fish like an eagle. This exercise is not only to train and develop speed and dexterity but more importantly to develop the precognizant intuition that separates the taijiquan fighter from other types. The vessel is the opponent's body. The water is their blood and the fish is their *qi* and intent. Routinely practice this exercise until proficient. "Starting late but reaching first".

3. Submerge Pumpkins—Using either two pumpkins or two bottle gourds or two basketballs (resembling pumpkins), step into a body of water until approximately waist deep. Place the two pumpkins or gourds on the water's surface underneath the palms at the sides. This is the starting position. Begin the exercise by submerging the pumpkins by pressing down with the palms until completely underwater and with controlled relax and let the vessels rise back up

to the surface. Maintain control of the vessels both while pressing down and releasing up so that they do not squirt away because although it is a press and release, yang and yin, there is still strong resistance occurring in both directions. This trains the practitioner in the action of forceful palm strikes and also trains the practitioner in the way of absorbing oncoming force or push-back. Repeat the exercise nine repetitions increasing this number over time.

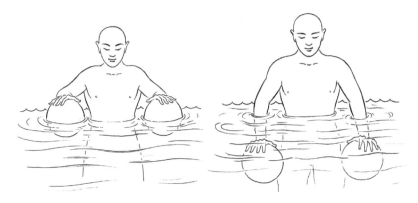

4. Kick the Pumpkin—Although the methods of kicking in taijiquan are limited to a few, they are very practical and direct action kicks nonetheless. Using two separate 6 foot lines, tether and tie the two ropes to a pumpkin, bottle gourd or basketball, leaving it centered halfway between the rope ends. Begin the exercise by grabbing hold the two rope ends with the right and left hands and the pumpkin laying on the floor. Using the ends of the toes, kick the pumpkin with force directly ahead. When the pumpkin reaches its furthest limit, time the return by pulling back the reins so that the pumpkin's return is fast. While still in the air, kick it back out. Practice and repeat this exercise using both feet doing ones best not to let the pumpkin touch the ground. This will strengthen the feet and legs, foot-eye coordination, reaction speed, and leg dexterity.

Relaxing the Thirteen Points

Light the Incense—The thirteen relaxed points, generally the opening of most Daoist practices of the White Cloud Monastery, are the thirteen original qigong movements developed by Lao Zi on Zhongnan Mountain, the origin of Daoism. When praying in Daoist and Buddhist temples, it is customary to light three incense (a flare), bow three times, so that Heaven recognizes your attendance and listens. Igniting the thirteen relaxed points (shoulders, elbows, wrists, hips, knees, ankles, and neck) gets you an audience.

Starting Position—Stand with the feet shoulder width apart. Turn the toes in slightly or at the absolute minimum, keep the feet paralleled. The shoulders should be relaxed. The chin one loose vertical fist from the upper chest. Elbows relaxed. Chest also relaxed and sunken or reduced. Waist should be relaxed so that the sacrum may relax and tilt gently forward like a hanging plumb bob. The knees and ankles are slightly bent. These exercises are done fluidly without pause and are not to be confused with stretching exercises.

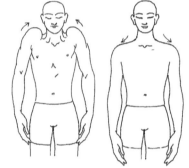

1. Shrug the Shoulders—Lift the shoulders up and try to touch the ears as if the shoulders are reaching for the moon. Do not hold. At the apex, release and drop the shoulders allowing them to fall, the weight of the arms creating separation at the base of the neck at the Dadui point (C-7). Lifting is yang and dropping is yin, the active and the inactive. Repeat 9 times.

2. Rotate the Elbows—Lift the left hand palm up while rotating at the elbow toward the body's medial line (conception vessel). Turn the left palm over with the fingers pointing downward at the center of the chest. Drop and let the left hand fall straight down past the navel and back to the left side of the body. Lift the right hand palm up while rotating at the elbow toward the body's medial line (conception vessel). Turn the right palm over with the fingers

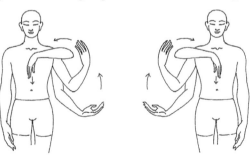

pointing downward at the center of the chest. Drop and let the right hand fall freely straight down past the navel and back to the right side of the body. Repeat 9 times each side. Lifting is yang and dropping is yin, the active and the inactive. Zhang Sanfeng saw this exercise as the movement of water inside the coconut, the sloshing inside able to move the sphere with force.

3. Rotate the Wrists—Interlock the fingers and hands, palms almost touching, elbows hanging relaxed nearly below hands. Alternate rolling each wrist forward (away from the body) so that a figure 8 motion is created, the hands and wrists remaining relaxed and pliable. After heat is felt in the wrists, reverse the direction of the rotations and alternate rolling each wrist backward (toward the body) so that a figure 8 motion is created, the hands and wrist remaining relaxed and pliable. After heat is felt in the wrists, the exercise is finished. In Chinese this exercise is called ruyi, a wishing practice.

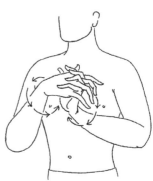

4. Flick the Fingers—Form two vertical hollow fist. Begin by flicking the index fingers from both hands off of the thumbs 9 times each. Repeat with the middle fingers 9 times. Repeat with the ring fingers 9 times. Repeat with the small fingers 9 times. Lastly, flick all fingers off the thumb at once 9 times. This exercise helps to open the 12 meridian channels of the body. The

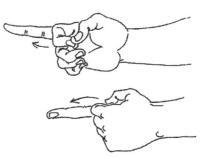

meridians begin and end on the hands and fingers-feet and toes.

5. Shake the Hands—Using gradually building force and speed, shake the hands out in front of the body to further open the meridians and bring qi and heat to the hands.

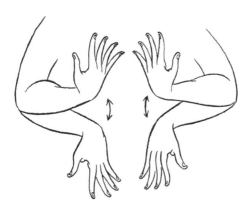

6. Rotate the Hips—While the hands are still warm, place the right hand in front of the left hip and the left hand behind the left hip. Begin rotating the left hip clockwise 9 times. Switch sides. Place the left hand in front of the right hip and the right hand behind the right hip. Begin rotating the right hip clockwise 9 times. This exercise not only loosens the hip joints but creates a yin and yang connection field between the palms, through the body to nourish the kidneys at the waist.

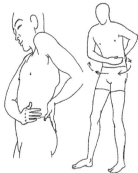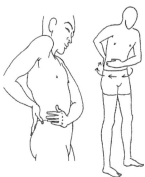

7. Rotate the Knees—With the hands still warm, place the right hand in front of the left knee and the left hand behind the left knee. Begin rotating the left knee clockwise 9 times. Switch sides. Place the left hand in front of the

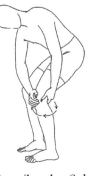

right knee and the right hand behind the right knee. Begin rotating the right knee clockwise 9 times. This exercise not only loosens the knee joints but creates a yin and yang connection field between the palms, through the knees to nourish the kidneys at the waist since the knees and kidneys are a direct correlation to one another, reflections if you will.

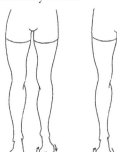

8. Inscribe the Soles and Ankles—Using the outer rim of the soles of the feet, rotate clockwise around the rim of the left foot first 9 times, imagine the left foot and lower leg are hollowed out. Rotate clockwise around the rim of the right foot 9 times, imagine the right foot and lower leg are hollowed out. Maintain contact with the ground at all times during the exercise.

9. Rotate the Ankles and Kick—Lift the left knee until the left upper leg is parallel to the ground keeping the lower leg portion loosely hanging. Begin to rotate the left ankle clockwise 9 times and gently kick out the left foot 3 times to further loosen the ankle joint. Lift the right knee until the right upper leg is parallel to the ground keeping the lower leg portion loosely hanging. Begin to rotate the right ankle clockwise 9 times and gently kick out the right foot 3 times to further loosen the ankle joint.

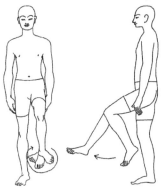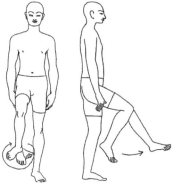

10. Loosen the Neck—Coming full circle to the top of the body, place the left palm under the chin with fingers pointing to the left ear. Place the right hand over the top left portion of the head, fingers pointing down toward the left ear. Very gently, push up and back the chin at a 45 degree angle with the left hand for a count of 3 push and release, assisted by the right hand gently tugging forward in the opposite direction. This is *not* a stretching exercise.

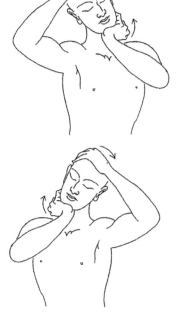

Place the right palm under the chin with fingers pointing to the right ear. Place the left hand over the top right portion of the head, fingers pointing down toward the right ear. Very gently push up and back the chin at a 45 degree angle with the right hand for a count of 3 push and release, assisted by the left hand gently tugging forward in the opposite direction. This is *not* a stretching exercise. Alternate left and right sides for 9 times each side. This exercise releases *qi* from the C-7 region of the body to form dragon bones, crystal-like formations that can survive cremation after death.

11. Move the Neck Front to Back—Lower the chin forward into the chest and extend the top of the head at the Baihui point (GV-20) forward and ahead and tilt the head back and extend the top of the head back and behind. This is one count. Repeat 9 times total. This is not a stretch.

12. Rotate the Neck—Beginning with the head at top center, let the head drop left, down and around to the right, and to top center 9 times. Reverse direction: let the head drop right, down and around to the left, and to top center 9 times. This is not a stretch and the circumference of the circles must not become taut. The neck and shoulders should remain relaxed and without stresses.

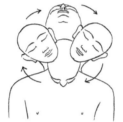
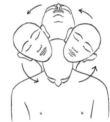

13. Lift and Release the Spine—Place the heels of the palms, fingers pointing up vertically, between the temples and the ears. Press and lift the head and spine upward, ideally until the heels of the feet raise, and release at the top. Do not hold at the top. This is *not* a stretching exercise. Repeat 9 times.

Original Daoyin

The daoyin warm-up exercises are designed to loosen the body, gather fresh *qi* from nature, and to calm, regulate, and harmonize the mind-body-spirit for practice. These exercises are done fluidly without pause and are not to be confused with stretching exercises.

1. Breathe into the Elixir Field/Zones—Start with the feet shoulder-width apart, turn the palms up, left hand over right, with the tips of the thumbs lightly pressed against one another, placed below the navel. Turn the toes from both feet inward by pivoting on the heels, followed by the heels moving inward by pivoting on the balls of the feet. Lastly, turn the toes from both feet inward once more by pivoting on the heels, and bringing the big toes in contact. The knees are bent, almost knock-kneed.

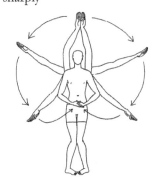

Inhale once sharply through the nose and lift the hands swiftly to the lower elixir field. Inhale sharply through the nose again and lift the hands to the middle elixir zone. Inhale a third time sharply through the nose and lift the hands to the upper elixir zone, palms facing the third eye and forehead. Continue the hands upward in transition until overhead and a long exhale once letting the hands separate to the flanks like a mushroom. Circle the hands back down to the waist into the starting position, palms up. Repeat 9 times. Rest in-between repetitions if needed. After completing the exercise, turn the toes to the outsides, the heels to the outsides, and the toes to the outsides, until the feet are once again shoulder width apart

2. Cleanse the Organs—Place the hands in front of the spleen and liver organs which are at the base of the left and right rib cage, with the palms facing the body. As if pinching two handfuls of cotton candy with all five fingertips, pull the toxins forward and away from the organs while slowly bending forward at the waist to 45 degrees, flicking away the toxins at full extension. Straighten the body by bending at the knees slightly and return the hands to the spleen and liver. Repeat the sequence 9 times. The hand transitions are like the actions of lap swimmers making their turns at the walls without stopping.

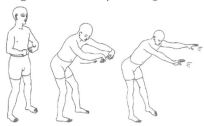

3. Gather the Q*i*—Open the arms and reach forward as if getting ready to give a big round hug as you gather in the *qi* from nature. Continue to close in the hug, bringing the palms all the way back to the chest, storing the *qi* in the middle elixir zone. Do not stop for nine gatherings. On the ninth gathering or hug, abruptly stop the hug mid-way in front of the body, fingers opposite and pointing at one another, the back slightly curved, while making the loud sound *ha*! That completes one repetition, inhaling back into middle elixir zone. Repeat the sequence 9 times. This exercise stores *qi* and helps clear the meridians.

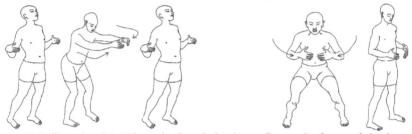

4. Pulling the Q*i*—Place the hands horizontally out in front of the lower elixir field, palms facing each other. Without the two palms ever touching one another try to get a sense of connection between them. Once the connection is established, expand and contract the space between the palms by moving the hands out and in, to the sides and back to the center. Look for sensations of *qi* between the palms of the hands while doing this. Feel if the *qi* thickens, changes temperatures (cool, hot, etc.), numbness in the hands, etc. It is useful to imagine you are pulling taffy or a large cotton ball to begin. Practice until there is a fullness between the hands and a thickness to the hands like a sponge that has absorbed water. The *qi* is ready to transition into the next exercise.

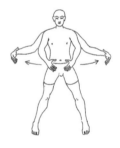

5. Move the Ball—Place the right hand, palm down, above the middle elixir zone and place the left hand, palm up, below the lower elixir field, while maintaining the connectivity already established during the previous exercise.

Relax the shoulders and close all ten fingers and round out the palms to form the shape an invisible *qi* ball that's being held between the middle and lower dans. Proceed to turn the waist to the right, being sure to leave the feet planted. At the end of the turn to the right side, switch the hand's positions so that the left hand is now over the right hand. Proceed to turn the waist to the left, being sure to leave the feet planted. At the end of the turn to the left side of the body, switch the hand's positions so that the right hand is now over the left hand. Proceed to turn the waist to the right in order to repeat. Right, left is one repetition. Repeat the sequence 9 times. When finished lower the hands to the lower elixir field, thumbs in the navel and the palms resting over the tummy with the two index fingers connected.

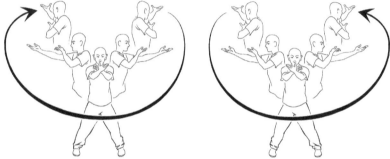

6. Roll the Ball—Start with the left hand above the right hand, out front the middle elixir zone, palms up. Turn the waist, torso, head, and eyes right, the right arm rising at a 45 degree angle, and the left hand gliding up the right arm to the right shoulder. Move the left hand under the right armpit. Turn the waist, torso, head, and eyes left, the right arm descending at a 45 degree angle, while gliding the left palm down, and under the right arm to out front the middle elixir zone, the right hand above the left hand, palms up. The feet remain rooted.

Turn the waist, torso, head, and eyes left, the left arm rising at a 45 degree angle, and the right hand gliding up the left arm to the left shoulder. Move the right hand under the left armpit. Turn the waist, torso, head, and eyes right, the left arm descending at a 45 degree angle, while gliding the right palm down under the left arm to out front the middle elixir zone, the left hand above the right hand, palms up. The feet remain rooted.

Right, left is one repetition. Repeat the sequence 9 times. When finished lower the hands to the lower elixir field, thumbs in the navel and the palms resting over the tummy with the two index fingers connected. This exercise develops arm sensitivity skills, even detecting a fly before landing.

7. Slap the Body—As if twisting a pellet drum or a monkey drum, turn the waist from side to side, left to right, back and forth, swinging or flailing the arms, and slapping the body with the palms and backs of the hands, moving up and down the body, head to toe. Repeat the sequence, up and down the body, as many as 9 times. This helps relax and dust the body off of turbidity.

8. Push-Hands Training (1)—Step into a left forward stance, and hold the hands, left in front of right, horizontally positioned out front of the middle elixir zone, palms facing the body. The shoulders and elbows are relaxed, forming a rounded empty space inside the arms. Shift the weight into the rear leg, pulling the hands down, in, and up in a circular pattern, then shift the weight back forward, pushing the hands up, out, and down in a circular pattern, out front of the middle elixir zone. Repeat the sequence a minimum of 9 times.

Switch stances and step into a right forward stance, and hold the hands, right in front of left, horizontally positioned out front of the middle elixir zone, palms facing the body. The shoulders and elbows are relaxed, forming a rounded empty space inside the arms. Shift the weight into the rear leg, pulling the hands down, in, and up in a circular pattern, then shift the weight back forward, pushing the hands up, out, and down in a circular pattern, out front of the middle elixir zone. Repeat the sequence a minimum of 9 times.

9. Push-Hands Training (2)—Step into a left forward stance, and hold the hands, left in front of right, extended. Turn waist right and shift the weight into the rear leg, pulling the hands overhead front to back, palms facing the sky, then shift the weight back forward, arms relaxed traversing the lower half, returning front. Repeat the sequence a minimum of 9 times.

Switch stances and step into a right forward stance, and hold the hands, right in front of left, extended. Turn waist left and shift the weight into the rear leg, pulling the hands overhead front to back, palms facing the sky, then shift the weight back forward, arms relaxed traversing the lower half, returning front. Repeat the sequence a minimum of 9 times.

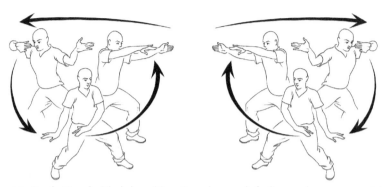

10. Push-Hands Training (3)—Step into a left forward stance, and hold the hands, left in front of right, extended. Turn waist right and shift the weight into the rear leg, pulling the hands around the body, front to back, palms facing away, then shift the weight back forward, arms relaxed traversing the lower half, returning front. Repeat the sequence a minimum of 9 times.

Switch stances and step into a right forward stance, and hold the hands, right in front of left, extended. Turn waist left and shift the weight into the rear leg, pulling the hands around the body, front to back, palms facing away, then shift the weight back forward, arms relaxed traversing the lower half, returning front. Repeat the sequence a minimum of 9 times.

11. Push-Hands Training (4)— Step into a left forward stance, and drop the hands. Then begin rolling the shoulders and hip joints circularly, front to back and back to front, at the same time shifting body weight, front to back and back to front, releasing every joint in the body in no fixed pattern. The body slippery and evasive like a cat or a snake. Repeat the sequence a minimum of 9 times.

Switch stances and step into a right forward stance, and drop the hands. Then begin rolling the shoulders and hip joints circularly, front to back and back to front, at the same time shifting body weight, front to back and back to front, releasing every joint in the body in no fixed pattern. The body slippery and evasive like a cat or a snake. Repeat the sequence a minimum of 9 times.

According to Daoists, when observing and evaluating martial arts skill, the focus does not fall upon the clean edges of the form, but instead pays careful attention to the malleability of the joints, a truer measure of attainment.

Static Postures

Static postures (*zhanzhuang* and *taiji zhuang*) are a rudimentary daoyin practice that requires little memory but needs a great deal of patience, time, and strength of spirit. A complete branch of daoyin at the White Cloud Temple, they work with external stillness to arrive at internal activity, i.e., *qi* and meridian development and internal organ generation. During the Yuan dynasty, the Complete Reality patriarch Qiu Chuji, although his expertise was in Five Centers Facing Heaven practice and *Yijing* fortune-telling, promoted static postures. The reason for this is that he did not sleep very much and not at all while lying down. Rather, he preferred to practice throughout day and night and accordingly slept standing up in static posture. He lived to 81, but, he practiced several lifetimes' worth of self-cultivation and good deeds. Under his influence, static postures became very popular and was extended to martial arts practices, and injected into the midst of their

Suggested Duration:
Stand for 2hrs
then practice Taiji

postures.

When Wu Baolin was young, Master Du challenged him to memorize an entire scripture before going to bed. This was a diversionary tactic, since Master Du never really expected his young acolyte to memorize that much in one evening but wanted him to learn how to sleep standing up. Wu Baolin would eventually fall asleep on his feet, wake-sleep-wake-sleep, before Master Du allowed him to rest on his round basket bed.

Suggested Duration:
Hold for 1 Hour to
Open the channels

Suggested Duration:
Hold until the
Temple Appears

Suggested Duration:
Hold until Rested

After he saw that Wu Baolin had gained the endurance and strength to stand for prolonged periods, Master Du would randomly stop him in certain positions during taijiquan practice, making him hold these postures for some time, even as long as an hour. These were somewhat advanced practices that took some getting used to. Still, they were very useful since static postures showed immediately where there might be a problem in the body, allowing great discomfort or pain to arise. The first inclination when this happens is to release the position and shake the limbs, but that is a mistake. Holding the posture until the discomfort subsides is the correct choice, lest there is no gain or improvement of the troubled areas.

Suggested Duration:
Hold for 10 Minutes

Practice Time

Life is a series of numbers and changes: counting heartbeats and footsteps, collecting memories, celebrating birthdays, adding and subtracting from piggy banks, change of address, classroom numbers, allowances, finances, disasters, and opportunities, fluctuating stock markets, the stars in the sky, minutes, hours, days and years. The *Yijing* deals primarily in numbers, and as its title, 'book of change' suggest, new calculations and modifications to any theorem are a pretext to new possibilities and providence, i.e., if individuals take part in managing the catalog of numbers in their own lives, good fortune can be met.

How can this be done? It can be done by adhering to *gongfu* principles. This has nothing and yet everything to do with martial arts. In the West, the term has come to mean fighting practices because many traditional Chinese fighting schools, popularized in the last century, have included it as part of their name, such as Wudang, Shaolin, Wing Chun Gongfu, etc. Yet, the true meaning is mastery gained over time, through effort, labor, and the acquisition of skills. Altogether, it indicates the right time and energy vested into a skill or cause to derive a dignified result. Therefore, *gongfu* is not limited to martial arts but can refer to any field of study or endeavor; whether medicine, engineering, writing, taijiquan, public service, fengshui, herbalism, music, and so on.

A writer who has won a Pulitzer Prize is said to have *gongfu*. A doctor who has come to treat successfully the most difficult diseases that human beings face today has *gongfu*. The immortal lady He Xiangu was granted magical wishing power after performing ten-thousand meritorious deeds, which was her *gongfu*. These executions of mastery cannot be met overnight. This requires time, consistent daily efforts for years and years, working and practicing the art to perfection. Those working with *gongfu* welcome pain and accept sacrifices. Self-discipline is a prerequisite to ward off the preoccupations that could lead one astray from one's goals: this is why Daoists prefer isolation in the mountains at least for some time in their training. The Eight Immortals promoted *gongfu* and praised learning a craft well, being able to feed the family. Master Du similarly reminded his students early and often to dedicate themselves and target the practice to a thousand times each day.

Taijiquan practice excites the *qi*, which excites the blood, which in turn excites the spirit in a peaceful and calm fashion. The more that taijiquan is practiced, the more these three life giving essentials gain force and stability. It is a process for irrigating thyself with *qi*. Proper irrigation of the body's internal landscape is no less important than tending to the gardens and the crops. If neglected, the full bounty will surely be missed; but with attentiveness there is always food and nourishment for the seasons. This illustrates how Daoist actively strive to commune with nature, follow nature, a philosophy proven to generate good health and longevity for ages. As they say, "When the student is ready, the teacher will appear."

The real power of taijiquan are revealed somewhere between 3,000 and 4,000 repetitions of the routine. As legend has it, after achieving these numbers, Zhang Sanfeng will appear to dedicated initiates and teach them the internal secrets of his fighting system. Master Du accordingly claims to have received Zhang Sanfeng Taijiquan first from his teacher at the Purple Cloud Temple, then from Zhang Sanfeng himself in the secret bamboo forest on Wudang. He in turn taught Wu Baolin and other Daoists at the White Cloud Temple. In both their experience, the legend holds true. Before he experienced it, though, Wu Baolin practiced each newly learned movement a thousand times and only then moved on to the next. If he was not full concentrated or worked in poor form, Master Du stood by with eighteen-inch chopsticks ready to thwack him across the hands if during opening wrists were not bent or other body parts he found out of position or not in rhythm. When the recursive loop of commitment reached 10,000, he found mastery, the real *gongfu* of taijiquan.

As Wu Baolin became more and more proficient in fighting, he swallowed each battle as a whet, each victory an inspiration and each loss a short unpleasant memory. The victors could always count on his return. He sought to hone his skills at every opportunity, night or day, never intimidated by age or experience, and most importantly, always willing to take instruction, learning from the village. It was the last road to personal autonomy as you may recall. Martial arts training at the monastery was generally practiced every morning at five o'clock and lasted for two hours, then breakfast. This class came immediately after chanting religious scriptures combined with daoyin exercises, the first-round lasting from 3 to 5 am, the hour of the tiger, after which a pissing contest would ensue. All of the monks of all ages would stand on a short wall and urinate into the open area. It was to measure internal *qi* power and kidney strength. The one who streamed the furthest was the strongest. Master Du was one of the oldest monks residing at the temple yet day in and day out he was far and away the clear-cut winner. The rest vied for second place.

Since Wu Baolin was not intimidated by anyone except for Master Du, he made passes around the temple with prodigious strength, keeping mostly to his own generation. On one occasion it cost him dearly. While fencing with steel swords, his Daoist brother's weapon broke through Wu Baolin's defense and sliced his neck accidentally, opening a long deep gash near the carotid artery. Using his bare hands, Master Du grabbed two handfuls of burning embers from an active incense urn and tossed them onto Wu Baolin's neck, cauterizing the wound in seconds, mitigating the bleeding. Master Du later applied a salve but the scar still remains today. Although traumatic, it did not slow anyone down. Accruing *gongfu* was sought after twenty-four hours a day.

One of Wu Baolin's older Daoist brothers was a committed taijiquan practitioner, but despite his seasoned age was already no match for Wu Baolin who was in the last of his teens. "The old respect the vigor of the young but are also inspired". During a push-hands match, two players tried to uproot and knock one another off balance. Wu Baolin could easily topple his partner and send some others flying violently into the air like a kite siphoned upward by a sturdy wind. It was not only his skill-set that was raising pulses but his relentless will to win, to gain his freedom from the temple, and by any resolve. Wu Baolin cultivated the Buddha's heart but his natural leadership let the others know when he meant business.

It was an essential part of monastic life where the wolf pack mentality was necessary to keep everyone's nature in focus and in good standing with the pack. It was easy to denote the absence of love and admiration, i.e., recognize friend or foe alike. It was customary to put the palms together and bless fellow monks and visitors of the temple. To do so the palms are joined in a praying gesture to mean wholehearted. A salutation. If the hands were held at the heart (middle elixir zone) or higher (upper elixir zone or above the head) it was a sign of sincere respect. If held below the heart the affections definitely were much less. If the hands failed to come together and with no return bow, perhaps it was the total absence of fondness and respect. As in any workplace, you have your allies and sometimes enemies. Many were simply not cutout for this level of competition so they just went with the flow to avoid confrontations; still every wolf in the pack is naturally compelled to try and compete, and gain rank and ravage their way to the alpha male. Wu Baolin was an old soul and managed to stay impartial knowing in the end the only person to beat was himself.

Like most young people Wu Baolin was forever in the mood to play. One evening Wu Baolin went promenading through the compound and came across his Daoist brother, again quietly playing taijiquan. He thought to himself, "Great! He's warmed-up and ready for action". He asked his Daoist brother if he wanted to play push-hands, and although it is a controlled sparring exercise, it often times escalated into a tussle. His Dao brother was faraway, deep in the clouds of meditation, his eyes closed and unresponsive, so Wu Baolin tried shoving him but mysteriously slipped off to the side. Nothing changed in his Dao brother's stance or play, continuing. He tried again using more strength but it was like trying to push or hug water, Wu Baolin was getting pushed down stream by an invisible current. He attempted to get close but again was repelled. This was terribly unusual. His Dao brother had never displayed such skill before. Wu Baolin came to respect his fellow monk's practice session and quietly exited the training ground.

He had questions, so he visited his teacher's study looking for an explanation. Wu Baolin went over every mystifying detail aloud, for himself and Master Du but he could not make sense of it. Master Du began to discuss the importance of *gongfu*. "Your Dao brother has time spent in the practice of taijiquan and has earned special counsel. When under this counsel not even a feather can alight on him because he is protected by the grace and power of Zhang Sanfeng. Your Dao brother practices at night because this is the precise time that Zhang Sanfeng practices taijiquan. Perhaps you should try doing the same from now on." Master Du then shared another extraordinary taijiquan accomplishment. Xu Benshan (1851-1932), Master Du's Daoist nephew from Wudang, was captivated by taijiquan, having no other interest whatsoever. He practiced day and night, drinking only water and hardly consuming any food. At age 81, he was found sleeping in *taiji zhuang*, the flesh still very warm, his spirit having already exploded out from his body, ascending to heaven.

It was some years later when Zhang Sanfeng would make contact with Wu Baolin in similar fashion. His message was clear, "Why are you not teaching my taijiquan to more people? It's a very good practice with many benefits." This interaction is one main reason for the release of this book.

Environmental Guidelines

Finding an ideal practice environment, a place where nature is present, was something Master Du stressed in his daoyin and martial arts classes. They were game changers. He made a list consisting of five uncomplicated naturally existing elements that if present during—could enhance the practice and progress of taijiquan. These were generally outdoor prescriptions but there were contingency plans and options for those that lived in crowded cities, desolate places, or in poor year round weather conditions. During poor weather, for instance, first look for a canopy of trees or a sheltered picnic area. If not available, try moving indoors into a basketball gym or a large hallway. If the backyard is your regular practice spot move into the house. Make sure there are plants to provide fresh oxygen, and make the room inside a room with a view of the outdoors with a door or windows, if convenient. Having running water, such as a kitchen sink nearby is a plus.

The Wisdom of Water—Flowing water is the most important element for a taijiquan practice area. Where there is movement, there is energy. Rivers, lakes, and oceans provide the best measures of qi in their waters since either they, run vigorously, rise or fall unexpectedly, gently rock and splash, and fill the air with their soothing sounds. Tired water, which is considered dead water, is usually found in man-made structures such as a swimming pool. Pools are saturated with chlorine, and rely on under-powered pumps for circulation so that the inevitable growth of pool algae can be avoided, maybe.

Go one step further, and practice taijiquan in water, either in the ocean or in a river. Wade in until the water comes up to the knees, or waist deep, depending on your experience and comfort level. As one of Dr. Wu's favorite practices, he stresses the importance of the legs flowing like water, a key principle of Zhang Sanfeng's taijiquan. While in the ocean, face the waves, so you can feel firsthand the forces of nature, and then rise to the level.

Taijiquan is always meditative. Water is patient and enduring, both characteristics essential to taijiquan growth. Modern living creates all sorts of mental and physical conditions that do not easily allow us the luxury of relaxing and letting go of our stresses, the senses often excited and accelerated up until the moment we go to sleep. Even this life pace can steal away our rest, when it causes insomnia. Whenever insomnia patients visited the White Cloud Temple, usually looking for an herbal prescription or acupuncture, Master Du took them to a stone slab laid across a rambling stream. He would let them lie down and rest for a duration and afterward send them home cured. Having running water in your practice area helps strike a balance between self-cultivation and daily life. Let water be of service and do part of this work for us.

Mountains Ethics—Mountains live forever. They are the over watch and part of the earth, yet remain high above it. The difficulty faced in developing living spaces in the mountains creates a deterrent for "progress". And there is the question of accessibility for extended family and friends as well as the threat of the seasonal elements in the higher elevations. Therefore, pristine nature is often protected and survived in these lowly populated areas. Because of the wilderness factor, mountain dwellers are won over by the honesty, reliability, and harmony of nature, thus are ethically grounded and come to possess right-eous energy. Water and mountains are the basic structures of yin and yang and are indeed complementary. Mountains are balanced and stable, firmly planted in their own separate ecosystem, far away from the lowlands. The base of the mountain is the stance of the tajiquan form, strong and unyielding. Many mountains are made of solid stone. This type of *qi* is the best kind for martial artist to develop within; as they become difficult to knockdown and even hard-er to stop like the avalanche.

Befriend Old Trees—Practicing taijiquan among old trees is an oppor-tunity to go to school, learning how to become more human. Trees are espe-cially known for their longevity and intelligence. One-thousand year old trees are quite common. Their energies are the healing catalyst for many difficult diseases. Cultivating *qi* from these deeply rooted ancient figures makes us stronger and healthier and if lucky enough, adds longevity to our life-cycle. Trees stand tall with their crowns in the sky. In Daoism they believe that hu-mans and trees are closely related kin and form a reciprocating pair. Humans inhale oxygen and exhale carbon monoxide. Tress inhale carbon monoxide and exhale oxygen. On land, humans would cease to exist without them.

Connect to Birds—With the exception of vultures and crows, any place where birds hang out, fly over, or nest, is a place of considerably good *qi*. Birds move and fly in more sophisticated patterns than other animals. They are communicators, the messengers of heaven's opinions according to Daoist. The trigrams of the *Yijing* supposedly go back to the flight patterns of birds, which are a barometer for testing the righteousness of your *qi*.

If birds hop within ten feet of you, no matter if you're standing still or moving, it implies that your *qi* has become cleaner and more serene. This is an accurate test. Another test, and one of the well-known achievements in taiji-quan, is if when a bird can finally alight on the palm of your hand, and this is where the real test begins. Without grasping, you must keep the bird in your palm. This can only be accomplished by having the acute sensitivity to some-one else's *qi*, to know when the bird is trying to take to the air.

Birds are extremely fast and light, since their bones are hollow and small. So when they squat down to push off, which happens in an instant, you must without thinking perfectly time gently and subtly to lower the hand and remove their springboard, careful to keep their legs extended and their power neutralized while the bird's feet barely stay in contact with the hand. This is a martial application that can be applied to bird or human. It's similar to the feeling of leaning over with an arm extended onto a wall that is not there, or the feeling of stepping off a curb you thought was still level ground. So Daoist believe that the combination of old trees and birds is auspicious. The more frequently that the birds visit a particular tree(s), the stronger and more gifted the tree's *qi* turns out to be. There are five different written forms for bird in Chinese. One such character is of a tree radical and a bird radical, joined together.

Cleanse the Body and Clear the Mind—If any of these criteria of the ideal environment can be fulfilled, it's a great start. Remember that human beings are the microcosm to the macrocosm, which is everything that is found outside ourselves. The positive within must also be addressed and prepared, then. The human body too contains water therefore before practicing taijiquan drink the highest quality water available and from a running water source whenever possible.

To become more like a tree, add to the daily diet a fair amount of fruits and vegetables and tea harvested from trees and plants, not necessarily consumed before exercise. And because of the role of the bird in Daoism, it is suggested never to eat birds that can fly for risk of losing favor and communication from above. The body itself represents the mountains where all of these things may thrive in abundance.

In further preparation for the practice of taijiquan, like any important event, we should consider our own level of heart, commitment and hygiene. Every time we practice represents a fresh start like preparing for the first day at a new job or a newly appointed position. Think of it like the first day of school, and striving for new heights. Practicing taijiquan can be viewed as a rebirth. When a baby is born, the most important step after initiating the baby's first breath, is to rinse off the amniotic fluid so that it does not dry inside and seal the newborn's pores, since the body depends on breathing through the pores. This illustrates that maintaining a clean body is valuable to the practice of taijiquan, so that skin free of debris can help the body open and receive oxygen.

Hygiene is also a sign of respect to the practice. In the mountains and during the cold winters in Beijing, it was not convenient or advisable for the monks to bathe every day due to extreme temperature change, which could lead to cold or pneumonia. However, cleanliness of the nine orifices (eyes, nostrils, ears, mouth, urethra, and anus) was strictly enforced, since they represent the gates connecting the nine palaces of heaven and those in the body. With these gates clear, it is easier to process and let go of emotions, thereby calming the mind and opening a greater connection with the universe, so that heaven, humanity, and earth can be one.

Maximizing Accomplishments

In the process of learning taijiquan, one question is always asked, "How does one excel?" Based on the experience of Masters Du and Wu Baolin's over for-ty-plus years of teaching, we can summarize the fundamental techniques and key practices of training.

The fundamental techniques constantly require review and improvement through practice in order to accomplish a desired benefit. They consist of two aspects, correct posture and fluid body movement.

Correct posture should be addressed before the mind-directed movement commences. In the beginning stage, the student is encouraged to imitate the postures that are structurally accurate. Only after the postures are structurally accurate and have become dynamically formed within taijiquan guidelines can the student gain insight into the martial art application. The guidelines for accurate movements and body attitudes are:

Head upright and relaxed—During practice, keep the head and neck in an upright position with the chin tucked-in slightly. The crown of the head, where the Baihui point (GV-20) is located, is held as if suspended by a string. The head and face should be relaxed, lively and in a natural state. This posture helps to keep the body straight and sturdy, and increases spiritual awareness.

Chest held in and back straight—The chest should be comfortably held inward with the shoulders relaxed and the elbows dropped downward. The back should be straight—the atlas and axis at the base of the skull should be held up and back, causing a slight sense of tightness. The held-in chest and straight back posture increases ability to exert and redirect forces.

Waist relaxes, pelvis tucked—In the held-in chest and straight back pos-tures, the waist must be relaxed. Only after the waist is relaxed and the torso firmly set can the feet be fully grounded, thus giving the lower limbs a solid foundation. The waist directs the movements of the entire body. The upper body posture including the chest, straight back and relaxed waist is established through a 'tucked-in' pelvis formed as the base. The pelvis is tucked-in as if to push the belly outward. This posture allows the qi to sink to the pelvis cavity (lower elixir field) and thus fill the abdominal cavity.

Buttocks rounded, thighs relaxed—The crown of the head must be aligned with the perineum in order to keep the body straight and allowing the qi to circulate freely. With the legs open and knees bent slightly toward each other, the whole structure will form and arch. With the lower belly filled with qi and with the perineum relaxed, the lower limbs can be on a solid foundation.

Shoulders sunk, elbows lowered—Sinking the shoulders means that the shoulders are to be relaxed and in a naturally downward position. Lowered the elbows means the elbows should be relaxed and dropped downward. This posture provides a stored energy in the body, which can potentially be directed to the palms.

Fingers relaxed, palms angled—The fingers are relaxed, and the palm is at a right angle to the wrist. During a palm pushing movement, the fingers are relaxed first. As the hand stretches and arrives at the intended position, the palm is bent to a right angle allowing the *qi* to penetrate through the fingers.

Body moving—Static postures demonstrate structure and form, while body movement represents concept of movement. In practice, not only is the correct posture essential, but proper body movement is also necessary to achieve the style and the technical aspects of taijiquan.

Torso upright and relaxed—While in forward or retreating movements, right or left turns, or in any direction led by the four limbs, the head and the torso must be aligned and straight to avoid any part of the body from being uncoordinated. Keeping the shoulders and lower limbs aligned and moving together is the key for the torso to follow appropriately. To achieve agility and body relaxation, it is essential that the waist, lower limbs and chest all move in harmony. With this achievement, the whole body will maintain a complete balance in all directions.

Legs moving—Leg movement or footwork is the foundation of keeping the body in balance. It is a determining factor in developing an agility of movement and a sturdy body. In a forward advancing movement, raise the thigh first and the calf, and the heel; all the while letting the foot relax naturally. Stretch the leg from a bent posture and step out slowly. At the time of stepping, let the heel land first and the rest of the foot. Whether one is advancing or retreating the front and rear legs should not be aligned in a straight line so as to avoid a loss of balance.

Hands and arms moving—Shoulders should be sinking and elbows lowered before hand movements begin. Only after shoulders and elbows are relaxed can the hand and arm move freely and with control. While reaching out the hand leads the elbow while the elbow leads the shoulder. To stop, the shoulder restrains the elbow while the elbow restrains the hand. When the arm is bent the shoulder ideally sinks down and allows the elbow to lead the hand. Allow the shoulder to rotate and move along with the wrist and allow the wrist to move along with palm, always forming an arc.

Eyes Focused—"Spirit emanates from the eyes; the eyes are the radiance of the mind." The focus of the eyes reflects the individual's spirit. The eyes follow the movements of the hand to look ahead, right, or left. This means initially the mind prepares for an intended movement, the eyes focus and look ahead into that direction. Subsequently, the body, hands and feet all follow and complete the movement. This represents a complete unification of spirit and form in taijiquan.

Mind directing—"All movements are directed by the mind." This is the most important technical aspect of taijiquan. This is to say, spirit (*shen*) and mind (*yinian*) should be unified and focused on the movements. To come to this the mind must be calm and concentrated. Just as the body movements are directed by the mind, so are the forces (energies) exerted by the hands resulting from the movements. This establishes a close relationship between movement and mind.

Breathing coordinated—All breathing should be in close coordination with movement. Generally speaking, one should inhale when the body is open and exhale when the body is closed; breathe in when the body is in elevated postures and breathe out when the body is in lowered postures. Whether breathing in or breathing out, always follow the *qi* to sink into the lower elixir field, the energy center located in the pelvis cavity.

Intrinsic energy—Taijiquan emphasizes the mind, not muscular or brute force (awkward force). Natural force results from a mind-directed movement with a proper and balanced posture. In this case, parts of the body's muscles are extremely relaxed while all the joints are loose and flexible. The resulting energy from this steady but lively movement, combined with a continuous and smooth force, is called intrinsic energy.

Martial Arts Training—To do well in taijiquan one must not only thoroughly understand the rationale of the fundamental techniques, but also develop mastery of the martial arts, which requires proper training. This involves internal coordination, i.e., mind-directed movements coordinated with breathing, as well as external coordination of the body form, that is, proper posture with accurate martial art application. The unification of internal and external coordination simply means a complete coordination of the body forms, movements and breathing.

In addition, dynamic movement is necessary, defined as combating motions, which consist of a series of special animated movements, following particular footwork and dynamic forms, while 'stillness' is defined as a static stance, which also consist of a series of particular stances with martial arts application. Therefore, the harmony of the 'dynamic movement' with 'stillness' is a complete balance of stance with movement, emphasizing the 'movement within stillness' and 'stillness within movement' balance. Once achieved, the quality of body forms and movements can be transcended to a realistic level.

Another dimension of martial arts training involves dynamic movements, and training concepts. They include Basic Stances, Wuji, Taiji, Open and Close, Up and Down, and Insubstantiality Stances; Basic Dynamic Movement, Repulse Monkey, Cloud Hands, Parting the Wild Horse's Mane, Golden Rooster Stands on One Leg, Brush Knee, Block, Parry, Punch (hollow fist), Kick with Right and Left Sole, as well as Grasp the Bird's Tail.

Agility and Awareness—This training consist of three stages, also called "three stages of *gongfu*." The first stage emphasizes basic training on individual postures combined with movements. Only through thoroughly understanding the rationale of fundamental techniques of hand movement, footwork, body movement and mastering the balancing of movements can one satisfy the taiji-quan guidelines.

The second stage emphasizes routine practice. It is important to master the transitions of movement within the routines while attending to the special techniques in the movement, which demands special attention. This is important so that the set of movement becomes smooth, natural and realistic.

The final stage emphasizes that the intrinsic energy exerted from body and hands is directed by the mind and coordinated with movements and breathing until it becomes agile yet sturdy, soft but firm, thereby unifying the whole being.

Taijiquan Stance Key

Horse Stance – Back View
Weight Dist: 50/50

Horse Stance – Front View
Weight Dist: 50/50

Left Forward (Bow) Stance

Weight Dist: 70/30

Left Empty Stance

Weight Dist: 90/10

Left One Leg Stance

Weight Dist: 100/0

Left Twist Stance

Weight Dist: 50/50

Right Forward (Bow) Stance

Weight Dist: 70/30

Right Empty Stance

Weight Dist: 90/10

Right One Leg Stance

Weight Dist: 100/0

Right Twist Stance

Weight Dist: 50/50

Chapter Seven

The Form

1. Wuji Position, Prepare to Enter Dao, Prepare *Qi*

Start by facing south with the heels together. Imagine standing in the center of a clock face as a pine tree, the left big toe set to 11 am, and the right big toe at 1 pm. The tips of the thumbs are over the navel at the Shenque point (CV-8), the index fingers joined at the Guanyuan point (CV-4) to close the circle, outlining the lower elixir field, representing Wuji, the Non-Ultimate and beginning of the universe. Meditate here to collect and concentrate the *qi* in the lower elixir field until ready to begin and becoming clear.

When ready, let the hands fall away from the center to a natural resting position. (If the hands reach to the lateral seam of the legs between the quadriceps and the hamstrings, there may be contact with the Fengshi point (GB-31) at the middle fingertip. Slowly lift the left heel off the ground so that body weight, blood, and *qi* begin pouring into the right leg while the left leg gradually empties. Maintain a steady and centralized one-legged stance, spine vertical, head and eyes looking straight ahead, careful to avoid leaning.

Once the right leg is stable and full, step the left foot to the left, touching down with the toes first to sense the ground's firmness. Once committed, drop the left heel, gently settling into a mild horse stance or mountain, feet slightly outside shoulder width, the knees slightly bent and foot angles remaining the same. Hands stay resting.

Return the left foot to the starting position, heels together, the left big toe set to 11 am and the right big toe set to 1 pm. Place the thumbs onto the navel and the index fingers reconnected again to form a circle over the lower elixir field, the source.

2. The Taiji Original Talisman

Lift the hands off the lower elixir field half an inch from surface, thumbs and index fingers in contact with one another in a ring. Connect the middle fingertips with the thumb tips, the four joined and curling together to form two perfectly round circles, the representation of the Taiji symbol, also the mathematical sign of infinity. The other three pairs of fingers are straightened.

Attach the third (ring) fingers to the thumbs in the same fashion as the middle fingers, doubling the thickness of the circles. Close the gap between the little and index fingers until contact is made at the fingertips, forming a bridge. Taiji is complete.

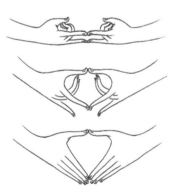

Keep the bridge connected with the two small fingers and the two index fingers, underlining the navel. Pull the two circles apart until the palms are facing up. This represents the one becoming the two, Taiji becoming yin-yang, independently.

Inhale through the nose, and lift the hands, bending at the elbows, keeping the shoulders down and relaxed, until the hands reach the center of the chest at the middle elixir zone or Tanzhong point (CV-17), actuating essence, *qi*, and spirit. Do not go above the transverse plane of the nipples.

Turn the hands over, palms down, and release the ten fingers: this represents the three becoming the myriad beings, all that exists. At the same time, lift the left heel, so that body weight, blood, and *qi* pour into the right leg.

Maintain a steady and centralized one-legged stance, spine vertical, head and eyes looking straight ahead, careful to avoid leaning.

Let the hands float downward in the shape of a shallow umbrella, left foot stepping left, touching down with the toes first. Once committed drop the left heel, gently settling into a mild horse stance, feet slightly outside shoulder width, the knees slightly bent, foot angles remaining the same. Let the hands slowly fall as if through the resistance of water or feathers over a light breeze, settling into the natural resting position in front of the body with shoulders relaxed and palms lightly resting on the front upper legs.

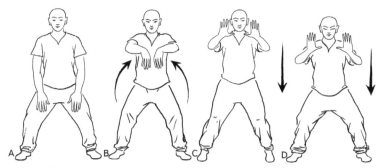

3. Release the Spirit

Imagine the sun rising under the arms, elbows, and armpits, the mind issuing orders to the *qi*. Let the arms rise effortlessly while the shoulders stay resting and the wrists bend at 90 degrees, so that all ten fingers point straight down toward the earth, vertically positioned.

As the arms ascend, they begin pulling up the whole body. The elbows gradually crease at the bend, both hands magnetically drawn toward one another to begin the forming of a circle. The hands should almost be touching just when the arms reach shoulder height, as if forming a halo over the imaginary sun. The legs have straightened and the heels of the feet gradually begin losing contact with the ground, as the sun lightens and lifts the body like hot air rising.

Just before the body is uprooted entirely at the feet, the body raised on the ten toes, flip the wrist upward one-hundred eighty degrees releasing out the Spirit to play, the ten fingers pointing upward toward heaven. The fingertips are never allowed to fly above the plane of the eyes. The elbows are naturally drawn downward.

The sun continues upward while the body sinks down, the heels touch the ground and the legs and knees lower, back into horse stance, bringing the hands down, careful to keep the fingers vertical. The palms face forward and away, the body upright, stable and relaxed.

4. Gathering Clouds, Ward-Off Southeast

As the lower half of the body sinks into the soft earth or permeable stone, and before the waist and hands begin to lean forward, turn the waist to the left throwing the hands and arms southeast in a curving circular motion. The right hand is following the left hand, the head and eyes now focused in the southeast direction. The entirety of the thirteen relaxed points and other joints kicked into action.

Circle back around to the torso, drawing the left foot heel to the inside-medial portion of the right heel. The left heel remains raised off the ground two to three inches, toes pointing southeast. The right hand assumes the superior position, palm down, with the Laogong (P-8) point at the middle elixir zone. The left hand, palm up, under the lower elixir field as if holding a ball. The fingers are tightly sealed together, and the body rests momentarily in suspension.

Drop the left heel weightily onto the ground, activating the kidney reflex area. The posterior tuberosity of the left heel lands approximately one inch away from the inside-medial portion of the right heel. When the left heel hits the ground the body sinks and turns from the waist to the right, distributing and directing the force of impact circularly around the body.

Continue to rotate to the right as far as possible, careful to stop before locking tension occurs, keeping the spine loose. The twisting wrings out the yang meridians on the back, opening the points and removing any excess moisture or toxins. Both feet remain fixed to the ground at all times.   Let the waist uncoil until the eyes and frontal torso are again facing southeast. Use this momentum to step southeast into a left forward stance, and separating the hands as if cradling a baby. The left arm is curved, shoulder relaxed, left hand and fingers angled down to the right at a forty-five degree angle. Thumb is opened. The right hand is held palm up, resting on the right rib cage, Wangu point (SI-4) on the ulnar border of the right hand resting on the Dabao point (SP-21) of the right rib cage.

5. Activate the Lung Channel via the Pericardium

The right hand forms a sword mudra, joining the thumb, ring finger, and little finger, thumb print covers the other two fingernails, acting as a clip. The index finger and the middle finger remain joined, straight like a sword's blade.

Inhale slowly through the nose, as the right hand sword mudra shoots forward, palm up, directly toward the tip of the left middle finger, at the Zhongchong point (P-9). The right hand banks in and follows the pericardium channel, traversing over the middle palm and medial aspect of the left forearm, over the bicep, until the middle finger of the sword mudra makes light contact with the Zhongfu point (LU-1) in the lateral aspect of the chest approximately one inch below the clavicle. The left hand remains in the ward-off position.

Step forward onto the ball of the right foot, heel raised, pausing next to the left foot, the waist slowly turning left, and the shoulder girdle in slow pursuit of this bearing. Follow the continuous motion, stepping out with right foot directly ahead of the left foot in the same southeast direction, and rotating to the left side of the body, aided by increasing deep pressure onto the Zhongfu point (LU-1) by the hand sword mudra.

Pivot the right foot toward the mid line of the body, both feet vectored inward opening the sacrum, and protecting against injury. Continue to press the Zhongfu point (LU-1), firmly pushing the body left. Continue left careful to stop before locking tension occurs, relaxing near the end, spine loose. Do not overstretch. Left hand remains in ward-off position shielding the anterior torso from shoulder to shoulder.

6. Lion Pushes the Ball

Reverse direction, from left to right, releasing the sword mudra. The right hand, palm down, moves under the left armpit, and the left hand turns palm down. Turn the waist right, as the hands rise and begin to separate like a pair of cutting-shears lightly brushing up against one another, until the body is turned facing southeast. The right foot pivots right mirroring the right hand, into a right empty stance. Imagine a large round stone ball out in front and begin outlining and contouring its shape using both hands beginning from the crown and around to the sides.

When the hands encompass the lower half of the stone ball, shift the weight into a right forward stance, arriving together with the hands, connecting the ulnar aspects, palms up, on the small intestine channel, completing the circle. The palms and forearms angled at 45 degrees downward, following the angulation of the right femur.

Shift the weight into the rear leg, drawing the hands up and back into the superior abdominal region. Do not lean backward. The hands then bend at the wrist diving the fingertips down the center of the abdomen following the conception vessel to the lower elixir field. Shift the weight into a right forward stance pushing the heels and palms of the hands forward. The wrist are bent to approximately ninety degrees from forearms, fingers pointed to the earth.

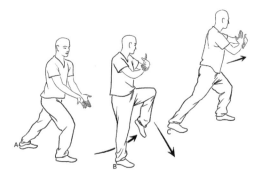

7. The Press

Press the body up, straightening the right leg and raising the left knee in a high step, knee pointing northeast, together with the head and eyes. Rotate the right hand so the fingers point up, palm facing front and the left hand horizontal, palm facing the body, left wrist relaxed. The Laogong point (P-8) in the right palm lays over and lightly presses on the Neiguan point (P-6) at the medial aspect of the left wrist. The elbows and shoulders are relaxed. [The large stone ball has been consolidated into a millet grain pressed between palm and wrist.]

Step northeast into a left forward stance, the hands pressing out, opening the space inside of the arms into roundness.

8. Black Dragon Activates Wind

Slide the right hand across the left palm until the tip of the right index finger contacts the tip of the left thumb, and left index finger contacts the tip of the right thumb to form a square window in front of the middle elixir zone. Square represents earth.

The right palm faces front and the left palm faces the torso. Hold this position and use your mind to draw a connection between the two Laogong points (P-8) of either palm by using an imaginary light, or thread or chain, some image that helps to create physical connectivity and sensation. Once connection is firmly established gently turn the waist right, pulling the right hand away from the left. The left arm, hand, and stance remain stationary. The eyes and head follow the right hand.

Turn the waist and torso until the right hand aligns over the right leg, fingers rotated vertically, the head and eyes fixed on the back of the right hand. Begin drawing down the right hand and arm toward the leg careful to keep the fingers vertical, creating a stretch and tension in the forearm. Release the tension forcefully whipping the Fengshi point (GB-31) on the lateral side of the right leg using the backs of the fingers and fingertips, striking front to back, for strengthening the legs, and alleviating hip and leg problems. Turn the hand up on the follow through moving in reverse, the eyes, and head following the back of the right hand back around the body until the tip of the right index finger contacts the tip of the left thumb, and tip of left index finger contacts the tip of the right thumb to form a square window in front of the middle elixir zone, northeast facing.

9. Window Peering through Heaven and Earth

Turn the left hand over so the palm faces away. Join the tips of the index fingers together and the thumb tips together to form a circle. Circle represents heaven. Move the hands and arms across the sky in an arch from left to right, northeast to southwest. The head is tilted upward so the eyes peer through the round window to frame the sun in passing.

Pivot the body one-hundred and eighty degrees into a right forward stance facing southwest. The hands separate, right hand leading the left hand. Follow through the hands sweeping down across the lower half of the body, palms turned down, and shifting the weight from right to left, the hands coming back to the left side, completing a 360 degree circle.

Reverse the hands direction back over the right foot, bringing the left foot next to the right foot, feet pointing southeast. The palms face away from the body, left above right, fingers pointing down.

10. Cranes Flying to the Moon

Take a step behind the body toward the northwest and pull the hands and arms directly overhead like cranes flying to the moon, followed by the eyes and head. The wrist are bent back so the palms are level and facing the sky.

Shift the weight into a left forward stance as the hands turn over, palms down, left leading the right, pointing and reaching northwest with every intention of touching the moon. Sweep the hands down across the body, left to right, while pivoting the feet toward east.

Step and place the left foot together with the right, facing east. The right arm is bent at the elbow, fist up and wrist bent, the back of the fist facing front away from the body. The left hand forms a cup, five fingers pressed together, underneath the right elbow to catch the qi drops. Meditate until cup is full.

11. Break the Lock

Lift the left cupped hand in front of right chest, then above the right shoulder. Turn the left hand over and pour the qi onto the right deltoid, while turning the right fist around. Lower the right arm, right wrist bent flexing backward, and step northeast into a left forward stance. The left palm cascades down over the right arm, and before reaching the wrist, the right wrist bends forward clearing the way for the left hand to pass over. The right arm mirrors the angulation of the left femur.

Press the fingernail of the right index finger with the right thumb so that the middle knuckle is pronounced, and press it onto the left index finger at the base of the fingernail Shangyang point (LI-1).

12. Face the Tiger

Plow upward on the large intestine channel with the middle knuckle of the right index finger pressing deeply, causing the left arm to curl. Pivot the left foot inward and turn the waist to the right. Continue on the channel over the left forearm and across the upper arm and left shoulder to the lateral aspect of the left side of the neck, onto the Futu point (LI-18). Press deeply for a millisecond, release.

Pivot the right foot out, dragging the middle knuckle, from left to right, across the throat over the laryngeal prominence (Adam's apple) onto the Futu point (LI-18) of the right side of the neck. Press deeply for a millisecond, release. The body has rotated one-hundred and eighty degrees facing southwest in a right twist stance.

Continue dragging the right hand around the back of the neck, to the left side. Move the right hand and forearm overhead, back to front, clearing obstructions, swiping over the left arm. From the inside-out, the left hand comes up and over the right arm fingers pointing upward guarding the head and torso, while stepping forward into a left empty stance, heel up. The right hand settles in front of the groin, fingers vertical. The left hand forms an L-shaped sight between the left thumb and index finger. Imagine a ferocious hungry tiger approaching you from the southwest, bringing out your inner force.

13. Strike Tiger's Ears (Twin Wind Filling Ears)

Lower the left heel to the ground, toes pointing southwest. Step forward onto the ball of the right foot, close to the left, turning the right foot, head, and torso west. The hands are set, palms down, at the sides, waist level, representing two swallows. The fingers are pointing forward and pulled upward to exercise hand strength and increase pounds of force.

Release the tension in the hands and forearms, thus launching the hands back, and circling them around from the flanks like two swallows taking flight. Transform the swallows into two hollow fist as the right foot and body lunge into a right forward stance. The fists strike Taiyang point (EX-1), at the level of the ears or temples, in front of the body, palms facing away.

14. Single Whip

Join the four fingers to the thumb of the right hand, fingers pointing down (eagle's beak), uniting the five phases. Open the left hand, horizontal, palm facing away. Lower the hands to shoulder level, bending at the elbows forming a circle with the arms. Turn the waist left, and into a horse stance facing southwest, lowering center of gravity, moving across to the left side of body. Right foot pivots inward and the left foot pivots outward for balance and symmetry. The eyes focused in the left hand.

Turn the waist right, lowering the center of gravity even deeper, until the upper legs are almost parallel to the ground, rotating back to the right side of body, the eagle's beak leading.

15. Buddha Pounds Mortar

Turn the waist left, and direct the body toward southeast, dropping the right arm alongside the body, palm pushing forward. At the same time, step forward with the right leg, towards southeast. The left hand remains horizontally positioned, palm facing away, guarding the body.

Continue stepping until the right foot is next to the left, heel off the ground, and the right inner forearm in the crook of the left hand between the thumb and index finger. Rotate the right arm counterclockwise a quarter turn, to slip around the left hand. The right hand and arm cut upward like a knife, overhead, the left hand, horizontal, dropping to the lower elixir field, palm down.

Close the right hand into a hollow fist, and turn the left palm up at the lower elixir field. Drop the right elbow down the center of the body, back of fist facing away, until elbow turns out to the right, right fist palm up at the middle elixir zone. Drop the right heel to the ground, and the back of the right fist into the left palm in unison, bending at the knees and sinking the body.

16. Golden Rooster Stands on One Leg

Inhale to inflate the body so it begins to straighten. The hands rise together to middle elixir zone, and then separate. Elevate and open the right fist so the palm faces the sky at around the upper elixir zone and the left hand palm down, at the middle elixir zone. Exhale sharply collapsing the body like a bellow, pushing the right hand up and the left palm down together with a forceful *ha* sound, clearing stress and leaving the mundane world behind.

Raise the right knee to the waist and pull the right elbow down above the knee, right hand vertical. The tip of the right middle finger is level with the pupil of the right eye. The left hand remains horizontal, palm down with the thumb pointed into the left inguinal canal at Chongmen point (SP-12). The right lower leg from the knee down is relaxed, the ankle and toes hanging freely.

17. Rolling Thunder Hammers and Push

Leap high and far, like a cat, toward southeast with the right leg, pushing off of the left, and hammer downward with the soft under portion of the right fist, on the midline. Elbow slightly bent. Immediately follow with a full lunging step into a left forward stance with a left hammer fist, punctuated by another right hammer fist. Elbows are bent, right fist ahead of the left, aligned with middle elixir zone (the three rolling punches are similar to the actions used in the speed bag training of western boxing).

Shift the weight into the rear leg and lift the wrist up and back to the shoulders in a circular pattern. The hands contour down the chest and abdomen with the fingers pointing up. Shift the weight into a left forward stance, pushing with the hands, wrists bent, the fingers pulled back. Use the heels of the palms to push upward (lifting under opponents ribcage), elbows bent, completing a perfect circle.

18. Cat Stretch (White Crane Spreads Wings), Brush Knee

Shift weight back into a left empty stance, floating the right hand, palm down, near the right temple, and lowering the left hand by the left knee. Turn waist left, fanning the right hand across the body as if swatting a fly [the fingertips no higher than the eyebrows]. Let the right hand set down on the left side, moving in a circular pattern, then back across to the right knee.

Turn the waist right, fanning the left hand across the body as if swatting a fly [the fingertips no higher than the eyebrows]. Let the left hand set down on the right side, moving in a circular pattern, then back across towards the left. At the same time, raise the right hand up near the right temple. Shift weight into a left forward stance and push from the middle elixir zone with the heel of the right hand, fingers pointing up, as the left hand brushes over the left knee, palm down, fingers pointing forward.

19. Repulse Monkey (1)

Step back with the left foot into the arch of the right foot, while floating the left hand, palm down, near the left temple. Right hand stays guarding the torso. Step back and out from the mid line into a right empty stance, completing left half of an X.

Turn the right palm up, arm gently extended, and push with the left hand, fingers pointing up, Wangu point (SI-4) following the small intestine channel of the right arm until the wrists' meet.

19. Repulse Monkey (2)

Step back with the right foot into the arch of the left foot, guiding the right hand, palm up, under the left arm to the armpit. Step back and out from the mid line into a left empty stance, completing right half of an X, while pulling the right hand across the chest to the right shoulder, turning fingers up, thumb over the right shoulder, palm facing front.

Turn the left palm up, arm gently extended, and push with the right hand, fingers pointing up, Wangu point (SI-4) following the small intestine channel of the left arm until the wrists' meet.

19. Repulse Monkey (3)

Step back with the left foot into the arch of the right foot, guiding the left hand, palm up, under the right arm to the armpit. Step back and out from the mid line into a right empty stance, completing left half of an X, while pulling the left hand across the chest to the left shoulder, turning fingers up, thumb over the left shoulder, palm facing front.

Turn the right palm up, arm gently extended, and push with the left hand, fingers pointing up, Wangu point (SI-4) following the small intestine channel of the right arm until the wrists' meet.

19. Repulse Monkey (4)

Step back with the right foot into the arch of the left foot, guiding the right hand, palm up, under the left arm to the armpit. Step back and out from the mid line into a left empty stance, completing right half of an X, while pulling the right hand across the chest to the right shoulder, turning fingers up, thumb over the right shoulder, palm facing front.

Turn the left palm up, arm gently extended, and push with the right hand, fingers pointing up, Wangu point (SI-4) following the small intestine channel of the left arm until the wrists' meet.

19. Repulse Monkey (5)

Step back with the left foot into the arch of the right foot, guiding the left hand, palm up, under the right arm to the armpit. Step back and out from the mid line into a right empty stance, completing left half of an X, while pulling the left hand across the chest to the left shoulder, turning fingers up, thumb over the left shoulder, palm facing front.

Turn the right palm up, arm gently extended, and push with the left hand, fingers pointing up, Wangu point (SI-4) following the small intestine channel of the right arm until the wrists' meet.

19. Repulse Monkey (6)

Step back with the right foot into the arch of the left foot, guiding the right hand, palm up, under the left arm to the armpit. Step back and out from the mid line into a left empty stance, completing right half of an X, while pulling the right hand across the chest to the right shoulder, turning fingers up, thumb over the right shoulder, palm facing front.

Turn the left palm up, arm gently extended, and push with the right hand, fingers pointing up, Wangu point (SI-4) following the small intestine channel of the left arm until the wrists' meet.

19. Repulse Monkey (7)

Step back with the left foot into the arch of the right foot, guiding the left hand, palm up, under the right arm to the armpit. Step back and out from the mid line into a right empty stance, completing left half of an X, while pulling the left hand across the chest to the left shoulder, turning fingers up, thumb over the left shoulder, palm facing front.

Turn the right palm up, arm gently extended, and push with the left hand, fingers pointing up, Wangu point (SI-4) following the small intestine channel of the right arm until the wrists' meet.

20. Activate the Elixir Field

Push and pivot the right foot open to widen the gate, settling into a relaxed horse stance, facing northeast. Reel both hands in so the palms turn to face the lower elixir field, fingers pointing down.

Continue circling up the left side of the abdomen until arriving at top center just below the sternum, marking one complete circle. Circle down the right side of the abdomen, past the lower elixir field and up the left side until top center, completing second circle. Circle down the right side of the abdomen, past the lower elixir field and up the left side until top center, completing the third and final circle.

Pause at top center inhaling, then forcefully drop the hands straight down between the legs lowering the body's center of gravity, keeping the torso and head upright, and sharply exhaling.

To enhance this exercise imagine the abdomen in a state of advanced pregnancy so that the palms may take on the contouring form of a large ball.

21. Shuttle Back and Forth, Side Strike Left

Turn the waist right, moving the right hand, palm down, above the right lung and the left hand, palm up, under the right ribcage. As the body's weight begins to favor the right side, lift the left knee and foot off the ground, straightening the right leg. Reverse rotation turning the waist left, and stepping northwest into a left twist stance, immediately followed by a low swinging right hook step into a right-weighted horse stance, facing southwest.

Shift into a left-weighted horse stance leading with the left latissimus and left hip, while executing a left rolling upward block (like a rolling pin) finishing above the head, forearm guarding the Baihui point (GV-20), palm up with the wrist bent. The right hand pushes, plowing across the chest, stopping on the outer edge of the left pectoral muscle. Head and eyes look southeast.

22. Shuttle Back and Forth, Side Strike Right

Turn the waist right, pivoting out the right foot into a right twist stance towards northwest, and moving the left hand, palm down, above the left lung and the right hand, palm up, under the left ribcage, immediately followed by a low swinging left hook step into a left-weighted horse stance, facing northeast.

Shift into a right weighted horse stance leading with the right latissimus and right hip, while executing a right rolling upward block (like a rolling pin) finishing above the head, forearm guarding the Baihui point (GV-20), palm up with wrist bent. The left hand pushes, plowing across the chest, stopping on the outer edge of the right pectoral muscle. Head and eyes look southeast.

23. Intercept, Punch

Turn the waist left, drawing both hands to the waist, while pivoting into a left forward stance facing northwest, executing a left brush knee block and a right low vertical punch.

24. Green Dragon Shakes Tail

Turn the waist right, pivoting into a horse stance, facing northeast (imagine straddling a water vessel). Place the right hand, palm open, over your heart (left chest) as if pledging allegiance to the flag, right middle finger in upper corner of chest, the thumb tucked over Zhongfu point (LU-1). Form a left hand sword mudra, and place the fingertips of left middle and index fingers onto Quchi point (LI-11), body relaxes and sinks.

Push forward with both palms like the breast stroke, circling around the inside of the water vessel, half formed by the inner legs. After stirring once around, turn the waist right, shifting into a right forward stance facing southeast, the right hand turning, palm up, to the front, shoulder height, and the left hand turning, palm up, to the rear, waist level.

25. Open the Heart Channel

Step forward onto the ball of the left foot next to right, bringing the left hand around to the front, horizontal, palm down with the thumb pointed into the left inguinal canal at Chongmen point (SP-12). Move the left hand to the ulnar aspect of right elbow, left middle finger pointing to the Shenmen point

(HE-7). Guide the middle finger along the heart meridian to its end at the small finger. Step southeast into a left forward stance and turn left hand, palm up, joining the hands on the ulnar aspects and pushing them forward, at shoulder height.

26. Turn the Stone Wheel

Turn the waist to the right pivoting 180 degrees to face northwest in a right forward stance. Shift the weight back onto the rear leg and draw the hands in toward the torso until the palms flip up to face the chest. Immediately pull down and turn the hands around [like a swimmers open turn], so the palms face front, fingers vectored inward, and thumbs opened to form a pyramid shape. Shift the weight forward into a right forward stance and push from low to high. The palms are molded as if holding a basketball, elbows slightly flared.

27. Cat Stalks and Pounces

Step forward onto the ball of the left foot, heel raised, next to the right. Sink low into the right leg, forming two relaxed cat paws (hands), the left hand higher than the right, palms neither facing one another nor facing forward. Switch the body weight from right to left, raising the right heel, the right hand now higher than the left, as if tipping scales.

Leap high and far toward northwest with the right leg, pushing off with the left, and pouncing down with the right cat paw, on the midline, immediately followed by the left leg, and pouncing down with the left cat paw, on the midline, settling in a left forward stance, punctuated by another pouncing right cat paw, on the midline. The left hand finishes palm down above the left knee, and the right hand centered above. These movements should contain the emotional excitement of a cat hunting, stalking, and finally, capturing its prey.

28. Parting Mountains Left

Turn the waist right, and bring the right hand to fall onto the left shoulder. Then bring the left foot next to the right foot, and bring the left hand across the body to fall onto the right shoulder, facing northeast [feel comfort holding one's self]. Open the arms positioning the hands vertically outside the shoulders, palms facing away. Lift the left knee to the waist forming a knife edge with the left foot. Let the body fall left (camel step) maintaining a fixed lower body position, while pushing out to the flanks with the palms as if parting two mountains. When the left foot hits the ground in a full horse stance facing northeast, the hands are reaching their complete extension, careful not to lock the elbows.

29. Parting Mountains Right

Turn the waist left, pivoting the left foot open, until the left hand falls onto the right shoulder. Swing the right leg 180 degrees, the sole of the right foot lightly grazing the ground, then circling around in front the body, finishing next to the left foot, at the same time, the right arm falling onto the left shoulder, the body facing southwest [feel comfort holding one's self]. Open the arms positioning the hands horizontally outside the shoulders, palms facing away, fingers pointing forward. Lift the right knee to the waist forming a knife edge with the right foot. Let the body fall right (camel step) maintaining a fixed lower body position, while pushing out to the flanks with the palms as if parting two mountains. When the right foot hits the ground in a full horse stance facing southwest, the hands are reaching their complete extension, careful not to lock the elbows.

Truth, Compassion, Embrace

Shakyamuni Buddha

30. Carry Tiger Back to Mountain, Pray to Buddha

Relax and gently sink, carving and lowering the knife edges of the hands to the center, joining and lifting the palms in prayer. The tips of the middle fingers are level with the apex of the nose, the elbows forming the base of a triangle or bridge.

The hands represent Truth (*zhen*), the left elbow is Compassion or more literally goodness (*shan*), the right elbow matches Embrace, literally beauty (*mei*), key principles of the Buddhist path. Repeat the mantra at least once in the posture. Either during or after the mantra, the practitioner should pray to someone or something they believe in wholeheartedly, and above their own level. It can be any deity from any religion e.g. Laozi, the Buddha, Zhang Sanfeng, Jesus Christ, the sun, the moon, a holy mountain or volcano, your teacher, etc., or just meditate on the nothingness of Dao.

31. Protect the Dharma

   Fix the eyes on whatever is directly in front of you in the distance. Turn the waist to the right, pushing the hands left, and lowering the left elbow to the rib cage for protection. The legs may incidentally move and turn at the joints, but the feet should remain grounded. Turn the waist to the left, pushing the hands right, the right elbow up striking horizontally. Turn the waist right and push the hands to the left, the right elbow up striking horizontally.

32. Spread the Dharma

   Step northwest with the left foot, laterally across and behind the right foot, setting it down perpendicular with the soles even on the ground (right twist stance). Tilt the hands 90 degrees right, forming a right angle with the left forearm, the hands set horizontally, and the right forearm set vertically. Eyes, head, and torso, turn facing southeast. Step northwest with the right foot into a left empty stance, separating the hands, pulling the right hand down alongside the right hip, palm down, and the left hand rotating a quarter-turn, the palm faces away.

33. Kite in Flight, Buddha Resting

Step northwest with the left foot behind the right. Begin turning the waist to the left, while lowering the left elbow slightly in the transition. The right hand remains fixed at the right hip. Continue turning the body 180 degrees into a left forward stance facing northwest, simultaneously rolling the left arm into an overhead block (like a rolling pin), palm facing the sky. In the turning, the right palm is propelled forward, pushing and rising like a kite, followed by the head and eyes, until the left hand catches inside the right elbow, and the right hand forms a hollow fist.

Begin turning the waist to the right, shifting the body weight into the right leg while outwardly turning and twisting the right fist, forearm, and shoulder (to include the spine), as far as possible, while the left hand holds the right elbow. The body leans right, head to the southeast. The head, neck, spine, and left leg are in alignment. Meditate and rest in this position if desired.

34. Uppercut Punch

Untwist the right arm and body, and step southeast with the left foot behind the right, turning the waist to the left 180 degrees into a left forward stance facing southeast. At the same time, bringing the right fist around in a 360 degree orbit, with an uppercut punch, top of the fist centered and level with the bottom of the nose, the left hand still holding the right elbow.

35. Block-Elbow-Palm

Shift the weight back into a left empty stance, pulling the right fist to the right temple turned horizontally, while lowering the left hand, palm down, guarding the left side, fingers angled in at a 45 degree angle.

Step forward into a right empty stance, hooking the right foot in, while executing a sweeping right inward block, right to left across the body, until the right fist reaches the left shoulder. The left hand remains fixed, palm down, outside the left inguinal canal. Transform the right inward block into a right elbow strike, while stepping forward into a left twist stance. Step forward again into a right forward stance, unlatching the right arm into a backhanded palm strike aimed at the bridge of an opponent's nose.

36. Circle the Body

Pivot the right foot in, and step southeast, laterally across and behind the right foot with the left, into a left twist stance, soles even on the ground. At the same time, form a right angle with the left forearm, horizontal, and the right forearm vertical, connecting the index fingers and the thumbs of both hands together to form a circle (heaven), palms facing away. The eyes, head, and torso now facing northwest.

Step back with the right foot into a left empty stance, and separating the hands. Pull the right hand down alongside the right hip, palm down. The left hand and arm stay in place. Relax all of the joints. Without lifting the feet off the ground, move forward bending at the knees, letting the entire body then rise like a wave upward, pitching back to the rear, and completing one full body circle. Continue the momentum and repeat the completion of a second full body circle.

37. Sleeping Buddha

Begin a third wave of circling. Halfway through, pivot the left foot inward, and turn the waist to the right, pivoting 180 degrees into a right empty stance facing southeast. The right foot is turned inward. At the same time, bend the elbows, and collapse both hands horizontally, right over left in front of the chest, the palms facing front in a defensive push. The angles of the hands, arms, shoulders and upper back take the shape of the eight trigrams. Pause with the body on guard like the tortoise.

Step northwest with the right foot into a left empty stance, lifting the right hand overhead, in an arch behind the body, the head and eyes following the hand. Draw the left foot next to the right, at the same time, pulling the left hand down alongside the right leg, meeting [but not touching], with the right wrist, between the left thumb and index finger.

Then step back with the left foot throwing both hands up and overhead, while pivoting 180 degrees into a left forward stance, facing northwest. The hands turn over, palms down, left leading the right, pointing and reaching northwest, until circling back down in front of the body. The right hand falls behind to the right hip, palm down, the thumb pointing to the head of the right femur at the Juliao point (GB-29). At the same time, form a hollow left fist, outwardly turning and twisting the left fist, forearm, and shoulder (to include the spine), as far as possible, so that the body leans, head to the northwest. The head, neck, spine, and right leg are in alignment. Sleep, meditate or rest in Sleeping Buddha position for as long as desired.

38. Exercise Weakest Body Part

Unwind the Sleeping Buddha posture, and flex the little fingers in on both hands, making two modified fist. Turn the left fist over, palm down, in front of the torso, and move the right fist forward, palm up. At the same time, step on-to the ball of the right foot, heel raised, next to the left foot, facing northwest.

Lower the left fist so the palm side of the fist covers the groin, and lift the right hand, palm up, in front of the body, to above the head. At the apex open the palm of the right hand, lowering it down the center of the body until the tip of the middle finger is level with the tip (apex) of the nose, sinking the body until the right heel touches the ground. Meditate in this position for as long as desired.

39. Cloud Hands

Take a step back with the right foot, turning the waist to the right, and pivoting into a relaxed horse stance, facing northeast. At the same time, float the right hand, positioned horizontally and palm facing away, across the body like slow moving clouds, from left to right, three vertical fist away from the tip (apex) of the nose. Do not let any part of the hand go above the eyebrows. The left fist remains covering the groin. When the right hand reaches the right side of the body, it freefalls, weightily slapping the outside of the right leg, middle finger striking the Fengshi point (GB-31).

Step the left foot to the right, joining only the heels of the feet, while lifting the left hand circularly across the body from right to left, like the minute hand on a clock, turning the waist and torso. The left palm faces the body, three vertical fist away from the tip (apex) of the nose, the tip of the middle finger never higher than the eyebrows. When the left hand reaches the left side of the body, it freefalls, weightily slapping the outside of the left leg, middle finger striking the Fengshi point (GB-31).

Step to the right with the right foot into a relaxed horse stance, while lifting the right hand circularly across the body from left to right, like the minute hand on a clock, turning the waist and torso. The right palm faces the body, three vertical fist away from the tip (apex) of the nose, the tip of the middle finger never higher than the eyebrows. When the right hand reaches the right side of the body, it freefalls, weightily slapping the outside of the right leg, middle finger striking the Fengshi point (GB-31).

Step the left foot to the right, joining only the heels of the feet, while lifting the left hand circularly across the body from right to left, like the minute hand on a clock, turning the waist and torso. The left palm faces the body, three vertical fist away from the tip (apex) of the nose, the tip of the middle finger never higher than the eyebrows. When the left hand reaches the left side of the body, it freefalls, weightily slapping the outside of the left leg, middle finger striking the Fengshi point (GB-31).

Step to the right with the right foot into a relaxed horse stance, while lifting the right hand circularly across the body from left to right, like the minute hand on a clock, turning the waist and torso. The right palm faces the body, three vertical fist away from the tip (apex) of the nose, the tip of the middle finger never higher than the eyebrows. When the right hand reaches the right side of the body, it freefalls, weightily slapping the outside of the right leg, middle finger striking the Fengshi point (GB-31).

Step the left foot to the right, joining only the heels of the feet, while lifting the left hand circularly across the body from right to left, like the minute hand on a clock, turning the waist and torso. The left palm faces the body, three vertical fist away from the tip (apex) of the nose, the tip of the middle finger never higher than the eyebrows. When the left hand reaches the left side of the body, it freefalls, weightily slapping the outside of the left leg, middle finger striking the Fengshi point (GB-31).

Step to the right with the right foot into a relaxed horse stance, while lifting the right hand circularly across the body from left to right, like the minute hand on a clock, turning the waist and torso. The right palm faces the body, three vertical fist away from the tip (apex) of the nose, the tip of the middle finger never higher than the eyebrows. When the right hand reaches the right side of the body, it freefalls, weightily slapping the outside of the right leg, middle finger striking the Fengshi point (GB-31).

Step the left foot to the right, joining only the heels of the feet, while lifting the left hand circularly across the body from right to left, like the minute hand on a clock, turning the waist and torso. The left palm faces the body, three vertical fist away from the tip (apex) of the nose, the tip of the middle finger never higher than the eyebrows.

When the left hand reaches to the left side of the body, reverse the direction of the left hand and arm back across the body from left to right, palm down, to the right hip and waist.

40. Monkey Presents Fruit to Heaven

Hook and drag the left palm across the waist from right to left, while stepping the left foot laterally across and behind the right to the southeast. When left hand contours around the left hip, it is mirrored by the right hand, the backs of the hands passing over the kidneys.

Turn the waist to the left, pivoting 270 degrees until the head and eyes come around to face northeast. Invert and slide the hands up the back, fingers pointing up. Move the hands forward under the arms and past the rib cage, merging the heels of the palms together at the middle elixir zone. Shift into a left forward stance, raising the hands in the shape of a chalice above the forehead.

41. Tiger Rips Apart the Heart (1)

Join the ulnar side edges of the palms and small fingers together. Maintaining contact, flip the hands up, in, and over until the fingers are pointed to the ground, each of the four fingers connecting to the thumbs, forming two crane's beaks. The radius side of the hands are touching, with arms fully extended forward, at shoulder level. Turn the palms up, laying right hand over left. Draw the hands and elbows tightly into the lower elixir field and shift the weight into the rear leg in a deep left empty stance. The eyes are looking upward at 45 degrees, the body is shaped in a V.

Turn the palms over, fingers pointing to the ground, with each of the four fingers connecting to the thumbs, forming two crane's beaks. Shift the weight into a left forward stance, lifting and extending the arms, shoulder width apart.

Join the ulnar side edges of the hands and small fingers, palms up, then flip the hands up-back toward the torso, turning 360 degrees until the fingers are back to back and pointing forward. At the same time, step up onto the ball of the right foot (heel raised), next to the left. Form two tiger claws, bending and curling-in all ten fingers, hands horizontally set, palms facing front. Sharply lift the right knee to waist level, foot relaxed, and separate the tiger claws and elbows as if tearing open a present. Step down into a right forward stance bringing the ulnar edges of the palms and fingers together, palms up, in front of the body at shoulder level.

41. Tiger Rips Apart the Heart (2)

Flip the hands up, in, and over until the fingers are pointed to the ground, each of the four fingers connecting to the thumbs, forming two crane's beaks. The radius side of the hands are touching, with arms fully extended forward, at shoulder level. Turn the palms up, laying right hand over left. Draw the hands and elbows tightly into the lower elixir field and shift the weight into the rear leg in a deep right empty stance. The eyes are looking upward at 45 degrees, the body is shaped in a V.

Turn the palms over, fingers pointing to the ground, with each of the four fingers connecting to the thumbs, forming two crane's beaks. Shift the weight into a right forward stance, lifting and extending the arms, shoulder width apart.

Join the ulnar side edges of the hands and small fingers, palms up, then flip the hands up-back toward the torso, turning 360 degrees until the fingers are back to back and pointing forward. At the same time, step up onto the ball of the left foot (heel raised), next to the right. Form two tiger claws, bending and curling-in all ten fingers, hands horizontally set, palms facing front. Sharply lift the left knee to waist level, foot relaxed, and separate the tiger claws and elbows as if tearing open a present. Step down into a left forward stance leaving the tiger claws in place, shoulder level.

42. Parading Tiger

Step onto the ball of the right foot (heel raised), next to the left, then execute a lifting right front kick, met and stopped by the right hand slapping the lower leg (shinbone). Bend knee to retract right leg and step into a left forward stance, right claw retracted.

Step onto the ball of the left foot (heel raised), next to the right, then execute a lifting left front kick, met and stopped by the left hand slapping the lower leg (shinbone). Bend the knee to retract the left leg and step into a right forward stance.

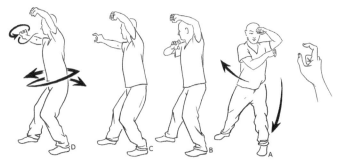

43. The Rooster Cries

Raise and change the left tiger claw into a hollow vertical fist outside the left temple, and lower the right tiger claw under the left armpit, and change it into the tiger's mouth by forming a C-shape with the index finger and the thumb. The remaining three fingers close.

Turn the waist to the right, pivoting 180 degrees into a right empty stance facing northwest. The right hand trails behind until the tiger's mouth reaches front. Turn the wrist right a quarter turn flipping the C-shape on its side at throat level. With speed and power, turn the waist three times, left-right-left, the tiger's mouth tearing away the throat of its prey. To maximize this energy, imagine a tiger in the belly, and the back and spine of a bear.

44. Subdue the Tiger (1)

Pivot the right foot out pointing the toes northeast, while lowering and changing the right hand into a hollow fist in front of the right inguinal canal, palm side facing the body. At the same time, lift the left fist overhead in a forward arching motion, pulling the left knee above the waist, then up and over as if mounting a tiger. The left leg is shaped in a floating horse stance, body now facing northeast.

Borrowing gravity, and with the weight and force of an elephant, let the body fall left a deep horse stance. The left leg hits the ground flatfooted and the left fist punches toward the waist, left to right, stopping in front of the left inguinal canal, palm side facing the body. The elbows are bowed.

44. Subdue the Tiger (2)

Pivot the left foot out pointing the toes southwest. At the same time, lift the right fist overhead in a forward arching motion, pulling the right knee above the waist, then up and over as if mounting a tiger. The right leg is shaped in a floating horse stance, body now facing southwest. The left fist stays fixed in front of the left inguinal canal, palm side facing the body.

Borrowing gravity, and with the weight and force of an elephant, let the body fall right into a deep horse stance. The right leg hits the ground flatfooted and the right fist punches toward the waist, right to left, stopping in front of the right inguinal canal, palm side facing the body. The elbows are bowed.

45. Bear-Monkey-Horse

Pivot the body into a right empty stance facing northwest, and form two monkey fist, by flattening the hollow fists. Drop the left hand to the left waist behind the body, palm up, and raise the right hand, palm down, in front of the body, shoulder level. Keep the elbows bent. Imagine your entire back and shoulders are of a bear. Harness this power

Draw back, and then leap forward off the rear leg, striking the ground first with the right foot, while executing a descending right monkey fist strike to the bridge of a nose, then the rear left foot again gaining purchase. With the feet fixed, follow through two more times with the body weight shifting from front to back to front circularly as if holding on to the mane of a horse in full gallop.

46. Snake Creeps through Grass

Stop with the weight over the right leg, and turn the waist, head, and eyes left 180 degrees, while pivoting the left foot open, toes pointing southeast. Release the left hand, palm open, so the back of the hand makes contact inside of the left upper leg. Slide the left hand down the leg, following the liver channel to the knee or slightly below if flexibility allows.

Step onto the ball of right foot, next to the left, and turn the left hand, palm up, under the lower elixir field. At the same time, change the right monkey fist into a horizontal hollow fist, executing a right overhead punch from the base of the skull, and diving straight down the front medial aspect of the body along the conception vessel, falling onto the left palm, knees bending.

47. Guard the Elixir Field

Open the right hand and rotate the wrist inward as if checking the time on a wristwatch, while pushing forward at navel level, palm facing away, and elbow bent. Then rotate the left wrist inward as if checking the time on a wristwatch, while pushing forward under the right hand to guard the lower elixir field, palm facing front, elbow bent.

With the hands fixed, begin walking in a square. Turn the waist left and tightly step across with the right foot, planting into a right angle, the right inner heel to the left great toe. Tightly step across with the left foot planting into a right angle, left outer heel to the right great toe. Tightly step across with the right foot planting into a right angle, right inner heel to the left great toe. Then step east with the left foot into a horse stance, facing south. Release the hands and arms in, turning the palms up, left fist, palm up, seated in the right, guarding the lower elixir field.

48. Winding Snake (1)

   Turn the head and eyes left to the east, while shifting the weight into the right leg, together with the right elbow as if rocking a baby. Push the left fist forward with the right hand, shooting the left elbow vertical, followed by the head and eyes, and the weight moving forward. At peak ascension, turn the waist left, with the coupled hands twisting overhead like a universal joint, at the same time pivoting the left foot out into a left twist stance, and dropping the left elbow to the left side, back behind the body as if rocking a baby.

   Step east into a modified right empty stance. Push the right hand forward with the left fist, shooting the right elbow vertical, followed by the head and eyes, and the weight moving forward. At peak ascension, turn the waist right, with the coupled hands twisting overhead like a universal joint, at the same time pivoting the right foot out into a right twist stance, and dropping the right elbow to the right side, back behind the body as if rocking a baby.

48. Winding Snake (2)

Step east into a modified left empty stance. Push the left fist forward with the right hand, shooting the left elbow vertical, followed by the head and eyes, and the weight moving forward. At peak ascension, turn the waist left, with the coupled hands twisting overhead like a universal joint, at the same time pivoting the left foot out into a right twist stance, and dropping the left elbow to the left side, back behind the body as if rocking a baby.

Step east into a modified right empty stance. Push the right hand forward with the left fist, shooting the right elbow vertical, followed by the head and eyes, and the weight moving forward. At peak ascension, turn the waist right, with the coupled hands twisting overhead like a universal joint.

Then drop both elbows in front of the body and separate the hands so the palms of the left fist and right hand face one another, in a right empty stance, facing east. Drop the hands forward, down, in and up, in a circular fashion.

49. Snake Spits Out Tongue

Place the tip of tongue on the roof of mouth, behind the teeth to activate the heart channel (tongue is heart's external reflection). Lower the left fist to cover the groin, palm facing in. At the same time, clip the right thumb close to the palm reinforcing hand strength, palm up, and strike out [spitting the tongue] to the eyes, pressing the right foot up, and pointing on the great toe.

Open the left fist and clip the left thumb close to the palm reinforcing hand strength, palm up. At the same time, step forward into a left empty stance, and strike out [spitting the tongue] to the eyes, pressing the left foot up, and pointing on the great toe. Simultaneously, pull back the right hand to guard the right ribcage.

Step forward into a right empty stance, and strike out [spitting the tongue] at eye level, with the right hand, pressing right foot up, pointed on the great toe. Simultaneously, pull back the left hand to guard the left ribcage.

Step forward into a left empty stance, and strike out [spitting the tongue] at eye level, with the left hand, pressing left foot up, pointed on the great toe. Simultaneously, pull back right hand to guard the right ribcage. Remain in left empty stance and strike out [spitting the tongue] at eye level, with the right hand, laying it over left hand.

50. Praying Mantis

After completing the fifth snake strike, roll the arms inward, palms down, joining the first and second fingers of each hand with the thumbs. The fourth and fifth fingers curl in. The wrist are bent, the arms straight, and shoulder width apart. Take a full step behind the right foot with the left, lowering the center of gravity, anchoring the elbows into the rib cages. Turn the waist left, pushing hands down and flipping the fingers pointing up, the backs of the hands passing over the kidneys, then forward under the armpits.

Turn the waist to the left, pivoting 180 degrees, into a left forward stance facing west, joining both palms together. Send the hands forward, down, in, and up, in a circular pattern, shifting the weight back to the rear leg and then front, the hands completing one full circle, fingers vertical, level with tip (apex) of the nose.

51. Swimming Dragon, Child on a Swing, Play Pipa

Tilt the hands 90 degrees left, forming a right angle with right forearm set horizontally, and left forearm set vertically. Turn the waist right, pulling the right elbow and level hands to right side of body, following with head and eyes. The spine and legs rotating slightly in transition.

Reverse directions, turning the waist left, and tilting the hands 90 degrees right, forming a right angle with left forearm set horizontally, and right forearm set vertically. Turn waist left pulling the left elbow and level hands to the left side of body, following with the head and eyes. The spine and legs rotating slightly in transition.

Reverse directions, turning the waist right, dropping and separating the hands in front of the body. Pull the hands and arms up over the head and right shoulder, in a circular motion, followed by the head and eyes. The wrist are bent so the palms face the sky.

Shift the weight into the rear leg, and pull the hands down behind the body to the waist. Turn the head and eyes facing west, and step forward into a right empty stance. Move the hands and arms in front of the body full circle, fingers pointing up, right hand higher than the left, palms turned in.

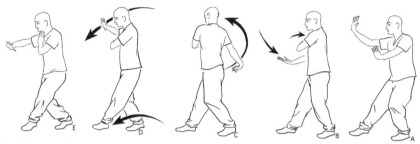

52. Trap and Press Right

Place the left palm over the right pectoral muscles, and drop the right hand, palm up, to the right hip, while turning the waist to the right. Pull the right hand behind the body, followed by the head and eyes. Lift the right hand up and over the right shoulder pushing down towards the navel zone, simultaneously stepping forward into a left transitional twist stance.

53. Push and Pull

Draw the right hand to the left ear, while closing the left hand into a hollow fist. Step into a right forward stance, and pull the left hand down to the left hip like a hammer, while pushing the right hand sword angled at 45 degrees, across the body, from left to right, neck level.

54. Trap and Press Left

Place the right palm over the left pectoral muscles, and release the hollow fist at the left hip, and turn the waist to the left. Lift the left hand up and over the left shoulder pushing down towards the navel zone, simultaneously step-ping forward into a left empty stance.

Lift the left hand in a hollow fist, and bring the right palm forward, so the palms of the left fist and right hand face one another, while stepping into a right empty stance, facing west. Drop the hands forward, down, in and up, in a circular fashion.

55. Bend the Bow-Shoot the Tiger

Imagine holding a bowstring with the left fist. Turn the waist to the left and draw the bowstring half the distance of the right arm [approximately to the elbow]. Relax the waist returning the left fist forward. Turn the waist left again, drawing and loading the bowstring fully, the left fist to the left shoulder creating tension.

Open the left hand and release the bowstring, launching the arrow (left hand opened-fingers up) forward, skipping off the right hand, while stepping into a left empty stance. The left hand inline and in front of the right hand.

Reach with the right hand to the left, and grab the imaginary bowstring, closing the right hand into a hollow fist. Turn the waist to the right and draw the bowstring half the distance of the left arm [approximately to the elbow]. Relax the waist returning the right fist forward. Turn the waist right again, drawing and loading the bowstring fully, the right fist to the right shoulder creating tension.

Open the right hand and release the bowstring, launching the arrow (right hand opened-fingers up) forward, skipping off the left hand, while stepping into a right empty stance. The right hand inline and in front of the left hand.

56. Needle at Sea Bottom

Point the fingers of the right hand downward, and follow the kidney meridian with the back of the hand, along the inside of the right leg to the arch of the right foot. The body sinks into the left leg to avoid bending too much at the waist. The left hand remains fixed at the middle elixir zone. Before touching ground with the fingertips, turn the right hand around, so the palm faces the arch, and push the hand forward with the palm, contouring around the toe tops to the lateral side of the right ankle, gathering earth qi. Turn the palm up, forming a cup.

Lift the right hand cupped along the gall bladder meridian, on the outside of the right leg, to the right ribcage, while straightening the body. Turn the right hand, fingers up, and push out from the middle elixir zone (solar plexus). Step forward into a left empty stance, while skipping the left palm off the right palm. The left hand inline and in front of the right hand.

Point the fingers of the left hand downward, and follow the kidney meridian with the back of the hand, along the inside of the left leg to the arch of the left foot. The body sinks into the right leg to avoid bending too much at the waist. The right hand remains fixed at the middle elixir zone. Before touching ground with the fingertips, turn the left hand around, so the palm faces the arch, and push the hand forward with the palm, contouring around the toe tops to the lateral side of the left ankle, gathering earth qi. Turn the palm up, forming a cup.

Lift the left hand cupped along the gall bladder meridian, on the outside of the left leg, to the left ribcage, while straightening the body. Turn the left hand, fingers up, and push out from the middle elixir zone (solar plexus). Step forward into a right empty stance, while skipping the right palm off the left palm. The right hand inline and in front of the left hand.

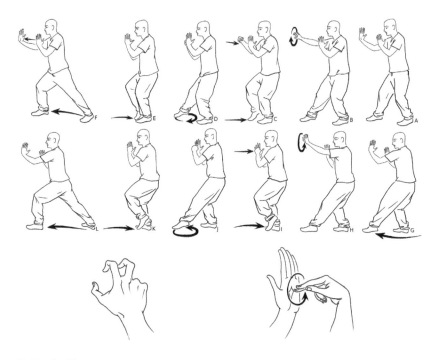

57. Eagle Claw

Form an eagle claw with three fingers of the right hand (index, middle, and thumb). From the right shoulder, turn the claw clockwise completing a circle. Then draw the right foot in on the toes, to the arch of left foot. At the same time, join the three fingers of the claw at the fingertips, pulling them to the left palm. Without touching, draw a clockwise circle on the left palm with the three fingers of the right hand, at the same time drawing a clockwise circle on the ground, right of the body, with the great toe of the right foot, leading back to the arch.

Step into a right forward stance, pushing the right hand ahead of the left, fingers pointed upward. Then quickly step forward into a left empty stance, while skipping the left palm off the right palm. The left hand inline and in front of the right hand.

Form an eagle claw with three fingers of the left hand (index, middle, and thumb). From the left shoulder, turn the claw counterclockwise completing a circle. Then draw the left foot in on the toes, to the arch of right foot. At the same time, join the three fingers of the claw at the fingertips, pulling them to the right palm. Without touching, draw a clockwise circle on the right palm with the three fingers of the left hand, at the same time drawing a counterclockwise circle on the ground, left of the body, with the great toe of the left foot, leading back to the arch.

Step into a left forward stance, pushing the left hand ahead of the left, fingers pointed upward.

Lohan Warrior Set

58. Child Worshipping Buddha

Step into a standing half lotus, crossing the right lower leg over above the left knee on Heding point (EX-38), and joining the hands together in prayer. Meditate in this posture for 1-10 minutes if desired.

Separate and lower the hands, palms down, past the waist, and bend the wrist, joining all four fingers to the thumbs, pushing as far up as possible, forming eagle's wings. At the same time, lean the torso forward from the waist at a 45 degree angle, the eyes following the same angle, staring into the distance, fixed on the crown of a tree or a distant mountain peak. As an independent meditation, hold this posture while gazing upward at a flame.

Lower the hands, while rotating the wrist inward, the fingers pointing up, passing under the armpits, forward in front of the chest. The torso is once again upright. Press the left palm down near the left waist, fingers pointing forward, and press the right palm skyward, horizontally positioned above the right shoulder, fingers pointing overhead. Elbows slightly bent.

Lift the left hand, palm up, to shoulder height, at the same time, press the right palm down near the right waist, fingers pointing forward.

59. Parting the Wild Horse's Mane

Step behind and across the left leg to the southeast with the right. Turn both palms over so the left hand remains above the right hand.

Turn the waist to the right, shifting into a right forward stance facing southeast, separating the hands and arms at 45 degree angles. The right hand angles upwards, circling the body, palm up, finishing in front of the right shoulder, and the left hand angles downward to the left waist, palm down, the fingers pointing forward. Elbows slightly bent.

Turn both palms over so the right hand remains above the left hand. Turn the waist to the left, shifting into a left forward stance facing northwest, separating the hands and arms at 45 degree angles. The left hand angles upwards, circling the body, palm up, finishing in front of the left shoulder, and the right hand angles downward to right waist, palm down, the fingers pointing forward. Elbows slightly bent.

60. Meeting the Eagle

Pivot the left foot outward 90 degrees, immediately followed by a low swinging right hook step into a right-weighted horse stance, facing southwest. Turn the waist to the left, shifting into a left forward stance facing southeast. At the same time, execute a left rolling upward block (like a rolling pin) finishing above the head, forearm guarding the Baihui point (GV-20), palm up with the wrist bent, and a right ascending palm thrust, at a 45 degree angle in front of the face [in defense of an attack coming from a high place: roof, wall, tree, etc.].

61. Separate Yin and Yang

Lower the elbows, opening the chest, and separate the hands and arms, palms horizontal and facing away. Turn the waist to the right, further separating yin and yang, the left hand trailing behind in the east. When the right hand, head, and eyes turn to the west, step forward into a left empty stance, bringing the left hand, low to high, in front of the body, palm up. The right hand circles around the right side, trailing in the east.

Step forward with the right foot, next to the left, executing a right uppercut punch. At the same time, turn the left hand over, palm down, across the chest with the left elbow bent, meeting and covering the right bicep at the elbow, right fist stopping below the right eye. Lower in the stance, sinking and concentrating the body's *qi* into the reproductive organs (men-testicles women-ovaries). Meditate as long as is necessary.

62. Lohan Personification of Force

Drop the right fist and left palm down to the waist. Step into a right emp-ty stance, and circle the hands upward around the flanks, meeting at the fore-head in front of Yintang point (GV-29), the right fist set in the left palm (palm the scholar, fist the warrior).

Pull the shoulders, elbows, and arms back, while stepping into a left for-ward stance, executing two upper cut punches, the fists finishing in front of the cheekbones.

Drop the fist to the waist, and step into a right forward stance, circling the fists around to the flanks, executing two outside–in vertical punches to the temples, palms facing front, the elbows bent.

Open the right hand and slap the top of the left fist, forcing the hands straight down to cover the groin, and shifting the weight back into the rear leg. Pull the hands in, flipping them over, inside to outside, palms up, completing a circle, while stepping forward into a left empty stance.

63. Swipe the Bear Claw

Lower the hands to the waist, left fist sitting on the right palm. Separate the hands, drawing the left fist, palm up, floating near the left lower rib cage. The right hand opens out, forming a bear claw, while stepping northwest into a transitional right forward stance. Turn the waist to the left and swipe with the bear claw, circularly, from right to left at neck height.

Shift the weight back, into a right empty stance, pulling the right handed bear claw in and across the chest, left to right, and completing a full circle. The right arm swings out again, from right to left, with the palm up and flat, drawing a medium circle. Quickly step forward into a left empty stance and swing the left arm out, from left to right, with the palm up and flat, at neck level, making three small finishing circles. The right hand is palm up, guarding the right lower rib cage.

64. Downward Block

Pivot left foot out, turning the waist to the left, while pulling the right hand in across the body, palm down, and lowering the left hand, palm up, to the waist. Step northwest into a right forward stance, turning the left palm to face and hover three inches above the lower elixir field, while executing a right downward block over the right knee, at a 45 degree angle, palm down, elbow slightly bent.

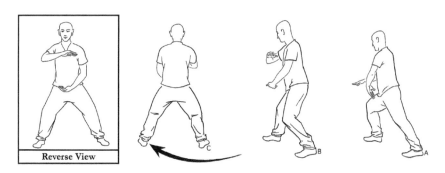

65. Taiji Ball

Turn the waist to the left shifting the weight back, and floating the right hand, palm down, at the middle elixir zone, and the left hand turned palm up at the lower elixir field. With the palms facing one another, in a low sweep, swing the left leg and body around, into a horse stance, facing north. The fingers are tightly sealed, and the hands rounded, as if holding a ball. Meditate.

66. Breaking the Snake

Pivot the left foot out, and turn the waist to the left. Beginning with the small fingers, roll and close the fingers [as if closing two fans] into fists. At the same time, lower the right fist near the right hip, twisting it inward, and raise the left fist to the left shoulder, twisting it outward. Continue turning left 180 degrees, lifting the right knee into a one-legged stance facing south. The right foot is flexed up from the toes and flex-tilted inwardly from the side. After maximizing all torsion, release it, dropping the right leg into a horse stance. The left fist drops like a hammer, stopping under the solar plexus, and the right fist swings outside-in to the middle elixir zone, above the left, the fists moving counterclockwise in small circles as if stirring porridge (3).

67. Rearing Horse

Turn the waist to the right leaving the feet firmly planted in a south facing horse stance, and execute a left horizontal punch to the west at the level of the solar plexus, and a right overhead block, fist closed. The inner right forearm is facing front, along with the head and eyes facing west. The upper and lower halves of the body are essentially perpendicular to one another, allowing for some joint tensions, especially from the waist down.

Release body torsion by pivoting the right foot out to the west, and execute a right overhead diving punch. Then immediately step forward into a left empty stance executing a left overhead diving punch. Step forward with the right foot, next to the left foot, at the same time, folding the left arm and fist across the solar plexus, palm facing the body, while executing a right diving punch over the right shoulder, down the front right half of the body, over the left fist. Sink.

68. Kick and Block

Spring the body upward lifting the right leg, toes pointing skyward, and strike the Heding point (EX-38) above the right knee cap with the heel of the right palm, creating a rebound. Immediately step back with the right foot into a left empty stance, and raise the left forearm up to just under the eyes with the inner forearm facing front, simultaneously pulling the right hand inside of the left forearm to the right waist. The right wrist is bent upward.

Step back with the left foot into a right empty stance, and raise the right forearm up to just under the eyes with the inner forearm facing front, simultaneously pulling the left hand inside of the right forearm to the left waist. The left wrist is bent upward.

69. Double Punch

Pivot the right foot inward, turning the waist to the left, roatating the body 180 degrees to face east, and vertically positioning the back of the right fist, at the right temple. Draw the left foot to right, on the toes, and pull the left fist, palm up, to the middle elixir zone. Lurch into a left forward stance, vectoring a vertical right punch down onto the bridge of nose level, and a lifting horizontal punch to the xiphoid process (dovetail below the sternum), each strike intended to break and snap the targets.

70. Hook and Throw (1)

Pivot the left foot out, while turning the head and eyes left, facing north. Turn the waist to the left, and step around with the right leg to the north in a transitional right empty stance, simultaneously dropping the right arm and fist down and across the body to the left side, elbow bent in a hook. Rotate the waist to the right, and shift into a right forward stance, at the same time, execute a right outward block/throw, while pulling the left fist down inside of the right forearm to the waist. The left wrist is bent upward.

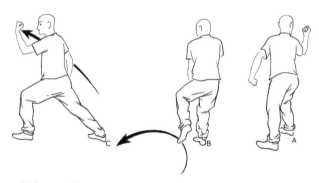

70. Hook and Throw (2)

Bring the left foot to the right foot, while turning the head and eyes to face west, simultaneously dropping the left arm and fist down and across the body to the right side, elbow bent in a hook. Rotate the waist to the left, and shift into a left forward stance facing west. At the same time, execute a left outward block/throw, while pulling the right fist down inside of the left forearm and to the waist. The left wrist is bent upward.

71. Cobra Hood

Step forward with the right foot next to the left, lowering the left hand, palm up, under lower elixir field. At the same time, execute a right overhead punch, back to front, climbing up behind the neck and over the top of the head, following the midline (conception vessel) of the frontal torso, ending in a horizontal punch into the left palm, covering the lower elixir field.

72. Reach-Pull-Throw (1)

Lift the right hand, palm up and flat, to underneath the chin, fingers pointing forward. Pivot the right foot out, and turn the waist to the right, while moving the right hand around the right side of the head to the nape of the neck. At the same time, lift the left heel, placing the weight onto the right leg.

Turn the waist to the left, and step into a left forward stance, forming a fist with the left hand, while throwing a right sword hand (as if throwing a baseball) down and across the body at a 45 degree angle, to the left hip, midway catching the left fist with the right palm (ball and mitt).

Turn the waist to the right, swinging the hands around together, to the right hip, shifting into a left empty stance, the left fist sitting on the right palm. Then shift the weight into a left forward stance [the knee passing ahead of the great toe], while executing a left elbow strike, hands still joined, palms up. (*The general rule is to keep the knee from going beyond the great toe at all times, but this is the exception to the rule.)

72. Reach-Pull-Throw (2)

Pivot the left foot out, and step forward into a long right empty stance with the toes slightly turned in, and the hands still joined, at the lower elixir field. Lift the left hand, palm up and flat, to underneath the chin, fingers pointing forward. Turn the waist to the left, while moving the left hand around the left side of the head to the nape of the neck.

Turn the waist to the right, shifting the weight into a right forward stance, forming a fist with the right hand, while throwing a left sword hand (as if throwing a baseball) down and across the body at a 45 degree angle, to the right hip, midway catching the right fist with the left palm (ball and mitt).

Turn the waist to the left, swinging the hands around together, to the left hip, shifting into a right empty stance, the right fist sitting on the left palm. Then shift the weight into a right forward stance [the knee passing ahead of the great toe], while executing a right elbow strike, hands still joined, palms up. (*The general rule is to keep the knee from going beyond the great toe at all times, but this is the exception to the rule.)

72. Reach-Pull-Throw (3)

Pivot the right foot out, and step forward into a long left empty stance, with the toes slightly turned in, and the hands still joined, at the lower elixir field. Lift the right hand, palm up and flat, to underneath the chin, fingers pointing forward. Turn the waist to the right, while moving the right hand around the right side of the head to the nape of the neck.

Turn the waist to the left, shifting the weight into a left forward stance, forming a fist with the left hand, while throwing a right sword hand (as if throwing a baseball) down and across the body at a 45 degree angle, to the left hip, midway catching the left fist with the right palm (ball and mitt).

Turn the waist to the right, swinging the hands around together, to the right hip, shifting into a left empty stance, the left fist sitting on the right palm. Then shift the weight into a left forward stance [the knee passing ahead of the great toe], while executing a left elbow strike, hands still joined, palms up.

72. Reach-Pull-Throw (4)

Pivot the left foot out, and step forward into a long right empty stance with the toes slightly turned in, and the hands still joined, at the lower elixir field. Lift the left hand, palm up and flat, to underneath the chin, fingers pointing forward. Turn the waist to the left, while moving the left hand around the left side of the head to the nape of the neck.

Turn the waist to the right, shifting the weight into a right forward stance, forming a fist with the right hand, while throwing a left sword hand (as if throwing a baseball) down and across the body at a 45 degree angle, to the right hip, midway catching the right fist with the left palm (ball and mitt).

Turn the waist to the left, swinging the hands around together, to the left hip, shifting into a right empty stance, the right fist sitting on the left palm. Then shift the weight into a right forward stance [the knee passing ahead of the great toe], while executing a right elbow strike, hands still joined, palms up.

Shift the weight back, joining the heels of the palms, right above the left, below the middle elixir zone. Shift into a right forward stance, pushing the palms out, right hand fingers pointing up, vertically, and the left hand fingers pointing down, vertically, forming a flat walled surface.

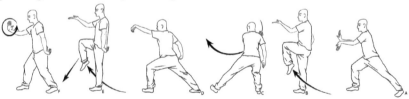

73. Crane's Crest

Press the right hand, palm down, to the right hip, while lifting the left hand, palm up, out in front of the left shoulder, while lifting the left knee into a one-legged stance, right leg straight. Circularly, pull the left arm back across the upper body to the right, while joining the four finger prints to the thumb.

Step into a left forward stance, leading with the back of the left wrist, rising up as the arm completes a full circle, finishing slightly above shoulder height, arm extended. Lift the right hand, palm up, in front of the right shoulder, while lifting the right knee into a one-legged stance, the left leg straight. The crane's head lowers to the left hip, with the wrist bent, five fingers pointing skyward. Leading with the right hand in prayer, step into a right empty stance, allowing all the weight and energy to move in a circular motion, front to back, forward-down-in-up-out, three times around.

74. Wave Right and Left

Wave the right hand to the right side of the body, fingers horizontally positioned, and palm facing out, then to the left, while turning the right palm up, across to the left side of body. Wave the right hand to the right side of the body again, fingers horizontally positioned, and palm facing out.

Following the right hand, pivot the right foot out, and step around with the left leg into a horse stance, facing north. The right wrist rotates, so are the fingers pointing up, and the palm facing front, at right chest. The left hand maintains the crane's head form (finger tips pointing down), at the left chest.

75. Discharge Power

Using the waist and the major joints for undulation, inhale and float the shoulders, arms, and hands back and in toward the chest, and exhale, gently pushing forward with the right palm and crane's head, deepening the stance. Inhale again returning to a relaxed horse stance, and float the shoulders, arms, and hands back and in toward the chest, and exhale, gently pushing forward with the right palm and crane's head, deepening the stance. Inhale for the third time, returning to a relaxed horse stance, and float the shoulders, arms, and hands back and in toward the chest. Then, with concentrated effort, using speed and internal power, exhale forcefully making a *ha* sound to powerfully expel the *qi*, while pushing forward with the right palm and crane's head, and grounding into a deep horse stance.

76. Dragon Ball

Pivot the right foot out, and turn the waist to the right, waving the right hand to the right side of body, fingers horizontally positioned, and palm facing out. Join the heels of the palms connecting Daling point(s) (PC-7) of the wrist, at the lower elixir field, left hand above the right hand, while stepping east into a left forward stance, pushing the hands out in front of the middle elixir zone. Each and every joint in the hands and fingers angling to form the shape of a stone ball or a large crystal ball.

Turn the hands over, pivoting at the wrist, and pull them into the lower elixir field, right hand above the left. Step east into a right forward stance, pushing the hands out in front of the middle elixir zone. Each and every joint in the hands and fingers angling to form the shape of a stone ball or a large crystal ball.

Pull the hands into lower elixir field, right hand remaining above the left, and step east into a left forward stance, pushing the hands out in front of the middle elixir zone. Each and every joint in the hands and fingers angling to form the shape of a stone ball or a large crystal ball.

77. Ox Gazes at the Moon

Step forward with right foot next to the left, rolling the right hand into a fist, to be wrapped and covered by the left hand. Begin bending the knees, and lowering the hands to the right hip, palms up. Turn the waist to the right side of the body while bending forward at the waist, so that the left elbow (ox's horn) points vertically to the moon, the head and eyes gazing upward over the right shoulder. This twisting motion wrings out the yang channels of the back. Do not hold.

78. Prancing Horse

Gently unwind, turning the waist to the left, slowly straightening the body, and floating the right hand, palm down, at the middle elixir zone and left hand, palm up, at the lower elixir field. Fingers tightly pressed and rounded as if softly holding a ball. Step straight back with the right foot to the west, and turn the waist to the right, pivoting into a mild horse stance, facing south. Keep the hands moving circularly, right hand down the right side to the lower position, and the left hand floats up the left side to the top.

Step west, crossing over the right foot with the left, and circularly reversing the hand positions, right hand above the left. The feet are flat on the ground. Step to the west with the right foot into a mild horse stance, circularly reversing the hand positions, left hand above the right. Step west, crossing over the right foot with the left, and circularly reversing the hand positions, right hand above the left. The feet are flat on the ground.

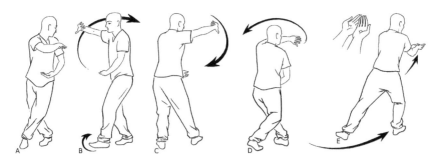

79. Begging Bowl

Turn the waist, head, and eyes to the left, looking over the left shoulder to the northeast. Unwind the waist to the right, waving the right hand around the upper body, fingers horizontally positioned, and palm facing out, while pivoting the feet 270 degrees, into a right empty stance, facing northeast. The left hand remains palm up at the lower elixir field.

As the right hand curves down the right side, taking the position at the lower elixir field, palm up, step forward into a left twist stance, and wave the left hand, right to left, across the upper body, fingers horizontally positioned, and palm facing out.

As the left hand curves down the left side of the body to the lower elixir field, join the hands together medially, palms up, to form a bowl, and step into a right forward stance presenting the bowl to the northeast, at the heart level.

80. Fan Through the Back

Turn the head and eyes towards the east, and draw the right foot to the left instep. At the same time, without disconnecting the hands, flip the fingers up, layering the right hand inside of left hand, then invert the hands inside-out. The left palm is horizontally positioned covering the back of right hand. The right hand is vertically positioned, fingers pointing up, palms facing out, guarding the left temple. Step east into a right forward stance, sliding the hands apart, in the arch of opening a fan, the right hand dropping forward, fingers pointing up, and the left hand pressing out laterally. Elbows bent.

81. Stir the Medicine

Lower the hands, sweeping them down front to back, across the lower half of the body, palms turned down, while shifting the weight front to back. Then shift the weight forward back into an east directed right forward stance, but with the head and eyes turned northeast. Set the left hand under the middle elixir zone and cupped, palm up, and the right hand centered above the left in a crane's beak, fingers pointing down. Keeping the left hand stationary, draw a clockwise circle just above the surface of the left palm with the right crane's beak.

82. Wrist Thrust and Cross Hands Push

Step with the left foot next to the right, while raising the left hand like a hood, over the back of the right wrist, horizontally positioned, and then palm facing front. The elbows are relaxed. Step northeast into a left forward stance, driving the back of the right wrist at an upward angle from the shoulder until fully extended, together with the left palm hovering above the right wrist, also pushing. Cross the hands at the wrist, left on the inside, and right on the outside, connecting Shenmen point (HT-7) and Yangxi point (LI-5). Shift the weight back into the rear leg, pulling the hands in and down the frontal torso. Continue lowering the crossed hands to the abdomen then shift the weight back into a left forward stance, pushing the crossed hands up ahead of the solar plexus.

83. Large White Peony

Turn the waist to the right, pivoting 180 degrees into a right empty stance, facing southwest, at the same raising the hands overhead. Separate and lower the hands to their sides, tracing a large circle in front of the body. At the half-way point, the arms parallel to the ground, shift the weight forward into the right leg. When the hands reach the circle's closure at the lower elixir field, join the ulnar edges of the palms, and lift the hands to shoulder height, while lifting the left knee into a one-legged stance, the right leg straight, and the left foot relaxed. Now visualize a very large white peony flower in the palms of your hands. Meditate.

84. Pneumatic Fingers

Flip the hands up, in and then over, palms down, with the fingers point-ing forward. Soar down southwest into a left forward stance, hands and fingers pushing straight out from the chest, rapidly vibrating like a pneumatic hammer or the ins-and-outs of a sewing machine needle. Before reaching full extension, open the arms out to the sides. Then turn the hands over, palms up, while leap-ing forward with the right leg, immediately followed by the left leg, stepping ahead into a left empty stance. The ulnar aspect of the palms join together flat at the level of the middle elixir zone.

85. Kicks, Swallow Returns to Forest

As if spring loaded, lift the right leg above the waist and slap the in-step/sole of the right foot with both hands, left to right, and from bottom up, in a circular pattern. Lower the kick, stepping into a right forward stance with the palms down, at waist level. Step onto the ball of the left foot next to the right, lowering the center of gravity. As if spring loaded, lift the left leg above the waist and slap the instep/sole of the left foot with both hands, right to left, and from bottom up, in a circular pattern. Lower the kick, stepping into a left forward stance, and upwardly extend the left arm, palm up, at a 45 degree angle, lightly covering the left palm with the right. As the left hand extends, slowly slide the right hand down to the elbow.

86. Orbit Extraordinary Meridians

Shift the weight into the rear leg, lightly grazing the right palm over the left upper arm and deltoid. Pivot the left foot inward and shift the weight again, while grazing the right palm back over the left arm to the left palm.

Turn the waist to the right, pivoting 180 degrees into a right empty stance facing northeast, with the palms flatly crossed in front. Separate the hands, so the left palm is up, and the right palm is down. Push the hands out to the sides, circularly, lowering the hands to waist level.

Step forward with the left foot, pausing close to the right, while joining the palms in front at the navel, the fingers pointing forward. Step into a transitional left forward stance, shooting the fingertips straight out. Lift the hands to circle back, with the fingers pointing up, while shifting back into a left empty stance. Complete the full circling of the hands to the navel, plus an additional quarter turn, with the hands and arms only, finishing in prayer in front of the middle elixir zone.

87. Windmill Strikes

Turn the waist to the right, separating the hands low and high. Pull the right hand deep into the right inguinal canal, fingers vertically positioned, and the left hand rising up, vertically positioned, fingertips at eye level. Then turn the waist to the left, pulling the left hand deep into the left inguinal canal, fingers vertically positioned, and the right hand rising up, vertically positioned, fingertips at eye level. There is tensity.

Release the tension, vaulting the right hand forward, circularly on the midline, with the fingers pointing up, together with the right foot stepping out. Then vault the left hand forward, circularly on the midline, together with the left foot stepping into a left forward stance. Then circle the right hand into the lead position ahead of the left, in a straight line, even height, fingers vertically positioned, and level with middle elixir zone.

88. Bird Lifts Up into the Air

Turn the waist to the right, pivoting 180 degrees facing southwest, while lightly filling the wings with air, by raising the elbows slightly. Trace a circle in front of the torso, separating the hands out and down to the sides, while shifting into a transitional right forward stance, joining the ulnar side of the hands, palms up, over the right knee.

Shift the weight back, pulling the hands up the inner right leg to the lower elixir field. Then lift the palms straight up the front of the body like an elevator, and spring forward into a left forward stance, pushing the fingers and hands out, at shoulder level.

89. Take Pulses, Eight Trigram Palms

Pivot the left foot inward, turning the right hand over so the pulses of the wrists' touch, right over left. Turn the waist to the right 180 degrees into a right empty stance, facing northeast, while positioning the hands horizontally, left over right, and pushing away from the chest, palms. The angles of the hands, arms, shoulders and upper back take the shape of the eight trigrams circle. Continue turning the upper body a quarter turn past the stance, scanning southeast.

90. Green Dragon Coils Body

Unwind the waist to the left, while crossing the arms, moving the right arm under the left, and pivoting the right foot inward 180 degrees, so the toes point southwest. Pivot the left foot outward, and perpendicular to the right,

into a tight left twist stance facing southwest, while the hands close-in underneath the armpits, the hands and fingers vertically positioned outside the torso,
palms facing the flanks. The great toe of the right foot is touching the outside
of the left heel. Continue coiling the upper body a quarter turn past the stance,
the eyes scanning northeast. The thumbs are tucked around behind the shoulders at Jianzhen point (SI-9), hugging tightly. The knees are slightly bent.

91. Three Throws

Unwind the waist to the right, while pivoting the left foot inward, and
lowering both hands to the waist, palms facing away. Quickly step with the
right, into a right forward stance facing north, throwing and arching the hands
overhead, palms skyward, the right hand leading the left. When the hands reach
waist level, flip the palms over like leaves turning, and throw them back overhead, in the opposite direction, palms skyward, left hand leading the right,
while shifting the weight into a left forward stance facing south.

When the hands reach waist level, flip the palms sideways facing right,
horizontally positioned, while turning the waist to the right, and pulling the
hands around the body. Pivot the right foot outward, swinging the left foot 225

degrees to the northeast, into a right empty stance, facing southwest. At the
same time, the right arm moves under the left, and the hands close-in underneath the armpits, fingers vertically positioned outside the torso, palms facing
the flanks. Continue turning the upper body a quarter turn past the stance,
scanning northwest. The thumbs are tucked around behind the shoulders at
Jianzhen point (SI-9), hugging tightly.

92. Heaven-Human-Earth United as One

Unwind the waist to the left 180 degrees into a left empty stance facing
northeast, while separating the arms and hands like scissors, outlining a tight
circle with the hands, in front of the chest. Near the bottom of the circle, when
the palms come to face one another, form a right hollow fist. Step forward into
a right empty stance and move both mirroring hands in a forward, down, and
up circle. At completion, form a left fist and open the right palm. Step forward
into a left empty stance and move both mirroring hands in a forward, down,
and up circle, stopping at the apex. The right hand, fingers pointing up, guards

the middle elixir zone, and the left fist is lowered to cover the left inguinal canal, the palm side facing the body.

93. Hook-Sweep-Step Through

Without adjusting the hand positions, step forward, hooking-in with the right foot at a right angle. Then turn the waist to the left, sweeping wide with the left leg 180 degrees to the northeast, the left foot lightly grazing the ground. Continue turning the waist to the left, and step straight through to the northeast into a right empty stance, the vortex of energy falling into the lead leg and hand, then bouncing back.

94. The Rooster

Raise the arms and shoulders, and the heel of the right foot. Spread all the fingers like curved winged plumage, with the small fingers bending and reaching closest toward the body. The right arm is pushing forward, pressing with the outer wrist, hand horizontally positioned. The left elbow and arm are pulling back, the palm of the left hand set in front of the left chest, horizontally positioned. The body is taut.

Claw deep, digging into the ground with the toes of the right foot, threatening to pull the body forward. Without restraint and almost recklessly, bound and shuffle forward with a left step, while pulling the right wing back under the advancing left wing, the two alternating circularly like a water wheel. This is immediately followed by stepping forward with the right foot into a right empty stance, while pulling the left wing back under the advancing right wing, the two alternating circularly like a water wheel. Put on the brakes.

Raise the arms and shoulders, and the heel of the right foot. Spread the fingers like curved winged plumage, the small fingers bending and reaching closest toward the body. The right arm is pushing forward, pressing with the outer wrist, hand horizontally positioned. The left elbow and arm are pulling back, the palm of the left hand set in front of the left chest, horizontally positioned. The body is taut. Push back on the ball of the right foot and resist this pushing with the left foot, creating resistance.

Without restraint and almost recklessly, bound and shuffle in reverse with a right step behind the body, pulling the right wing over the advancing left wing, the two alternating circularly like a water wheel. This is immediately followed by a step backward with the left foot into a right empty stance, while pulling the left wing over the advancing right wing, the two alternating circularly like a water wheel. Put on the brakes.

95. Shielding Evil

Relax the right hand so the fingers realign, while lowering the left hand, palm up, to the lower elixir field. Turn the waist to the right, moving the torso, head, and eyes, waving the right hand, left to right, across the body, palm facing in, and horizontally positioned. As the right hand curves down to take the position at the lower elixir field, palm up, turn the waist left, waving the left hand across the body, right to left, palm facing in, and horizontally positioned.

As the left hand curves down to take the position at the lower elixir field, palm up, turn the waist to the right, waving the right hand across the body, left to right, palm facing in, and horizontally positioned, until reaching outside the right shoulder.

96. Cat Whiskers

Position the right hand behind the right side of the face, the thumb set under the jawline, with the palm facing forward. Push the hand forward and down contouring the jawline and face, the index finger brushing the eyebrows. Before the fingers hit the nose, tilt the head down and away to the left to avoid its contact. The right hand lowers meeting the left hand at the lower elixir field. The hands do not touch.

Lift the head, and position the left hand behind the left side of the face, the thumb set under the jawline, with the palm facing forward. The right hand is palm up, at the lower elixir field. Push the hand forward and down contouring the jawline and face, the index finger brushing the eyebrows. Before the

fingers hit the nose, tilt the head down and away to the right to avoid its contact. The left hand lowers meeting the right hand at the lower elixir field. The
hands do not touch.

Lift the head, and position the right hand behind the right side of the face,
the thumb set under the jawline, with the palm facing forward. The left hand is
palm up, at the lower elixir field. Push the hand forward and down contouring
the jawline and face, the index finger brushing the eyebrows. Before the fingers
hit the nose, tilt the head down and away to the left to avoid its contact. The
right hand lowers meeting the left hand at the lower elixir field. The hands do
not touch. (There is an ancient Chinese phrase, "If a cat washes its face, it will
bring rain." meaning prosperity.)

Turn the waist to the left, pivoting the body 180 degrees to face southwest, while taking a half step into a left forward stance, and separating the
hands. The left hand, palm up, shoots out from the shoulder, and the right
hand, palm down, remains directly in front of the groin, fingers pointing
straight.

97. Cover

Cross the chest with the left arm, placing the left palm over the right pectoral muscle. Then cross the chest with the right arm, placing the right palm
over the left pectoral muscle [forming an X], while stepping into a right empty
stance. Lower the right hand to the right hip, and brush the right arm down to
the wrist with the left palm. Then lift and rotate the right forearm in and up,
forming a right fist covered by the left hand (knuckles aligned), at the same
time stepping southwest into a transitional low left twist stance.

98. Rocking the Moon

Quickly step forward with the right foot, then shuffle the left foot ahead of the right, the weight and hands falling forward. Shift the weight back into a left empty stance, rocking the hands to the right hip, striking behind with the elbow. The eyes remain fixed to the southwest. Step behind the body with the left leg, and turn the waist to the left, pivoting 180 degrees into a left forward stance, facing northeast, while swinging the hands up under the chin, the left hand covering the right fist (knuckles aligned). The forearms and elbows are pulled in close.

99. Swirling Water, Wading in Pool

Unlock the hands and push them forward, palms down, at waist level, the hands and arms shoulder width apart. Turn the waist and upper body to the right, moving the hands around the right side of the body as if swirling water, until reaching the right hip. Reverse directions, turning the waist to the left, moving the hands around to the left side of the body as if swirling water, until reaching the left hip. Step into a right forward stance, and turn the waist and upper body to the right, moving the hands around the right side of the body as if swirling water, until reaching the right hip. Step into a left forward stance, and reverse directions, turning the waist to the left, moving the hands as if swirling water, until directly in front of the body.

100. Meet the Tidal Wave

Shift the weight back into the rear leg, lifting the hands, arms, and shoulders, up and in, wrist bent, in a large circular motion. When the hands reach the chest, pull and bend the fingers back, shift the weight forward, pushing ahead with the palms, up to chest level.

Shift the weight back into the rear leg, lifting the hands, arms, and shoulders, up and in, wrist bent, in a large circular motion. When the hands reach the chest, pull and bend the fingers back, and step into a right forward stance, pushing ahead with the palms, up to chest level.

Shift the weight back into the rear leg, lifting the hands, arms, and shoulders, up and in, wrist bent, in a large circular motion. When the hands reach the chest, pull and bend the fingers back, and step into a left forward stance, pushing ahead with the palms, up to chest level.

101. Clearing the Great Vertebrae

Flip the palms up, redirecting the hands over the shoulders, while shifting the weight back into a left empty stance. Join the palms behind the neck at Dazhui point (GV-14), then point and lift straight up and overhead. At the apex, lower the hands straight down in front of the chest. Slide the right hand down off the left, like a glacier splitting, palm down, directly in front of the groin, fingers pointing straight.

102. Cotton Palm

Lift and turn the right palm up and the left palm down, in front of the middle elixir zone, while turning the waist right. Pivot 180 degrees into a right forward stance, facing southwest, extending the right arm forward from the shoulder, lightly covering the right hand with the left hand, which slowly slides down to the elbow.

103. Prepare to Turn

Shift the weight into the rear leg, and continue sliding the left palm up along the right arm, over onto the right deltoid. Shift the weight back into a right forward stance, and slide the left hand back, to cover the right palm.

Turn the waist to the left, pivoting the right foot inward, into a mild horse stance facing southeast, as the right hand slides under the left arm, palm up. Continue rotating the waist, torso, head, and eyes to the left, until the right hand reaches the left armpit. The left arm remains slightly bent at the elbow.

104. Green Dragon Turns Its Body

Unwind, turning the waist to the right, while reversing the direction of the right hand, sliding under the left arm to the palm. Pivot the right foot outward, and swing the left foot around, turning the body 180 degrees to face northwest in a mild horse stance. Extend the right arm, palm up, moving it around the body to the right, the left hand sliding up the right arm, over onto the deltoid muscle. The head and eyes are fixed on the right hand.

Unwind, turning the waist to the left, while reversing the direction of the left hand, sliding over the right arm to the palm. Pivot the left foot outward, and swing the right foot around, turning the body 180 degrees to face southeast in a mild horse stance. Continue turning the waist to the left, as the right hand slides under the left arm, palm up. Rotate the waist, torso, head, and eyes to the left, until the right hand reaches the left armpit. The left arm remains slightly bent at the elbow.

Unwind, turning the waist to the right, while reversing the direction of the right hand, sliding under the left arm to the palm. Pivot the right foot outward, and swing the left foot around, turning the body 180 degrees to face northwest in a mild horse stance. Extend the right arm, palm up, moving it around the body to the right, the left hand sliding up the right arm, over onto the deltoid muscle. The head and eyes are fixed on the right hand.

Unwind, turning the waist to the left, while reversing the direction of the left hand, sliding over the right arm to the palm. Pivot the left foot outward, and swing the right foot around, turning the body 180 degrees to face southeast in a mild horse stance. Continue turning the waist to the left, as the right hand slides under the left arm, palm up. Rotate the waist, torso, head, and eyes to the left, until the right hand reaches the left armpit. The left arm remains slightly bent at the elbow.

105. Grasp Sparrow's Tail, Concluding Breath

Turn the waist to the right, sliding the right hand under the left arm to the palm. Gently raise the right hand aside the right shoulder at a 45 degree angle, sliding the left hand down onto the right forearm, fingers in line, and eyes up. Step with the right foot next to the left, feet together. At the same time, invert the right hand, palm facing the sky, above the upper elixir zone, and the left hand, palm down, at the middle elixir zone. Sharply exhale with a powerful *ha* sound, collapsing the body like a bellow, pushing the right palm up and the left palm down in unison (mind, body and spirit cleared of distractions).

106. Bow Out

Slowly straighten the legs, while bringing the hands together in prayer, the middle finger tips leveled at the third eye. Take a step backward with the left foot, followed by a step backward with the right foot, and a final step backward, left foot next to the right, feet together. Bend forward at the waist and bow, then return to the upright position. Finally, lower the hands to the Wuji position, with the thumbs in the naval and the index fingers connected, closing the circle.

About the Authors

Dr. Wu Baolin is a senior master of Daoist taijiquan, Chinese medicine and *qi* cultivation. From an early age he learned the most comprehensive system of taijiquan, studying with Master Du Xinling, a legendary Wudang fighting monk, and abbot of the White Cloud Monastery, which for almost a thousand years has been one of the most respected centers in China for the study and practice of Daoist philosophy, medicine and martial arts. Daoist style taijiquan is comprised of three main components: martial arts, qigong, and *Yijing* (Book of Changes) philosophy, a supreme health and longevity practice. Dr. Wu's achievements in the three categories, rank him one of the monastery's highest initiates. In addition, Dr. Wu Baolin is an expert in Daoist swordplay, Baguazhang, Xingyiquan, Chinese herbal medicine, and more, reaching the highest pinnacle, making accurate predictions and excelling in martial practice.

Dr. Wu is nationally recognized as an authority in the practice of Traditional Chinese Medicine and also has a thorough understanding of Western Medicine, as evidenced by his training and experience. Dr. Wu received his medical degrees from the most esteemed schools in China. He graduated from the National College of Traditional Chinese Medicine in Beijing, holds a master's degree from the China Academy of Traditional Chinese Medicine and became an Attending Physician at Guang An Men Hospital (China's foremost combination Western/Chinese medical institution). Several years later, he went to Japan to take part in government-sponsored research and earned his PhD. in Neurophysiology from prestigious Kyoto University. He then served as Director of Qigong and Traditional Chinese Medicine at Takua Hospital in Kildore, Japan.

To understand Dr. Baolin Wu's excellence in his field, one must go beyond academic credentials. He hails from one of the most prominent medical families in China. His renowned ancestor Wu Qian, an imperial doctor of the

Qing Dynasty, was the author of "The Mirror of Medicine", the encyclopedia work that stands today with the "Materia Medica" (1590) as the basis for all modern Chinese medicine. Wu Xizhi, Dr. Wu's paternal grandfather, was the personal physician of Pu Yi, the last emperor of China. Dr. Wu's mastery has been shaped by the wisdom of seven generations, passed down to him by his family. In addition, the Daoist principles instilled in his young days have given Dr. Wu a sensitivity towards his patients as well as a holistic understanding of the nature of healing.

After working as a physician at Guang'anmen Hospital in Beijing for many years, he emigrated to the U.S. in 1990. Since then, Master Wu has served as a teacher of Daoist exercise and TCM practitioner in Santa Monica, Calif. He has three earlier books: *The Eight Immortals' Revolving Sword of Pure Yang* (Three Pines Press 2011), *Qi Gong for Total Wellness: Increase your Energy, Vitality and Longevity with the Ancient 9 Palaces System from the White Cloud Monastery* (St. Martin's Press, 2006), and *Lighting the Eye of the Dragon: Inner Secrets of Taoist Feng Shui* (St. Martin's Press, 2000). See https://beijingchinesemedicalcenter.com/

Michael McBride is a native of Los Angeles. For the past 24 years, has studied the Daoist arts under the guidance of Master Wu Baolin. He trained in qigong, taijiquan, Daoist swordplay and Chinese medical massage. He has traveled extensively in and around China for more than two decades. He is a coauthor of *The Eight Immortals' Revolving Sword of Pure Yang* (Three Pines Press 2011).